EFFECTIVE MEDIATION ADVOCACY
FOURTH EDITION

Discourage litigation. Persuade your neighbours to compromise whenever you can. Point out to them how the nominal winner is often a real loser – in fees, expenses, and waste of time. As a peacemaker the lawyer has a superior opportunity of being a good man. There will still be business enough.

Abraham Lincoln
Notes for a Law Lecture, July 1, 1850

Good lawyers must have the skills required for professional competence. But this is not enough. They must know how to carry the burdens of other people on their shoulders. They must know of pain, and how to help heal it. Lawyers can be healers. Like physicians, ministers, and other healers, lawyers are persons to whom other people open up their innermost secrets when they have suffered or are threatened with serious injury. People go to them to be healed, to be made whole, and to regain control of their lives.

James D Gordon III
Arizona Law Review and the Modern Mind
(1991) vol 33 no.2

EFFECTIVE MEDIATION ADVOCACY
A Guide for Practitioners
FOURTH EDITION

ANDREW GOODMAN

LLB MBA PhD FCIArb FInstCPD FRSA Barrister
CEDR Mediator and IMI Mediation Advocate

Professor of Conflict Management and Dispute Resolution Studies, Rushmore University

Convenor, Standing Conference of Mediation Advocates

Director, College of Mediators

Director, Association of Mediation Assessors, Trainers and Instructors

Distinguished Fellow, International Academy of Mediators

Of the Inner Temple, a Master of the Bench

With Forewords by

Rt. Hon. Lord Dyson

Irena Vanenkova
Formerly Executive Director, International Mediation Institute

SCMA Standards and Competencies in Mediation Advocacy

MEDIATION PUBLISHING

International Mediation Institute

Disclaimer

This work is not intended to be comprehensive. It is not a substitute for appropriate legal advice. Neither the author not the publisher accept any responsibility for loss occasioned to any person acting or refraining from acting as a result of material contained in this publication.

ISBN 978-1-85811-608-2
Ebook ISBN 978-1-85811-609-9
Printed and Designed in the UK

Mediation Publishing,
Suite 74, 17 Holywell Hill
St Albans
AL1 1DT, UK

www.mediationpublishing.com

Foreword

In 1996 it was noted that one of the most pressing questions relating to mediation was whether it formed part of the 'practice of law.'[1] It was a question that could barely be raised with any real credibility ten years later when I had the welcome opportunity to write the foreword to the first edition of this extremely valuable book. A proper understanding of mediation, its practices and techniques, was – or at the very least ought to have been – an essential component of every lawyer's arsenal. Moreover its central importance to dispute resolution was firmly a part of the wider dispute resolution landscape: the Civil Procedure Rules, Pre-Action Protocols, and a number of significant Court of Appeal decisions had helped to achieve that end.

Mediation has not stood still since 2006. Its importance, and utility to parties seeking to resolve their disputes amicably at proportionate cost and in a reasonable time, has been emphasised on innumerable occasions, not least by Sir Rupert Jackson in his far-reaching Report on the Costs of Civil Justice. The need for all lawyers to have a proper grounding in mediation was strongly emphasised in that Report. If the first edition of this book was timely, the publication of this edition is timelier still. Mediation is an essential. This book is an essential too. It provides the clearest possible grounding in the skills and practice of mediation, and the role of the advocate throughout the mediation process. It is compendious in scope and thoroughly practical in its advice. It should be seen to be the pre-eminent guide to practitioners who wish to develop and hone the specialist skills required of effective mediation advocates. It will continue to prove to be of real benefit to practitioners and, most importantly, to their clients.

The Right Honourable Lord Dyson
Formerly Master of the Rolls and Head of Civil Justice
January 2016

1 C. Menkel-Meadow, Is Mediation the Practice of Law, (1996) 14 Alternatives to the High Cost of Litigation (5) 57, 60.

Foreword

Increasingly in this complicated world, disputes are being seen as problems to be solved, not battles to be won. Ever anxious to replace risk with certainty, and to avoid the vortex of the cost spiral, disputants are increasingly intolerant of professional advisers obsessed with winning at all costs, utterly fixed on their positions, blind to their clients' underlying needs.

Driven by user demand, mediation has therefore become a mainstream dispute resolution process. However, too many advisers apply their litigation mindset even in settlement negotiations, unable to extract themselves mentally from the cut-and-thrust of the courtroom or arbitral tribunal. They need to apply quite different attitudes and approaches, and a different bank of knowledge and skills, when assisting their clients to resolve disputes in mediation.

Mediation is most successful when the parties' advocates or advisors are knowledgeable and skilled in the principles of the mediation process and negotiation theories. Mediations can fail when party representatives act as gladiators rather than as negotiators. Since mediation presents unique problem-solving opportunities in which representatives can assist their clients to reach faster, cheaper and better outcomes with the assistance of a mediator, any extension to the literature on the subject is to be warmly welcomed.

Party representatives can play a pivotal role in helping their clients get to the negotiating table, select the most suitable mediator acceptable to the other party, and achieve outcomes that are often unattainable in a courtroom or arbitration tribunal. But to do that, they need a very different bank of knowledge and a very different set of skills than they would apply in litigation or arbitration. This is accentuated in the many jurisdictions around the world that have yet fully to normalise mediation as a mainstream process.

To meet this challenge Andrew Goodman, in this edition of his popular work on mediation advocacy, helps professional practitioners extend their toolbox of techniques and processes to enable their clients to satisfy their needs.

This is an important and practical contribution to the mediation revolution that is sweeping the world. This is one of the authoritative books recommended by the International Mediation Institute - IMI – for professional advisors wishing to qualify as IMI Certified Mediation Advocates, a mechanism providing the professional and technical basis for enabling disputing parties to identify professionals experienced in advising and representing clients in the resolution of disputes through mediation and related dispute resolution processes.

IMI will continue to recommend this book to all aspiring mediation advocates.

Irena Vanenkova
formerly Executive Director
International Mediation Institute
December 2015

Preface to the Fourth Edition and Acknowledgments

It is my pleasure to introduce this fourth edition of *Effective Mediation Advocacy - A Guide for Practitioners* which is accompanied by a separate second student edition, and complemented by *Advanced Mediation Advocacy*. Its predecessor had local editions produced in Hong Kong, Nigeria and India, and in the Turkish language. I am open to help develop this work in any jurisdiction and in any language.

This book was first published as *Mediation Advocacy* in 2005 at a time when the idea of specialist representation in mediation was in its infancy. As the contents have grown in length, so has the field of practice developed to become normative. Only nomenclature appears to be left as a matter of serious debate. Judiciaries around the world now encourage mediation as a mainstream method of dispute resolution. Governments are doing so as a means of cutting cost, with increasing control and regulation brought about by statute, most recently in Nigeria, Turkey and India.

Mediation is with us to stay, and practitioners need to learn the process and the skills necessary to protect their clients' best interests, and to add value to their professional practice. This book is intended to contribute to that knowledge and takes in the November 2023 Court of Appeal decision in Churchill v Merthyr Tydfil CBC which effectively frees the courts to mandate mediation, and the consequences of both delays caused by the pandemic and the lacuna in EU cross-border enforcement of English court judgments that was caused by ministerial inattention to detail in Brexit.

I now practice in mediation as a mediator, advocate, trainer and adviser in over 20 jurisdictions. In the year of writing alone I have worked in the jurisdictions of England and Wales, Guernsey, Jersey, Cayman Islands, British Virgin Islands, France, the Netherlands, Austria, Turkey, Nigeria, India, the United Arab Emirates, Thailand, India, Singapore and Hong Kong. Although this work is grounded in and necessarily governed by the law of England and Wales, I hope the principles discussed travel reasonably well and the concepts understood and problems grappled with by the courts in England will have a strong resonance elsewhere, particularly in jurisdictions where litigation is slow, expensive, subject to political interference or control, caught up in a military conflict or post-conflict situations, and broadly where access to justice is a diminishing right.

Having said that, and despite its great strengths, advantages and convenience, practitioners will recognise that mediation is not a substitute for access to justice. But it may be the best thing presently available. And it is therefore something we should all know about.

I am very grateful to my colleagues at the Standing Conference of Mediation Advocates, Roger Levitt, Douglas Beckworth, John Burgess and Paul Rose against whom I bounce my ideas. In the wider mediation community, I have always looked to Michel Kallipetis KC, Colin Manning, Iain Christie and other members of the Bar ADR Panel and Civil Mediation Council for stimulating conversation and thought, and I acknowledge with thanks the use I have been offered of papers prepared for Bar ADR events. Practising mediator Karena Ellis-Greenway allowed me to publish her private standard mediation agreements, and the ADR Group their agreement and rules.

Lord Dyson, formerly Master of the Rolls and Head of Civil Justice, has very graciously taken an interest in this publication since its inception, and for this edition I reproduce his kind foreword. He was and remains a real force for good in the development of mediation, and I also wish to associate such sentiments with Lord Neuberger, Sir Rupert Jackson, Dame Sue Carr, the Lady Chief Justice, Sir Alan Ward, HH Judge Bartle KC and HH Judge Alastair Hammerton, each of whom has shown me great kindness (and great indulgence).

The International Mediation Institute has endorsed my work, and I am grateful for the contribution of a foreword by its former executive director, Irena Vanenkova. I commend the work of IMI to mediation practitioners everywhere, and in particular invite you to consider the IMI decision tree on selecting a mediator, and the IMI's Olé Case Management Tool which is designed to help running mediated disputes, both of which I have been given kind permission to include.

It seems to me that this area of practice can only expand. Economic conditions and the rapid development of digital technology in this area suggest that it will now do so quickly. I invite all those who wish to engage as practitioners to be prepared.

Andrew Goodman
81 Chancery Lane, London
May 2024

Contents

Foreword, The Right Honourable Lord Dyson, formerly Master of the Rolls........ v

Foreword, Irena Vanenkova, International Mediation Institute........................... vii

Preface.. ix

Table of Cases.. xvii

Table of Conventions, Rules and Statutes.. xxi

Introduction.. 1

The Growth in Mediation 2
What is Mediation? 9
When Mediation Might be Inappropriate 11
The Benefits of Mediation 28

Part I: The Role of the Mediation Advocate.. 31

Meeting the Demands of a Modern Law Market 33
The Development of Mediation 33
The Adjudicative Model and Historic Professional Psyche 37
Why, then, use a Lawyer as an Advocate in Mediation? 43
The Changing Role of the Lawyer 48
Lawyer or Non-lawyer Advocate? 49

Part 2: The Decision to Mediate... 53

Is the Case Suitable for Mediation? 56
Is the Case Ripe for Mediation? 57
Getting the Client to Mediate 58
Dealing With the Client's Questions 60
Key Points to Explain 61
Getting Your Instructing Solicitor or Principal to Agree to Mediation 63
Getting the Other Side to Mediate 64
Arguing Against Mediation 67

Part 3: Choosing A Mediator.. 71

Choosing the Right Mediator 74
The IMI Decision Tree 79
Mediation Service Providers 81

Part 4: The Pre-Mediation Process 83

Choosing the Venue 85
The Mediation Agreement 86
Document Preparation 88
The Written Position/Participation/Interest Statement 90
Working with the Mediator in the Pre-Mediation Phase 92
Decisions as to Strategy 94
Who Should Attend? 94
Who Should be Contactable? 96
Role of the Attendees 97
Preparing the Attendees 99
Ethics and Other Matters 100
What Does the Client Want to Achieve? 101
Obtaining Authority to Settle 103
Working up the Mediation Brief 104
Pre-Mediation Preparation 108
The Advice on Mediation for the Client 109
Fixing the Mediation Date 110
Getting it Wrong 110

Part 5: The Mediation Day 115

Timetabling 117
Practical Considerations 117
Procedure 118
The Opening Statement 121
Private and Open Sessions 123
The Role of the Advocate at the Mediation 126
Working with the Mediator – Tactical Considerations 128
Team Strategy 130
Working Towards a Settlement 133
Effective Mediation Management 134
Negotiation Processes and Strategies Within Mediation 135
The Momentum to Expect 139
Traits of Effective and Ineffective Negotiators 141
Ten Rules for Effective Negotiation Within Mediation 143
Negotiating Phases 145
Opening Negotiating Positions 145
Movement 146
Crisis and Deadlock 147
Dealing with Obnoxious Opponents 148
Dealing with Overly Aggressive Opponents 149
Using Tit-for-Tat as a Model Negotiating Strategy 150
Forensic Skills of Mediation Advocates 151
Control of the Client 154
The Settlement Agreement 155
Time-limited Mediations 156

Part 6: Mediation Privilege and Confidentiality 159

The Existence of Mediation Privilege 161
Challenges to Mediation Privilege 164

Part 7: Costs Issues 175

Mediation Costs 171
Litigation Costs and ADR 172
The Recoverability of Costs 174
Costs of the Mediation in the Litigation 174
Litigation Costs in the Mediation 175
Mediation Costs and Public Funding 176
Mediation Costs and Conditional Fee Agreements 176
The Relevance of Court-directed Mediation 178
Adverse Costs Awards for Unreasonable Failure to Mediate 179
Potential Difficulties 189

Glossary of Mediation Terms 197

Appendices 207

I. The SCMA Mediation Advocacy Standards 209

II. Sample ADR Group Standard Mediation Agreement 237

III. Example Private Mediation Agreement 253

IV. Example Settlement Agreement 257

Bibliography 259

Index 265

Table of Cases

Balfour Beatty Construction Northern Ltd v *Modus Corovest (Blackpool) Ltd* [2008] EWHC 3029 TCC, 31,42,47
Brown v *Patel* [2007] EWHC 625 (Ch), 31,42,160
Burchell v *Bullard* [2005] EWCA Civ 358, 9,14,64,184

Cable & Wireless Plc v *IBM United Kingdom Ltd* [2002] EWHC 2059 (Comm), 31,42,48,49,178
R G Carter Ltd v *Edmund Nuttall Ltd* (2002) BLR 59, 62
Cattley v *Pollard* [2007] Ch 353, 161
Chantrey Vellacott v *The Convergence Group PLC and Others* [2007] EWHC 1774 (Ch), 174
Corenso v *Burnden* [2003] EWHC 1805 (QB), 66
Cumbria Waste Management v *Baines Wilson* [2008] EWHC 786, 31,42,162
Churchill v *Merthyr Tydfil CBC* [2023] EWCA Civ 1416, 1,5,26-27,31,63,159, 178,179
R (Cowl and others) v *Plymouth City Council* [2001] EWCA Civ 1935; [2002] 1 WLR 803, 176,178,180

Re D (A Child) (Hague Convention: Mediation) [2017] EWHC 3363 (Fam) [2018] 4 WLR 45, 167
Re D (Minors) (Conciliation: Disclosure of Information) [1993] Fam 231, 165
Re D. In Re E (A Child) (Mediation Privilege) [2020] EWHC 3379 (Fam), 167
Daniels v *Commissioner of Police For The Metropolis* [2005] EWCA Civ 1312, 184
DSN v *Blackpool Football Club Ltd* [2020] EWHC 670 (QB) at [28], 24
Dunnett v *Railtrack* [2002] 1 WLR 2434, 5,65,180
Dyson v *Leeds City Council (No.1)* [2000] CP Rep 42, 179,180

Eagleson v. *Liddell* [2001] EWCA Civ 155, 175
Earl of Malmesbury v *Strutt and Parker* [2008] EWHC 424 (QB), 162

Faidi & Anor v *Elliott Corporation* [2012] EWCA Civ 287, 3,15,64
Farm Assist Ltd (in Liquidation) v *DEFRA* (No.2) [2009] EWHC 1102 (TCC), 31,42,59,83,162,163,166
Forster v *Friedland* C.A. (Civil Division) Transcript No. 205 of 1993, 158

Gaith v *Indesit Company UK Ltd* [2012] EWCA Civ 642, 23,64
Garritt-Critchley and Others v *Ronnan and Solarpower PV Ltd* [2014] EWHC 1774 (Ch), 5,22,32,42,63,186,187

Halsey v *Milton Keynes General NHS Trust* [2004] EWCA Civ 576, [2004] 1 WLR 3002, 1,5,9,11,12,13,14,16,18,23,24,26,28,65,159,176,178,179,182
Henderson v *Henderson* (1843) 67 ER 313; [1843-1860] All ER Rep. 378, 57
Henry Construction Projects Ltd v *Linton Fuel Oils Ltd* 9578 of 2012, 32
Hickman v *Blake Lapthorn* [2006] EWHC 12 (QB), 185
Hodgkinson & Corby Ltd v *Wards Mobility Services Ltd* [1997] F.S.R. 178, 158
Holloway v *Chancery Mead* [2007] EWHC 2495 (TCC) [2008] 1 All ER (Comm) 653, 31,42,48
Hurst v *Leeming* [2003] 1 Lloyd's Rep 37, 5,11,12,22,65,66,181,183

In Re a Company [2005] EWHC 3317 (Ch), 32

Interactive Technology Corporation Ltd v *Ferster & Ors* [2015] EWHC 3895 (Ch), 168

Kinstreet Ltd v *Balmargo Corporation Ltd* [2000] CP Rep 62, 178

Lakehouse Contracts v *UPR Services Ltd* [2014] EWHC 1223 (Ch), 32
Laporte v *Commissioner of Police for the Metropolis* [2015] EWHC 371 (QB), 5,24,32,42,63,188

Muller v *Linsley & Mortimer* [1996] PNLR 74, 161
Muman v *Nagasena* [1999] EWCA Civ 764 [2000] 1 WLR 299, 178

N v *N* [1999] Fam. Div LTL Lawtel AC7800507, 62
Neal v *Jones Motors* [2002] EWCA Civ 1730, 181
Nigel Witham Ltd v *Smith* [2008] EWHC 12 (TCC), 13

O'Callaghan v *Coral Racing Ltd* [1998] EWCA Civ 1801, 62
Oliver v *Symons* [2012] EWCA Civ 267, 15

PGF II SA v *OMFS Co. 1 Ltd* [2013] EWCA Civ 1288, [2014] WLR 1386, 4,5,24,32,42,58,64,185

Reed Executive Plc v *Reed Business Information* [2004] EWCA Civ 887; [2004] 1 WLR 3026, 59,65,159,184
Rolf v *De Guerin* [2011] EWCA Civ 78, 14,63,64
Royal Bank of Canada v *Secretary of State for Defence* [2003] EWHC 1841 (ChD), 181
Rush & Tompkins Ltd v *GLC* [1989] AC 1290 HL, 59,159

Shirayama Shokusan v *Danovo* [2003] EWHC 390 (Ch); [2004] 1 WLR 2985, 176
SITA v *Wyatt* [2002] EWHC 2401 Ch, 66,182
Stoney-Andersen v *Abbas & Ors* 2 [2023] EWHC 2964 (Ch), 25
Sulmerica CIA Nacional de Seguros SA v *Ensa Engenharia SA* [2012] EWCA Civ 638, 31,42,48,178
Swain Mason & Others v *Mills & Reeve* [2012] EWCA Civ 498, 5,20,32,42,64

Tomlin v *Standard Telephones and Cables Ltd* [1969] 1 W.L.R. 1378, 158,161

Underwood v *Cox* (1912) 4 D.L.R. 66, 158
Unilever plc v *Proctor and Gamble* [2000] 1 WLR 2436, 158,160

Valentine v *Allen, Nash & Nash* [2003] EWCA Civ 1274, 182
Vedatech Corpn v *Crystal Decision UK Ltd and Crystal Decision (Japan) KK* [2003] EWCA Civ 1066, 31,42,97
Venture Investment Placement Ltd v *Hall* [2005] EWHC 1227 (Ch), 59,65,117,160
Vernon v *Bosely* (No 2) [1999] QB 18 CA., 96
Virani v *Manuel Revert Y CIA SA* [2003] EWCA Civ. 1651; [2004] Lloyd's Rep 4, 181

Walker v *Walker* 23 Q.B.D. 335, 159
Colin Wright v *Michael Wright Supplies Ltd* v *Turner Wright Investments Ltd*, [2013] EWCA Civ 234, 24

Table of Conventions, Rules and Statutes

Civil Procedure Rules, 3
1, 96
1.1, 180
1.3, 58
1.4(2)(e), 5,58
1.4(2)(f), 5
3.1(4), 58
7.3, 59
26.4(2)(b, 24
36, 10,14,16,21,185
44, 109,176
44.4, 10,179
44.5(3), 58
Practice Direction 4.3(f) and 4.6(e), 4

Companies Act 2006
s994, 168

EU Directive 2008/52/EC, 6
EU Directive (EU) 2013/11/EU, 6,32
EU Regulation (EU) No 524/2013, 32
European Convention on Human Rights,
Art 6, 179
Senior Courts Act 1981
s51, 174

Singapore Convention - United Nations Convention on International Settlement Agreements Resulting from Mediation ("the Singapore Convention") 2019, 6,7

Introduction to the Fourth Edition

Despite recent developments in the field, and in particular the recent Court of Appeal decision in *Churchill v Merthyr Tydfil CBC*[1] which removed in England and Wales the obstacle to Court-mandated mediation established by the previous decision of *Halsey v Milton Keynes General NHS Trust,*[2] for the intending practitioner advocacy in mediation remains relatively still in its infancy. Some consider the word advocacy itself to be incompatible with a settlement driven narrative. But there is no reason to suppose that as mediation becomes normalised in the minds of both clients, lawyers, and the general public, as the Ministry of Justice scrapes together a few pence to launch its awaited mandatory small claims mediation scheme, and as court-annexed schemes worldwide develop, mediation will not come to be regarded as just another form of dispute resolution in which legal representation is required as a matter of course.

The advocate's particular expertise will need to be developed so that mediation advocacy becomes a specialist and desirable skill, which adds value to professional practice at a time when many are worried about a shrinking market brought about by the conflation of significant rises in court fees, the reduction in litigation funding and the reduction of capital expenditure on the court estate. Added to the delays in courts around the world as a result of the global pandemic, and the difficulty in recognising and enforcing England and Wales court judgments in EU countries as a result of the lacuna in Brexit negotiations, there should be a substantial and growing demand for mediation as appropriate dispute resolution in most circumstances.

For those engaged in professional practice, the study of mediation advocacy is to adopt new and effective practice skills, perhaps (and still) on the margin of orthodox advocacy training. As a subject it cannot yet pretend to have any substantial academic hinterland, but juridification is coming, and in its wake the theoretical study of judicial decision making in the field. There is already a growing body of authorities in many jurisdictions which concern the scope of an advocate's role in mediation, the enforceability of both contractual mediation clauses and mediation settlement agreements, and this will have a growing impact on strategy to be adopted in support or defence of the client's

1 [2023] EWCA Civ 1416

2 [2004] EWCA Civ 576, [2004] 1 WLR 3002

interests. Mediation advocates should know current authorities in this area (see Appendix 1 SCMA Standards).

Both primary and delegated legislation are now in place in this area in many civil law jurisdictions, such as Turkey, Romania, Greece, Italy and Brazil, and in a growing number of common law jurisdictions, for example India, Singapore, Hong Kong and Ireland. Institutional or professional regulation is growing across the United States and Canada and in Australia, Singapore and New Zealand. These can only expand in number and degree of regulation.

Mediation is not a soft option for the advocate. The contents of this book concern what advocates should anticipate and how they should prepare, and also seeks to engage those more seasoned advocates wishing to specialise in mediation advocacy and who want to develop the particular skills that it requires.

There has been a clear move in recent years away from the generalist mediator to the lawyer specialist mediator. It has been recognised by sophisticated commercial parties with complex disputes that both lawyer and subject-matter expert mediators with experience in the field of the dispute give mediation a better chance of success. Informed commercial parties look for sensible reasons, based on proper risk analysis of the litigation in question, to found a recommendation for settlement. They settle because there are sound commercial reasons for doing so, usually based, at least in substantial part, on a careful analysis of the strengths and weaknesses of the case.[3]

But beyond knowing his client's case, the lawyer or other professional acting as a practitioner in mediation must know his client's wider commercial, financial, social, relationship or any other factors that drive him or her towards or away from settlement. Lawyers are trained to focus narrowly on a formatted case, regulated by the process of the court. Mediation forces them to take a much wider view and adopt an approach for which they have yet to be trained in any serious manner.

This book is therefore designed to help prepare advocates to use the mediation process to their and their clients' best advantage.

The Growth in Mediation

In recent years the use of mediation in the United Kingdom has increased exponentially. This reflects a global trend, extending across Europe into southeast Asia and to the Far East. Although the modern practice of civil

3 *New Sophistications in Commercial Mediation*, Elizabeth Birch, ACI newsletter issue 9 Spring/Summer 2004.

mediation only reached the UK from the United States and Pacific Rim countries in April 1989, by 1995 alternative dispute resolution started to enter the mainstream as courts began making directions proposing it. However, it was the introduction of the new Civil Procedure Rules (CPR) in 1999 that transformed mediation in England and Wales from a minority pursuit to an integral part of the pre-trial process, and one that any party to litigation can no longer afford to ignore. In his review of costs in civil proceedings, culminating in major changes to the CPR after 1st April, 2013, Lord Justice Jackson's Final Report wholly endorsed the use of mediation, short only of making it compulsory.

Jackson accepted that mediation is highly efficacious in all areas of work, including personal injury and clinical negligence, while still unappreciated and under-used. His preferred strategy was to be one of educating judges and others to encourage its use, by structuring the costs regime to incentivise doing so, accepting that it can itself save costs.[4] Courts subsequently and very quickly took on board the Jackson view, referencing the usefulness of mediation in delivering what courts often cannot. Lord Justice Jackson himself led the charge towards mediation in *Faidi & Anor v Elliott Corporation:*[5]

> "[35]....The courts stand ready to deliver such a service to litigants and must do so as expeditiously and economically as practicable. But before embarking upon full blooded adversarial litigation parties should first explore the possibility of settlement. In neighbour disputes of the kind now before the court (and of which I have seen many similar examples) if negotiation fails, mediation is the obvious and constructive way forward.
>
> [36].In the present case a mediator would not have been concerned about the interaction between the various leases and the licence to carry out works. Nor would he have been concerned about the other interesting points of construction, which first the county court judge and now this court have been called upon to decide. Instead, he would have been helping the parties to find a sensible resolution of the practical problem which had arisen. I have little doubt that such a mediation would have been successful. The points of law upon which the litigation has turned are not easy ones and at the time of the hypothetical mediation neither party could have been confident of victory.
>
> [37].As it is, neither side wrote to the other proposing mediation until shortly before the hearing in the Court of Appeal. By then huge costs had been incurred. The claimants' costs up to the end of trial were £23,195. The claimants incurred a further £34,609 costs on the appeal. The defendant's costs up to the end of trial were £32,798. The defendant incurred a further £49,532 costs on the appeal. Thus, the total costs thrown away amount to £140,134. If the parties were driven by concern for the well being of lawyers, they could have given half that sum to the Solicitors Benevolent

4 See: The Jackson Report amendments to the CPR – What do they do to encourage settlement (if anything?) Tony Allen Solicitor, Mediator and Senior Consultant to CEDR, www.cedr.com 26 Mar 2013.

5 [2012] EWCA Civ 287

> Association and then resolved their dispute for a modest fraction of the monies left over."

One of Lord Woolf's aims for the CPR was to encourage and promote settlement at as early a stage as possible, and to streamline procedures to facilitate the negotiation of settlements before trial. These rules envisaged that parties ought to embark on meaningful dispute resolution negotiations at soon as litigation is contemplated, long before the issuing of a claim form. To this end Pre-Action Protocols were introduced, governing conduct in the early stages to require the parties to consider whether a form of alternative dispute resolution, often mediation, might be appropriate. Further, the Practice Direction on Pre-Action Conduct required parties in cases not covered by a Protocol to show a willingness to consider mediation.[6]

The Practice Direction – Pre-Action Conduct and Protocols sets out the following:

> Settlement and ADR
>
> 8. Litigation should be a last resort. As part of a relevant pre-action protocol or this Practice Direction, the parties should consider whether negotiation or some other form of ADR might enable them to settle their dispute without commencing proceedings.
>
> 9. Parties should continue to consider the possibility of reaching a settlement at all times, including after proceedings have been started. Part 36 offers may be made before proceedings are issued.
>
> 10. Parties may negotiate to settle a dispute or may use a form of ADR including—
>
> (a) mediation, a third party facilitating a resolution;
>
> (b) arbitration, a third party deciding the dispute[7];
>
> (c) early neutral evaluation, a third party giving an informed opinion on the dispute; and
>
> (d) Ombudsmen schemes.
>
> 11. If proceedings are issued, the parties may be required by the court to provide evidence that ADR has been considered. A party's silence in response to an invitation to participate or a refusal to participate in ADR is

6 Practice Direction 4.3(f) and 4.6(e)

7 (Information on mediation and other forms of ADR is available in the Jackson ADR Handbook (3rd edn Oct. 2022 available from Oxford University Press) or at—

•http://www.civilmediation.justice.gov.uk/

•http://www.adviceguide.org.uk/england/law_e/law_legal_system_e/law_taking_legal_action_e/alternatives_to_court.htm)

capable of being considered of itself unreasonable by the court and could lead to the court ordering that party to pay additional court costs.[8]

At the Allocation Questionnaire stage, the first Case Management Conference, and the Costs Management Conference, parties are expected to report to the court on the practical steps they have or are taking to engage in some form of ADR. This is reinforced by the professional duty of solicitors to explain ADR and within it, mediation, to their clients.

Once a claim is issued, the court's duty actively to manage cases includes "encouraging the parties to use an alternative dispute resolution procedure if the court considers that appropriate and facilitating the use of such procedure" (CPR 1.4(2)(e)) and "helping the parties to settle the whole or part of their case" (CPR 1.4(2)(f)). Courts now take upon themselves the possibility of mediation at an early stage in the proceedings, particularly where the parties appear shy of doing so, and increasingly make strong recommendations.

From the Court of Appeal, Civil Division to small claims mediation in the County Court, court-annexed mediation schemes at entry-level management have an element of compulsion about them, and automatic referral will increasingly be contemplated. With the removal of the impediment that was *Halsey* by *Churchill,*[9] the court can now impose a stay of proceedings and mandate the parties to mediate, albeit exercising such a discretion on a case-by-case basis so that it does not impair the very essence of the claimant's rights under Article 6, European Convention on Human Rights, in pursuit of a legitimate aim, and in such a way that it is proportionate to achieving that legitimate aim.[10]

The flip side of a CPR designed to promote early settlement is that courts will, in certain circumstances, impose costs sanctions on parties who unreasonably refuse to mediate. All advocates must be aware that unsuccessful litigants who refuse mediation can face indemnity costs, while even those who win at trial risk an adverse costs order if the court considers their behaviour to have been unreasonable. What emerged with the early implementation of the CPR in *Dunnett v Railtrack,*[11] *Hurst v Leeming*[12] and *Halsey v Milton Keynes NHS Trust*[13] has found its highest expression in *PGF II SA v OMFS Company 1*

8 See *PGF II SA v OMFS Co. 1 Ltd, op.cit*
9 *Op.cit @ [19-21]*
10 *Churchill, op. cit @* [50]
11 [2002] 1 WLR 2434
12 [2003] 1 Lloyd's Rep 37
13 [2004] 1 WLR 3002

Ltd[14] where declining to respond to a request for mediation will be taken by the courts to be an unreasonable refusal, with costs consequences following.

Both the British Government and the European Union have also recognised the value of mediation and sought to increase its use. Since 2001 the Government has been committed to using alternative dispute resolution (the "ADR" pledge, repeated in 2012 and 2016) in all appropriate cases where the other side agrees. In addition the European Commission is keen to encourage the use of mediation, particularly in cross-border disputes where mediation can be far easier and cheaper than negotiating the complexity of another jurisdiction's legal system. To that end a Directive on Cross-Border Mediation was not only produced[15] in 2008 and brought into operation in 2011 for cross-border disputes, the European Parliament established a reporting process to monitor implementation after 2013. For a reason that seems inexplicable, the operation of the EU Directive on Cross-Border Mediation was among the first to be removed from England and Wales after Brexit. Whether that was a symbolic gesture, or part of the wider lacuna of government in dealing with post-Brexit cross-border civil justice recognition and enforcement remains to be seen, unless the MoJ was remarkably perspicacious in its view of the long-term effectiveness of the Singapore Convention on Mediation 2019.

Thus far, and for most of this book, I have assumed that the mediation will occur live on a face-to-face basis with the mediator and other parties. It is possible and becoming increasingly common for parties to smaller claims to have their mediation conducted over the telephone, in a series of calls with the mediator. Automatic referral to Small Claims Track Mediation in the County Court, when available, will rely heavily on telephone mediation to make it cost effective for all parties, and for HM Courts and Tribunals Service (HMCTS).

In addtion, it was as a result of the huge changes forced upon the mediation industry by the pandemic that online dispute resolution (ODR) has become normalised. What may have been a fringe activity in the latter half of the last decade is now mainstream, led by practitioners such as Stephen Walker. He sees no difference in the process whether one is mediating live or online, although there are plainly advantages and disadvantages to each method.[16] Formats involving the physical absence of the mediator can succeed, but the task for both the mediator and mediation advocate is likely to be much harder

14 [2013] EWCA Civ 1288 [2014] 1 WLR 1386; see also *Swain Mason & Others v Mills & Reeve* [2012] EWCA Civ 498; *Garritt-Critchley and Others v Ronnan and Solarpower PV Ltd* [2014] EWHC 1774 (Ch); *Laporte v Commissioner of Police for the Metropolis* [2015] EWHC 371 (QB)

15 Directive 2008/52/EC 21 May 2008

16 Discussed in more detail in *Advanced Mediation Advocacy*

in the absence of being able to study reaction in body language and consider what the nuancing means. A major change from January 2016 concerned the implementation of the EU Directive for the use of online mediation,[17] or ODR, and an EU Regulation[18] to solve consumer disputes, and this has been developed to run alongside the existing complaints procedures of such e-commerce giants as Amazon, E-bay and Alibaba. In this jurisdiction *Churchill* has now paved the way for non-judicial consumer complaints schemes to be recognised as an active precursor to litigating claims.

The UK response to the Directive on online dispute resolution for consumer disputes was announced by Lord Dyson, then Master of the Rolls, in February 2015 following the report of the advisory group to the Civil Justice Council which was established to look at the wider potential for the use of ODR for resolving civil disputes of value less than £25,000 in England and Wales. The group explored its limitations and drawbacks, and the issues that need flagging up to protect consumers and businesses. The principal recommendations of the report were that HMCTS should establish a new, internet-based court service, known as HM Online Court (HMOC) discussed in Chapter 1. It still remains to be seen whether resources to be committed by government to meet these recommendations will be adequate, involving the development of technical infrastructure and training. If so it will herald much innovation in the civil justice system, but also set against a background of reducing the physical estate of HMCTS while at the same time coping with the substantial delays caused by Covid 19.

On a larger scale the International Mediation Institute threw its weight behind a multi-national treaty in relation to the enforceability of settlement agreements resulting from international commercial conciliation. This took the form of the adoption of the United Nations Commission on International Trade Law (UNCITRAL) Working Group II proposal for the enforcement of mediation settlements along the line of the 1958 New York Convention on the Recognition and Enforcement of Foreign Arbitral Awards. Until the introduction of the proposed treaty an often-cited challenge to the use of mediation in commercial disputes was the lack of an efficient and harmonised framework for cross-border enforcement of settlement agreements resulting from mediation. It was in response to this need that the Singapore Convention on Mediation was developed and adopted by the United Nations.

17 Directive 2013/11/EU

18 Regulation (EU) 524/2013

The Convention was finalised at the fifty-first UNCITRAL Commission session, which came to a close in July 2018[19]. The amended Model Law (the UNCITRAL Model Law on International Commercial Mediation and International Settlement Agreements Resulting from Mediation (2018)) was also adopted at the same session.

In December 2018, the United Nations General Assembly, by consensus, passed a resolution to adopt the United Nations Convention on International Settlement Agreements Resulting from Mediation, recommended that the Convention be known as the "Singapore Convention on Mediation", and authorised the signing ceremony of the Convention to be held in Singapore on 7 August 2019.

46 countries, including the world's two largest economies – the United States and China – as well as three of the four largest economies in Asia – China, India and South Korea – signed the Convention on the day it opened for signature. Another 24 countries attended the signing ceremony in Singapore to show their support for the Convention.

On 25 February 2020, Singapore and Fiji became the first two countries to deposit their respective instruments of ratification of the Convention at the United Nations Headquarters in New York. With the third instrument of ratification deposited by Qatar on 12 March 2020, the Convention entered into force on 12 September 2020.

As of March 2024, the Convention has 55 signatories, of which eight are parties to the Convention. The United Kingdom became a signatory on 3 May, 2023 but at the time of writing has not yet ratified.

So in the present legal landscape, whether on a small or large scale, and whether domestic or international, it is essential for all lawyers to have a good understanding of the mediation process, although the use of mediation is certainly not the sole prerogative of the legal profession, and, save for jurisdictions where mediation is heavily regulated, representatives in mediation may be surveyors, architects, engineers, accountants, company officers, trades union officials, human resources professionals, clinicians and other subject matter experts.

19 For this et seq see https://www.singaporeconvention.org/convention/about

What is Mediation?

There is no single definition of mediation agreed by either mediation service providers or mediation institutions. The Singapore Convention offers a very broad approach, which expressly includes conciliation:

> Mediation is a process for discussing and resolving disputes. It is a party-driven process whereby the mediator's role is not to adjudicate, but rather to facilitate discussions between disputing parties to arrive at a mutually acceptable solution. The nature of the process promotes the preservation of relationships between the parties. The mediation process is also flexible, confidential, and in many instances, more cost and time efficient than other dispute resolution processes such as litigation and arbitration. For States, the process can help relieve pressure on the state court system.

For our purposes let us start with the basics. Mediation is a voluntary, non-binding, and private dispute resolution process in which a neutral person helps the parties try to reach a negotiated settlement.[20]

Voluntary

In most cases mediation cannot take place unless the parties agree to enter the process, although this may only be after a strong judicial recommendation, with an associated risk of cost sanctions against a party who refuses to mediate, and the possibility of a procedural stay requiring the parties to at least try mediation.

Mediation is not possible without the participation of all parties, and will cease if one party walks out, which they are free to do at any time.

Non-binding

Mediation is also truly voluntary, as entering the process does not bind the parties to reaching settlement. Settlement can only come about on the authority of the parties concerned. As the mediator has no authority to make a binding determination, if the parties cannot agree, then there will be no settlement and the case will proceed to the next stage in the litigation process. However, if settlement is reached the agreed terms will form part of an enforceable contract. Mediation is merely a process which acts as a catalyst for settlement: many of those cases that do not settle at the mediation itself in fact settle shortly afterwards.

---

20 See Brown and Marriot, *ADR Principles and Practice*, 4th Edition, Sweet and Maxwell 2018.

Private

Although refusing to mediate can have adverse costs consequences, the mediation process is both "without prejudice" and confidential to the extent the law permits.[21] This means that parties can conduct themselves in the mediation, for example by disclosing information, expressing views, making suggestions or offering concessions, safe in the knowledge that this will not preclude them arguing a different position should the matter proceed to trial. Similarly, a party is free to refuse offers made in mediation, or even to walk out, without the risk of this being held against them if a court determines costs in the future.[22] That is the position even if an automatic referral to mediation becomes more normative, or if mediation is mandated by a judge in the exercise of a management discretion. You can take a horse to water, but you cannot make it drink.

The confidential nature of mediation negotiations stands in clear contrast to the courtroom, where the trial of the issues, including the conduct of the parties, is in public and potentially extremely embarrassing. Of course, should mediation break down a party is free to formalise an offer made during mediation as a CPR Part 36 offer which would carry the usual costs implications of that Part, or a *Calderbank* letter or open correspondence which would attract the court's discretion under CPR Part 44.4.

The terms of any settlement agreed in mediation are usually also confidential. However, this need not necessarily be so. In certain disputes one of the parties may be seeking some kind of public vindication (e.g. in a defamation case) or apology for past conduct and there is no reason why a public declaration cannot form part of a mediated settlement. For example, in the Alder Hey Hospital retained organs litigation while the core element of the claim was compensation, the settlement extended to the creation of a garden of remembrance, a public apology by all institutions involved, a public statement by the relevant government minister, and a plaque to be fixed on the wall outside the hospital.

Neutral mediator

The role of the mediator is key to the success of any mediation, and it is essential that the advocate knows how to select the best person for the job and work with him or her. The mediator must be a truly neutral person having no association with either of the parties nor any interest in the outcome. Mediation requires all parties to trust and give authority to the mediator.

21 See the discussion in Chapter 6.

22 See *Halsey* op.cit and *Burchell v Bullard* [2005] EWCA Civ 358.

Should any party withdraw that authority, the mediation will come to an end. Likewise, should trust in the mediator be broken for any reason, it is unlikely that a settlement will be reached.

The mediator's role is to assist the parties in their negotiations with each other and help the parties work towards a consensual resolution to the dispute. However, the parties themselves remain responsible for their own decisions and answerable for the terms of any settlement that may be agreed.

A settlement, negotiated by the parties

As highlighted above, a settlement is only possible in mediation with the consent of the parties, and it is they who are responsible for the terms of any agreement. While mediation certainly aims for a resolution that maximises all parties' interests (often called "win-win" outcomes), by its very nature it should never achieve an outcome with which one party cannot live. As the onus of arriving at the terms of settlement rests with the parties, the flexibility of the process allows for more ingenuity and extra-legal solutions than would ever be possible from a determination imposed by a court or other arbitral process. That is why the scope of the advocate's role is not confined to the part he or she would ordinarily play simply in the conduct of the legal case.

When Mediation might be Inappropriate

Since the courts are likely now to impose sanctions on a party who unreasonably fails to mediate, this begs the question when is it reasonable to refuse mediation, or in which cases is mediation inappropriate? After *Churchill*, it can be said that much the same reasoning will apply to applications for mediation to be mandated, or such applications resisted.

This issue was first considered in detail in *Halsey v Milton Keynes General NHS Trust*[23] where the Court of Appeal was more sympathetic to parties who refuse to mediate than Lightman J had been in the earlier case of *Hurst v Leeming.*[24] In that case, Lightman J suggested that to escape a sanction for refusal, the refusing party would have to show that mediation would have no reasonable prospect of success. In *Halsey* the Court of Appeal took a more subtle approach: the starting point is that to deprive a successful party of all or part of their costs, (or, presumably, to impose a sanction on an unsuccessful party) the other side must show he has behaved unreasonably in failing to mediate.

23 [2004] EWCA Civ 576 [2004] 1 WLR 3002

24 [2003] 1 Lloyd's Rep 37

Dyson LJ, as he then was, considered[25] that a number of factors should be taken into consideration when assessing whether a party behaved unreasonably, and these included:

- The nature of the dispute;
- The merits of the case;
- The extent to which other settlement methods have been attempted;
- Whether the costs of the mediation would be disproportionately high;
- Whether any delay in setting up and attending the mediation would have been prejudicial; and
- Whether the mediation had a reasonable prospect of success.

Dyson LJ acknowledged that a small number of cases are intrinsically unsuitable for mediation, and gave a number of examples of these:[26]

> (1) Where the parties wish the court to determine issues of law or construction which may be essential to the future trading relations of the parties, as under an on-going long term contract, or where the issues are generally important for those participating in a particular trade or market.
>
> (2) Similarly, where a party wants the court to resolve a point of law that arises from time to time, and one or more parties consider that a binding precedent would be useful.
>
> (3) Cases involving allegations of fraud or other disreputable conduct against an individual or group, which are unlikely to be successfully mediated because confidence is lacking in the future conduct of that party.
>
> (4) Cases where injunctive or other relief is essential to protect the position of a party.

The judge went on to consider that where a party actually does have a watertight case, a refusal to mediate can be reasonable, pointing out that otherwise there would be scope for claimants with a weak case to use the threat of a costs sanction to force a party into a mediated settlement even where the claim or defence is without merit. However, the party's belief that his case is watertight must be reasonable.

The Court of Appeal held that the costs of mediation can be a factor of particular importance where the sums at stake in the litigation are small. This is because a mediation can sometimes be as expensive as a day in court, as the parties will often have legal representation and the mediator's fees and

25 at [17]-[24]

26 at [18]

other disbursements are usually to be borne equally by the parties regardless of the outcome. In addition, the possibility of the ultimately successful party being required to incur the costs of an abortive mediation is a relevant factor that a court may take into account in deciding whether the successful party acted unreasonably in refusing to agree to ADR.

This is an important consideration bearing in mind the increasing trend for courts to promote automatic referral to mediation in small claims, and the exercise in future of the power to stay and order mediation. Remember, mediation is not a panacea. *For a legally represented client, a small claims mediation is likely to cost at least the same as the hearing itself, but with no guarantee of an outcome at the end of it.* An unsuccessful mediation in a small claim will effectively double a legally represented client's costs, whether or not this client is eventually successful, due to the "no costs" rule of the small claims track.

When considering whether mediation stood any reasonable prospect of success, the Court of Appeal in *Halsey*, in contrast to *Hurst v Leeming*, held that the burden was on the party seeking to prove the other side had behaved unreasonably to show that mediation would have had a reasonable prospect of success. By and large judges are still unwilling to deprive a successful party of its costs.

Halsey spawned considerable debate among practitioners, and for many it was merely a matter of time before its principal point of contention was reviewed. In the nearly two decades that followed the courts have heard argument about reducing the scope of what may amount to a reasonable refusal to mediate[27].

In *Nigel Witham Ltd v Smith,*[28] HH Judge Coulson QC (afterwards Mr Justice Coulson) was asked to reduce the successful party's costs on the basis of the novel proposition that, although there had been a mediation, it had taken place too late in the dispute with the result that considerable costs had been wasted. The judge decided (at paragraph 36) that the principles in *Halsey* might, in an exceptional case, be applicable so that there might be an adverse costs order if there was a very late mediation and its chances of success were very poor and if it could be shown that the successful party unreasonably delayed in consenting to the mediation.

27 I am very grateful to Colin Manning and to Michel Kallipetis KC, as both past Chairman of the Bar ADR Panel, for permission to draw respectively on notes prepared for the July, 2015 Bar ADRP Mediation Training Day, and the SCMA Mediation Matters Day in March, 2014 in this and the subsequent pages.

28 [2008] EWHC 12 (TCC)

However, the judge decided that the contention failed on the facts because there was nothing to demonstrate that the defendants unreasonably delayed in consenting to the mediation. Also, he concluded that, even if there had been an earlier mediation, the claimant's uncompromising attitude meant that it would not have had a reasonable prospect of success.

The judge made the following general remarks about premature mediations (at paragraph [32]):

> "It is a common difficulty in cases of this sort, trying to work out when the best time might be to attempt ADR or mediation. Mediation is often suggested by the claiming party at an early stage. But the responding party, who is likely to be the party writing the cheque, will often want proper information relating to the claim in order to be able to assess the commercial risk that the claim represents before embarking on a sensible mediation. A premature mediation simply wastes time and can sometimes lead to a hardening of the positions on both sides which makes any subsequent attempt of settlement doomed to fail. Conversely, a delay in any mediation until after full particulars and documents have been exchanged can mean that the costs which have been incurred to get to that point themselves become the principal obstacle to a successful mediation. The trick in many cases is to identify the happy medium: the point when the detail of the claim and the response are known to both sides, but before the costs that have been incurred in reaching that stage are so great that a settlement is no longer possible."

The judge found the documents in that case made plain that, at the very start of the dispute, the claimant had adopted an extremely uncompromising attitude to the defendants in his claim against them. The claimant's pre-action correspondence was littered with references to his intention to pursue an entitlement to every penny of the claim. Compromise and reconciliation did not feature prominently. As a result, in accordance with one of the key principles in *Halsey*, the judge concluded that an early mediation had little or no chance of success.

In fact cases applying or arguing *Halsey* in the first few years after it was decided were rather rare, perhaps either because parties were encouraged to mediate where mediation had a reasonable prospect of success or because, where a party had lost at trial, its advisers may consider that it would afterwards be difficult to persuade the judge that mediation had had a reasonable prospect of success. However, since 2011, there have been a number of cases in the Court of Appeal where judges were called upon to apply *Halsey*, with different outcomes and which on their face do not necessarily clarify the likely approach of the courts to a refusal to mediate. One of the factors affecting the exercise of the court's discretion can be the class and nature of the claim.

In *Rolf v De Guerin* [29] a building dispute for damages in the sum of £90,000 had resulted in an award of only £2,500, and an award of costs in the defendant's favour. On appeal, the Court of Appeal decided to exercise its own discretion on costs and, applying *Halsey*, concluded that offers to mediate early in the proceedings had been unreasonably rejected and that the reasons given by the defendant, including wanting to have his "day in court" "do not seem to hold water", even if he had been proven correct. It described such disputes as this as "wasteful and destructive" and referred to the observations of the same court in *Burchall v Bullard* [30] that "a small building dispute is par excellence the kind of dispute which lends itself to ADR". Although the claim was particularised at £90,000, the claimant had made a Part 36 offer of £14,000 and offered to mediate or have a round table meeting to discuss settlement. These offers were refused. The defendant did subsequently agree to mediate, but subject to a maximum sum he would pay.

The trial judge had decided that up to the Part 36 offer there should be no order as to costs, but ordered the claimant to pay the defendant's costs thereafter. The Court of Appeal held that the judge had been wrong to take account of the Part 36 offer and decided there should be no order as to costs. It held the proposed mediation or negotiation would have had a reasonable prospect of success and the defendant had been unreasonable in refusing to mediate, and that "ought to bear materially on the outcome of the court's discretion, particularly in this class of case."

As to the argument that the defendant could refuse to mediate because he wanted his "day in court", Lord Justice Rix commented:

> "As for wanting his day in court, that of course is a reason why the courts have been unwilling to compel parties to mediate rather than litigate, but does not seem to me to me to be an adequate response to a proper judicial concern that parties should respond reasonably to offer to mediate or settle and that their conduct in this respect can be taken into account in awarding costs".

The defendant could not have known what might have been the claimant's bottom line unless and until he "entered into the spirit of a settlement or mediation".

Faidi, Hameed and Faidi, Inam v Elliot Corporation [31] was a dispute between neighbours in a block of flats in London SW1 about vertical noise transmission through floors. The lease required carpets to be laid. The upstairs flat had

29 [2011] EWCA Civ 78
30 [2005] BLR 330
31 *Op.cit*

had timber floors installed (under a licence for alterations) rather than carpet, but with what were said to be appropriate noise insulation arrangements that produced better soundproofing than carpet. The case occupied two days at first instance and then came to the Court of Appeal. It was found that the licence for alterations was a waiver of the requirement to lay carpets, so carpets did not have to be laid. All three Court of Appeal Lord Justices expressed the view that mediation would have been a better route here. In particular Lord Justice Jackson said

> "In the present case a mediator would not have been concerned about the interaction between the various leases and the licence to carry out works. Nor would he have been concerned about the other interesting points of construction, which first the county court judge and now this court have been called upon to decide. Instead he would have been helping the parties to find a sensible resolution of the practical problem which had arisen. I have little doubt that such a mediation would have been successful. The points of law upon which the litigation has turned are not easy ones and at the time of the hypothetical mediation neither party could have been confident of victory.

Lord Justice Ward said:

> "I wish enthusiastically to associate myself with the observations of my Lords on the desirability of mediation in neighbourhood disputes. To repeat what I recently said in *Oliver v Symons*[32], a boundary dispute:
>
> > "I wish particularly to associate myself with Elias L.J.'s pointing out that this is a case crying out for mediation. All disputes between neighbours arouse deep passions and entrenched positions are taken as the parties stand upon their rights seemingly blissfully unaware or unconcerned that they are committing themselves to unremitting litigation which will leave them bruised by the experience and very much the poorer, win or lose. It depresses me that solicitors cannot at the very first interview persuade their clients to put their faith in the hands of an experienced mediator, a dispassionate third party, to guide them to a fair and sensible compromise of an unseemly battle which will otherwise blight their lives for months and months to come."
>
> Not all neighbours are from hell. They may simply occupy the land of bigotry. There may be no escape from hell but the boundaries of bigotry can with tact be changed by the cutting edge of reasonableness skilfully applied by a trained mediator. Give and take is often better than all or nothing."

As has been said above, the high point of the decisions favouring the approach of *Halsey* in the Court of Appeal came with *PGF II SA v (1) OMFS Company*

32 [2012] EWCA Civ 267

and (2) Bank of Scotland PLC [33] in which the first instance judge applied *Halsey* in favour of the losing party's costs.

In that case the claimant landlord claimed dilapidations from the defendant tenant. On 9 January 2012, the day before trial, the claimant accepted the defendant's Part 36 offer of £700,000 made on 11 April 2011. This ended the proceedings except for the question of costs. The defendant accepted that the claimant should be paid its costs for the period up to 2 May 2011 – 21 days after the Part 36 offer. The only issue that the judge had to decide was the costs order to make for the period from 3 May 2011 to 10th January 2012 ("the relevant period").

The claimant argued that it should have its costs for this period alternatively that it should not have to pay the defendant's costs. One of the reasons relied on was that the defendant had unreasonably refused to mediate. It was accepted that the claimant was the losing party and that it had the burden of proving the defendant's unreasonableness.

By way of general comment, the judge stated that the court should be wary of arguments only raised by the successful party in retrospect as why that party refused to mediate or as to why it cannot be demonstrated that a mediation would have had a reasonable prospect of success. Such assertions are easy to put forward and difficult to prove or disprove. Also, it is clear that the courts wish to encourage mediation and whilst there may be legitimate difficulties in mediating or successfully mediating these can only be overcome if those difficulties are addressed at the time. The judge added (at paragraph [44]):

> "It would seem to me consistent with the policy which encourages mediation by depriving a successful party of its costs in appropriate circumstances that it should also deprive such a party of costs where there are real obstacles to mediation which might reasonably be overcome but are not addressed because that party does not raise them at the time".

The judge decided that the defendant had unreasonably refused to mediate and made the following points:

(i) Although the burden was on the claimant to establish that the defendant had acted unreasonably, this was not an unduly onerous burden as all that had to be shown was that the mediation had a reasonable prospect of success and not that it would have been successful.

33 [2013] EWCA Civ 1288 reported at first instance at [2012] EWHC 83 (TCC) per Mr Recorder Stephen Furst QC sitting as a Deputy High Court Judge.

(ii) There was a reasonable prospect of success because these were well advised commercial parties who, with the benefit of experienced lawyers, would have been able to reach an accommodation.

(iii) It was reasonable to infer that the defendant was refusing to mediate in view of its failure to respond to the suggested mediation. There was nothing to suggest that the claimant was merely going through the motions and would not have engaged in a mediation had the defendant responded positively.

(iv) The date at which the court should consider the impact on costs of the refusal to mediate was the date of the refusal not the date when the hypothetical mediation would have taken place.

This was a robust judgment and a clear warning to those parties who choose not to mediate. Not surprisingly the decision was appealed (in fact by both the claimant and the defendant OMFS).

The backdrop to the appeal was Jackson LJ's Review of Civil Litigation Costs – Final Report, the *Jackson ADR Handbook* published in response to Jackson LJ's invitation as set out in that Report, and the latest amendments to the Civil Procedure Rules, with its emphasis on proportionality. This decision, being from a strong Court of Appeal, and following the Jackson review is worthy of quite detailed consideration.

Briggs LJ, who gave the judgment in the Court of Appeal, said, at paragraph [1]:

> "This appeal raises, for the first time, as a matter of principle, the following question: what should be the response of the court to a party which, when invited by its opponent to take part in a process of alternative dispute resolution ("ADR"), simply declines to respond to the invitation in any way?"

In *Halsey* itself and in subsequent cases, the argument in support of an adverse award of costs had arisen in circumstances where a party had expressly communicated its refusal to the other party. The Court of Appeal, at paragraph [22], went on to summarise the principles established by *Halsey*, which were not disputed on the appeal.

The justification for any extension to the *Halsey* principles fell to be considered against factors identified in the Court of Appeal, namely:

(i) The perceived levels of success of mediation in resolving disputes;

(ii) The focus in Jackson upon achieving proportionality between the cost of litigation and the value of that which is at stake, and his endorsement of ADR as a dispute resolution process which is "still insufficiently understood and under-used";

(iii) The constraints affecting the provision of state resources for the conduct of civil litigation and the need to ensure that court time and resources is proportionately directed only to those disputes that need it, and the need for parties to behave responsibly and to engage in ADR wherever that process offers a reasonable prospect of securing a just settlement at proportionate cost. In this context: "it is a waste of its resources to have to manage the parties towards ADR by robust encouragement, where they could and should have engaged with each other in considering its suitability, without the need for the court's active intervention".

The *Jackson ADR Handbook* was published in 2013[34], after the decision of Mr. Recorder Furst QC but before the case went to the Court of Appeal. In Chapter 11 at paragraph 11.56 of the Handbook the editors offered advice as to the practical steps that a party should take to avoid sanction by the court, including the following:

(1) Do not ignore an offer to engage in ADR. Failure to respond is likely to be treated as an outright refusal.

(2) Respond promptly, in writing, giving clear and full reasons why ADR is not appropriate at this stage of the dispute or proceedings. The reasons given, where possible, should be justified in the light of the relevant principles derived from Halsey and subsequent cases ...

(3) If lack of evidence or information is an obstacle to a successful ADR process being undertaken at that time, this must be canvassed with the other party to the dispute in the correspondence, and consideration should be given to whether that evidence or information can be obtained during the ADR process or in advance of the process...

(4) Letters replying to requests to engage in ADR should be written with care. A party may have a good reason to refuse ADR at that point in time, but the correspondence should not be written in such a way that closes off exploration of ADR processes at a later date. An outright refusal to use ADR at any time is more likely to be construed as unreasonable.

34 Now in its 3rd edition 2022

In his judgment (paragraphs [34] to [37]), Briggs LJ (with whom both Maurice Kay and McFarlane LJJ concurred) stated that:

> " ... the time has now come for this court firmly to endorse the advice given in Chapter 11.56 of the ADR Handbook, that silence in the face of an invitation to participate in ADR is, as a general rule, of itself unreasonable, regardless whether an outright refusal, or a refusal to engage in the type of ADR requested, or to do so at the time requested, might have been justified by the identification of reasonable grounds..."

In so saying, he accepted that this was a general and not invariable rule, as there could be "rare" cases where it was obvious that ADR was so plainly inappropriate that it would be wrong to characterise silence as unreasonable. Nevertheless, even in such cases, the burden would be on the recipient of the invitation to make good any such justification. Briggs LJ continued:

> "There are in my view sound practical and policy reasons for this modest extension to the principles and guidelines set out in the *Halsey* case, which concerned reasoned refusals, provided in prompt response to the request to participate in ADR. The first is that an investigation of alleged reasons for refusal advanced for the first time, possibly months or even years later, at the costs hearing, where none were given at the time of the invitation, poses forensic difficulties for the court and the inviting party including, in particular, the question whether the belatedly advanced reasons are genuine at all. The manner in which this issue was debated both before the judge and on this appeal is illustrative of those difficulties."
>
> "Secondly, a failure to provide reasons for a refusal is destructive of the real objective of the encouragement to parties to consider and discuss ADR, in short to engage with the ADR process. There are many types of reasonable objection to a particular ADR proposal which, once raised, may be capable of being addressed."

Any difficulties could and should be discussed between the parties so as to resolve or narrow the issues between them, as happens routinely in the course of litigation generally, for example with expert evidence. This should apply to ADR with the advantage of saving valuable court time in case management and addresses the policy of proportionality, and to save the time and resources of both the parties and the court.

The court concluded that, on the face of the correspondence between the parties, the defendant's silence in the face of two requests to mediate was itself unreasonable conduct of litigation sufficient to warrant a costs sanction. There was no need to engage in a point by point analysis of the *Halsey* guidelines. The defendant's silence amounted to a deemed refusal to mediate. The judge at first instance had determined that the refusal had been unreasonable and the Court of Appeal agreed following the reasoning of Mr. Recorder Furst QC at paragraphs [42] to [46] of his judgment.

The only reservation expressed by Briggs LJ was that he found it surprising that the claimant had made no complaint at the time to the failure by the defendant to respond to its invitation in circumstances where such failure was plainly a refusal.

The order made by the trial judge had been to deprive the defendant of all its costs entitlement between the relevant dates. This was challenged by the defendant as being mechanistic and not approached by weighing all other factors in the balance, including that of the claimant's responsibility for failing to accept the defendant's offer until the eve of the trial. Briggs LJ said that a finding of unreasonable conduct by a refusal to accept an invitation to engage in a discussion about ADR did not produce an automatic result in terms of costs penalty. It was simply an aspect of the parties' conduct which needed to be addressed in the context of the wider balancing exercise. The judge has a wide discretion and the proper order in any case can range between disallowing the whole or only a modest part of the otherwise successful party's entitlement to costs.

Briggs LJ was of the view that had the matter been for him he would not have ordered that the defendant should be deprived of all of its costs for the relevant period, but only some proportion of them. As the discretion was that of the judge, and a broad discretion at that, the court did not interfere with the order that the defendant be deprived of the whole of its costs, which was within the range of proper responses to the "seriously unreasonable" conduct identified by the judge.

Although, in principle, a court could order an otherwise successful party to pay all or part of the unsuccessful party's costs, such a draconian sanction should be reserved for only the most serious and flagrant failures to engage in ADR, as for example, where the court had taken it upon itself to encourage the parties to do so, and which encouragement had been ignored.

The courts have been called upon to deal with a variety of cases where adverse orders as to costs have been sought[35]. Often, and, inevitably, they are fact specific. In the case of *Swain Mason & ors v. Mills & Reeve (a Firm)*,[36] decided before the appeal in *PGF*, the Court of Appeal overturned the decision of the judge at first instance on costs, when he found that the successful defendant firm (M) had acted unreasonably in refusing to mediate the claim. He had ordered the claimants (C) to pay only 50% of M's costs of the proceedings, partly because of M's refusal to mediate. The Court of Appeal stated that,

35 See the discussion at Chapter 7.
36 [2012] EWCA Civ 498

where a party reasonably believed that he had a watertight case, that might well be a sufficient justification for a refusal to mediate, even when on some issues the defence did not succeed. The Court of Appeal held that it had not been shown by C that M had acted unreasonably in refusing to agree to mediation and ordered C to pay 60% of M's costs.

At various stages during the course of the litigation, C had proposed mediation or some other form of ADR. The Judge, at interlocutory hearings had also suggested that the parties should consider mediation. At all times, however, M had refused to mediate on the basis that the claim was entirely without merit. It had, however, offered a "walk away", and to negotiate over its own costs if the proceedings were withdrawn (in response to a Part 36 offer). Thus far, but no further, was M prepared to move.

The Court of Appeal referred to *Halsey* where it had been made clear that parties were not compelled to mediate. In particular it had been stated that where a party reasonably believed that it had a watertight case, that might well be a sufficient reason to refuse to mediate. As had been stated, if that were not the case, then there is the real risk for a party to threaten costs sanctions to extract a settlement of an unmeritorious claim.

In *Swain,* it was said that: "the fundamental question remains as to whether it has been shown by the unsuccessful party that the successful party had acted unreasonably in refusing to agree to a mediation". Lord Justice Davis, who made that comment concluded that that had not been shown in the instant case.

One matter relied upon at first instance was that if mediation had been attempted and was successful, the risk of collateral reputational damage would be avoided, Davis LJ took a contrary view:

> "A settled professional negligence claim is capable, in some instances, of leaving behind reputational damage. Some professional defendants may, entirely reasonably, wish to publicly vindicate themselves at trial in respect of claims which will have been publicly aired by the commencement of proceedings. It is a matter for them. It would be unfortunate – speaking generally – if claimants in cases of this kind could be encouraged to think that such a consideration as identified by the judge could enhance their bargaining position."

The Court also did not agree that it was correct to describe M's refusal to mediate as "intransigent". Nothing had changed in the course of this case "(unlike many cases) to necessitate a re-evaluation on the question of liability. A reasonable refusal to mediate does not become unreasonable simply by being steadfastly, and for cause, maintained."

It is clear from *Swain* that the Court of Appeal emphasised the particular circumstances of that case, namely the justifiably certain belief that the claim had no merit and M's desire to be vindicated at trial on the issue of liability, and for professional reputational reasons for this to occur.

There is anecdotal evidence that this case has been used by solicitors acting for defendants, particularly in professional negligence litigation, to support a refusal to mediate, when they believed that their clients had a strong case on the merits. It is argued that the decision indicates that on certain facts-specific occasions the Court of Appeal can be more sympathetic on costs to a party who refuses to mediate.

If litigators consider that the Court of Appeal in *Swain* has shifted its ground, and given fresh encouragement to parties who refuse to mediate, they are wrong. In reality, the Court of Appeal was doing no more and no less than following the guidance in *Halsey* where it was stated:

> "[18] ...The fact that a party unreasonably believes that his case is watertight is no justification for refusing mediation. But the fact that a party reasonably believes that he has a watertight case may well be sufficient justification for a refusal to mediate."

In *Phillip Garritt-Critchley & Ors v Andrew Ronan and Solarpower PV Ltd*,[37] His Honour Judge Waksman QC, sitting as a judge of the High Court, ordered indemnity costs as a sanction for a refusal to mediate. In that case, the defendants made plain that they were not prepared to engage in any settlement activity, as "the parties are too far apart at this stage". When challenged for reasons, they said they considered that there was no reasonable prospect that the claimant would succeed and, therefore, the defendants' rejection of mediation was entirely reasonable. The claimant persisted throughout the litigation process with the same response from the claimant, effectively stating their "extreme confidence" in the outcome.

Briefly, the issues in the case were whether or not a binding agreement had been made, and, if so, a quantum issue on any compensatory award – essentially questions of fact. The judge endorsed the comment of Mr Justice Lightman in *Hurst v Leeming* that "The fact that a party believes that he has a watertight case again is no justification for refusing mediation. That is the frame of mind of so many litigants."

In respect of the argument that the parties were too far apart, the judge commented that: "Parties don't know whether in truth they are too far apart unless they sit down and explore settlement. If they are too far apart, then

37 [2014] EWHC 1774

the mediator will say as much within the first hour of mediation. That happens rarely in my experience." The defendants sought to rely on a number of *Halsey* grounds to resist the claimant's application, all of which were dismissed by the judge. One of these grounds was that the costs of the mediation were disproportionately high against a final offer to settle the claim for £10,000. The cost of a day's mediation might cost as much as the offer. The judge rejected this argument saying that the correct comparison should be to the costs of a trial, not the offer.

There will be few cases where parties can be certain of the outcome, possibly on liability or, more likely, on quantum. The Courts, and indeed the CPR, still robustly encourage the parties to engage in mediation during the course of the litigation process, or, where appropriate, before proceedings are commenced, with possible costs sanctions if they unreasonably refuse. As Sir Anthony Clarke said, when he was Master of the Rolls, the parties must assist the court in furthering the over-riding objective by taking proper part in the mediation process.

Judge Waksman QC also made reference, among others, to a dictum of a further Court of Appeal case in which Lord Justice Ward (one of the judges in *Halsey*) stressed the value of mediation in the following terms:

> "The opening bids in a mediation are likely to remain as belligerently far apart as they were in correspondence, but no-one should underestimate the new dynamic that an experienced mediator brings to the round table. He has a canny knack of transforming the intractable into the possible. That is the art of good mediation, and that is why mediation should not be spurned when it is offered[38]".

Judge Waksman QC concluded by reference to *PDF*

> "This decision of the Court of Appeal is of obvious importance to all practitioners. If a party should decide not to mediate, it must be clear and state in writing precisely why this is the case. In particular, any response should explain why, if so, it is considered that a mediation would not have any reasonable prospect of success. Serious thought should be given to the factors, such as inadequate disclosure, or the need for experts' reports or any other further information which might alter that party's view so as to give any mediation a reasonable hope of succeeding, and keep an open mind as to the possibility of mediating at an appropriate time. On no account should an invitation to mediate be ignored, for that is likely to be held to be a refusal to mediate and the chances of justifying that refusal at a later date are likely to be slim indeed."

Whilst the thrust of the principles in *Halsey* was not challenged in general in the *PGF* case, it should not be thought that this represents the end of the on-going debate about the applicability of all those principles, not least the extent to

38 *Gaith v Indesit Company UK Ltd* [2012] EWCA Civ 642

which the courts should "robustly" encourage mediation. Subsequently Ward LJ, in *Colin Wright v Michael Wright Supplies Ltd v Turner Wright Investments Ltd,*[39] suggested that perhaps it may be time to review what he described as the "rule" in *Halsey* for which he accepted he was partly responsible, where at paragraph [9] of the judgment of Dyson LJ said:

> "It seems to us that to oblige truly unwilling parties to refer their disputes to mediation would be to impose an unacceptable obstruction on their right of access to the court."

At paragraph [3] of his judgment, Ward LJ questioned whether this part of the judgment was obiter, as some have argued, and whether CPR 26.4(2)(b) allows the court of its own initiative:

> "at any time, to direct a stay for mediation to be attempted, with the warning of the costs consequences, which *Halsey* did spell out and which should be rigorously applied, for unreasonably refusing to agree to ADR? Is a stay really "an unacceptable obstruction" to the parties' right of access to the court if they have to wait a while before being allowed across the court's threshold? Perhaps some bold judge will accede to an invitation to rule on these questions so that the court can have another look at *Halsey* in the light of the past 10 years of developments in this field."

In the context of the extension of the courts' powers of case and costs management, with the emphasis on the need for proportionality in the conduct of litigation, *PGF* may be only a first step, not only to extend the principles in *Halsey*, but for the courts to be much more pro-active in its encouragement of mediation, if not to the point of compulsion, at least by making referrals to mediation automatic in all courts. Parties would still be able to refuse to mediate, albeit subject to the risk of being made subject to an adverse order as to costs.[40]

The reasons for refusing mediation must be cogent and compelling. In *DSN v Blackpool Football Club Ltd.*[41] Griffiths J was unimpressed by the defendant and awarded indemnity costs against it:

> "The reasons given for refusing to engage in mediation were inadequate. They were, simply, and repeatedly, that the Defendant "continues to believe that it has a strong defence". No defence, however strong, by itself justifies a failure to engage in any kind of alternative dispute resolution. Experience has shown that disputes may often be resolved in a way satisfactory to all parties, including parties who find themselves able to resolve claims against them which they consider not to be well founded. Settlement allows solutions which are potentially limitless in their ingenuity and flexibility, and they do not necessarily require any admission of liability, or even a payment of money. Even if they do

39 [2013] EWCA Civ 234

40 See also Chapter 7 and *Laporte v Commissioner of Police for the Metropolis* [2015] EWHC 371(QB) (19 February 2015)

41 [2020] EWHC 670 (QB) at [28]

> involve payment of money, the amount may compare favourably (if the settlement is timely) with the irrecoverable costs, in money terms alone, of an action that has been successfully fought. The costs of an action will not always be limited to financial costs, however. A trial is likely to require a significant expenditure of time, including management time, and may take a heavy toll on witnesses even for successful parties which a settlement could spare them. As to admission of liability, a settlement can include admissions or statements which fall short of accepting legal liability, which may still be of value to the party bringing a claim."

In *Stoney-Andersen v Abbas & Ors*[42] HH Judge Paul Matthews (sitting as a High Court judge in the Bristol District Registry), in depriving an executor of indemnity costs from the estate, considered the repercussions that might follow from refusing mediation in inheritance disputes. The case arose from a relatively modest estate, valued at £491,154, where family disagreements over inheritance led to legal proceedings. The claimant's solicitors initially proposed mediation in March, 2021. Despite subsequent acceptance by the first defendant, the claimant withdrew the offer in August 2021, citing clear liability. The court highlighted the importance of considering mediation and ADR in such cases, referring to the claimant's initial willingness to engage in alternative dispute resolution. The court ruled in favour of the claimant as the "successful party" but while awarding costs on the standard basis, also expressed disapproval of the claimant's initial refusal to mediate, and denied an indemnity from the estate for those costs of issues lost by the defendants.

The judge said at [56]

> "I am satisfied that the first and second defendants were right to pursue the possibility of mediation, and that the claimant was wrong, no matter how much she was being told that she would be likely to win, to ignore it. It is a commonplace that both sides are told by their lawyers that they will win. But they cannot both be right. Indeed, sometimes, both sides are wrong. The combination of litigation risk and irrecoverable costs almost always makes it worthwhile considering mediation and other ADR. On the (admittedly limited) material before me, the claimant did not give enough thought to this. In accordance with the case law, I consider it appropriate to mark the court's disapproval of the claimant's failure to take up the mediation/ADR suggestions of the first and second defendants..."

I now turn to consider *Churchill v Merthyr Tydfil CBC*[43] which many commentators are already seeing as the most significant development in the juridification of mediation for two decades. This arises from the fact that a particularly strong Court of Appeal comprising Baroness Carr LCJ, Sir Geoffrey Vos MR and Birss LJ invited the participation of intervention from The Law Society, The Bar Council of England and Wales, The Civil Mediation Council, The Centre for Effective Dispute Resolution, The Chartered Institute

42 [2023] EWHC 2964 (Ch) on November 24, 2023

43 [2023] EWCA Civ 1416

of Arbitrators, the Housing Law Practitioners' Association and the Social Housing Law Association.

In addition to scrutinising the first instance tribunal's decision concerning whether or not to stay proceedings in order to require the appellant to undertake the local authority's complaints process prior to bringing his claim, there were three issues of policy before the Court with which it was concerned:

(1) Was the judge right to think that *Halsey* bound him to dismiss the Council's application? This involves a consideration of whether the passages in *Halsey* relied upon by the judge were part of the main reasoning of that decision.

(2) If not, can the court lawfully stay proceedings for, or order, the parties to engage in a non-court-based dispute resolution process?

(3) If so, how should the court decide whether to stay the proceedings for, or order, the parties to engage in a non-court-based dispute resolution process? This involves a consideration of the relevance of the kind of non-court-based dispute resolution process being considered.

The first question was really concerned with whether or not the Court could mandate mediation. It concluded that any observations to the contrary made in *Halsey* were *obiter dicta* and not binding. This opens the way for mandatory mediation in circumstances where a court considers in appropriate to lawfully stay proceedings, or order the parties to engage in a non-court-based dispute resolution process, subject to the proviso that the order made: (a) did not impair the very essence of the claimant's right to a fair trial, (b) was made in pursuit of a legitimate aim, and (c) was proportionate to achieving that legitimate aim of settling the dispute fairly, quickly and at reasonable cost.[44]

In response to submissions made by the interveners which mirrored the *Halsey* factors to be taken account of in determining whether it was reasonable to refuse to mediate, the Master of the Rolls, delivering the judgment of the Court, said at [66]

> "I do not believe that the court can or should lay down fixed principles as to what will be relevant to determining those questions. The matters mentioned by the Bar Council and Mr Churchill, and by the Court of Appeal in *Halsey* are likely to have some relevance. But other factors too may be relevant depending on all the circumstances. It would be undesirable to provide a checklist or a score sheet for judges to operate. They will be well qualified to decide whether a particular process is or is not likely or appropriate for the purpose of achieving the important objective of

44 At [23,24,58 and 65]

> bringing about a fair, speedy and cost-effective solution to the dispute and the proceedings, in accordance with the overriding objective."

Thus *Churchill* paves the way for more fact-based decisions on the appropriateness in any particular case on the imposing of a stay, the making of adverse cost sanctions or the express mandating of mediation. The power of the Court to do so is no longer in doubt.

The Benefits of Mediation

Facts and figures for the effectiveness of mediation are limited since by and large the outcome remains confidential, and in some cases the existence of both dispute and mediation is also confidential – one of its benefits. Anecdotal evidence from those involved in mediation suggests that a very high proportion of mediated cases do settle at the mediation appointment, with a further considerable proportion settling soon afterwards. For example, the Centre for Effective Dispute Resolution ("CEDR") reports on its website that over 70% of cases referred to it settle. The mediation industry often – again anecdotally – claims up to an 85% success rate.

In addition to its success rate, whatever that may actually be, and the scope for potential cost savings, mediation has other benefits of which you should be aware when called upon to explain these to your client. Such benefits can best be seen merely by comparing traditional litigation with ADR in general, and mediation in particular.

Litigation is formal. It imposes a binding solution where inevitably one party or the other is likely to be dissatisfied with the outcome, often highly dissatisfied. The expense and costs regime may make even the winner dissatisfied. It removes control of the dispute from parties, first by vesting it in the lawyers and then in the court's administration and management system. It addresses issues in a purely legal context, in the public eye, with fixed pre-determined remedies that you either obtain or fail to obtain. It is slow, expensive, and destroys relationships.

By contrast ADR/mediation is an informal (even if structured), and very flexible procedure with no imposed solutions – particularly suited to imaginative problem solvers. It gives better and more supple results because control remains directly in the hands of the parties as decision makers. Win or lose, it is comparatively quick and can still be relatively cheap as a self-contained process. It saves management time. It is private and confidential. And as a dynamic it actively promotes renewal and reconciliation because it is designed to restore relationships. Litigation looks to find fault and attribute blame. Mediation does not. This makes mediation a particularly attractive route where parties are likely to continue to have dealings and to interact in the future, whether in business, as neighbours or within the confines of some close personal relationship or physical proximity.

In *Halsey* Dyson LJ also took the opportunity to promote the advantages of mediation

> "We recognise that mediation has a number of advantages over the court process. It is usually less expensive than litigation which goes all the way to judgment .... Mediation provides litigants with a wider range of solutions than those that are available in litigation: for example, an apology; an explanation; the continuation of an existing professional or business relationship perhaps on new terms; and an agreement by one party to do something without any existing legal obligation to do so.[45]"

ADR, and in particular mediation, is here to stay. All litigators must have a basic understanding of its principles and practice to be able to act in an advisory role. As advisers, litigators must be able to identify cases, both pre- and mid-proceedings, for which mediation is appropriate, and to explain the mediation process to clients and other legal professionals. As advocates, they must be able to prepare cases for mediation in a manner that best represents the client's interests, and to engage in strategies that will ensure their clients' cases are presented as effectively as possible. The adversarial approach in mediation is very different to that used in litigation. It calls for a much more collaborative approach since in order to be successful both parties must be satisfied with the outcome, and not just your own client. You must not kick against it simply because it goes against the orthodoxy of your training but learn to recognise the value of the mediation process as a legitimate and routine method of case management and disposal and look for the value in having a satisfied client.

45 *op.cit.* @[15]

Part 1

The Role of the Advocate in Mediation

Chapter 1
The Role of the Advocate in Mediation

Meeting the Demands of a Modern Law Market

Over the past 25 years the growth of mediation in England and Wales, as elsewhere, has been encouraged by the courts and broadly by the insurance industry, recognised by commerce, gained acceptance by forward-minded practitioners, and has become a trusted alternative to litigation by those users who have come to learn of its existence and its sophistication. Progress remains slow and incremental. But set against the aggressive reduction by governments of public funding for civil justice, the enormous rise in court fees for litigants, the huge expense of bringing claims to trial, significant timetabling delays caused by the pandemic and in EU cross-border enforcement by Brexit, and the uncertainty of recovering costs after the UK's Woolf and Jackson Reforms, those in dispute resolution practice can reasonably expect significant increases in mediation business, and in awareness of mediation by the public. The long-awaited rise in market demand for mediation as a product should, by any logical measure, be upon us, with the Courts and MoJ signalling mandated mediation and automatic referral after *Churchill.*[1]

The Development of Mediation in England and Wales

What was originally intended as a flexible, procedure-free (and, to an extent, lawyer-free), unregulated dispute processing method, has been the subject of increasing juridification (or 'law creep') over the last twenty years as state endorsement or sponsorship of mediation has increased. The courts have busied themselves with examining the enforceability of mediation clauses,[2] the extent of confidentiality and privilege attaching to the process,[3] the

1 *Op.cit.*

2 *Cable & Wireless Plc v IBM United Kingdom Ltd* [2002] EWHC 2059 (Comm); *Holloway v Chancery Mead* [2007] EWHC 2495 (TCC) [2008] 1 All ER (Comm) 653; *Balfour Beatty Construction Northern Ltd v Modus Corovest (Blackpool) Ltd* [2008] EWHC 3029 TCC; *Sulmerica CIA Nacional de Seguros SA v Ensa Engenharia SA* [2012] EWCA Civ 638;

3 *Cumbria Waste Management v Baines Wilson* [2008] EWHC 786; *Farm Assist Ltd (in Liquidation) v DEFRA (No.2)* [2009] EWHC 1102 (TCC).

enforceability of mediated settlement agreements,[4] the liability of participants and non-parties when things go wrong,[5] ongoing intervention by use of costs sanctions for parties who unreasonably ignore requests to mediate[6], or refuse to participate[7], and the introduction of mediation into new areas, such as insolvency, and specifically early use to prevent the winding-up process[8] with a view to delivering better outcomes for creditors. The mediation practitioner must therefore at least be aware of the existence of a growing body of authority attaching to the mediation process.

The growth of Online Dispute Resolution may eclipse in volume standard models of civil/commercial mediation in the face of the EU legislative proposals on ADR in consumer disputes and a supporting regulation on online dispute resolution (ODR). On 8 July 2013 both the ADR Directive[9] (now no longer a matter for the United Kingdom jurisdictions) and the ODR Regulation[10] came into force.

Within the EU the ADR Directive sought to promote ADR in the consumer sphere by encouraging the use of approved ADR entities that ensure minimum quality standards. In particular, it required Member States to ensure that their approved ADR entities are impartial and provide transparent information about their services, offer their services at no or nominal cost to the consumer, and hear and determine complaints within 90 days of referral. The Directive applies to domestic and cross-border disputes concerning complaints by a consumer resident in the EU against a trader established in the EU. It does not apply to traders' complaints against consumers (such as claims for payment) or to trader-to-trader grievances.

The ODR Regulation provided for the EU Commission to establish a free, interactive website through which parties can initiate ADR in relation to disputes concerning online transactions (offline transactions are excluded). National ADR entities will receive the complaint electronically and seek to resolve the dispute through ADR, using the ODR platform exclusively if they wish.

---

4 *Vedatech Corpn v Crystal Decision UK Ltd and Crystal Decision (Japan) KK* [2003] EWCA Civ 1066; *Brown v Patel* [2007] EWHC 625 (Ch); see also Foskett QC, David *The Law and Practice of Compromise* Thomson Sweet & Maxwell 8th edn 2015 4-37/4-50

5 E.g. *In Re a Company* [2005] EWHC 3317 (Ch)

6 *PGF II SA v OMFS Company 1 Ltd* [2013] EWCA Civ 1288 [2014] 1 WLR 1386

7 *Swain Mason & Others v Mills & Reeve* [2012] EWCA Civ 498; *Garritt-Critchley and Others v Ronnan and Solarpower PV Ltd* [2014] EWHC 1774 (Ch); *Laporte v Commissioner of Police for the Metropolis* [2015] EWHC 371 (QB)

8 *Henry Construction Projects Ltd v Linton Fuel Oils Ltd* 9578 of 2012; *Lakehouse Contracts v UPR Services Ltd* [2014] EWHC 1223 (Ch); *In Re A Company* 3177 of 2015.

9 Directive 2013/11/EU

10 Regulation (EU) 524/2013

Nothing in the legislative package imposes any form of mandatory ADR on any party. The use of ADR entities or the ODR platform will require the agreement of both the consumer and the trader.

In January, 2015 the UK Government in furtherance of its interest in creating an online court, announced broad plans for compliance with the Directive and Regulation, following a consultation on promoting the use of ADR schemes in disputes involving consumer complaints. These included:

- the creation of a new 'residual' ADR scheme to fill the current gaps in the existing consumer ADR landscape;
- the appointment of the Trading Standards Institute (TSI) as the UK's competent authority to monitor ADR providers in the non-regulated sectors;
- an 8 week extension to the standard 6 year limitation period for bringing court proceedings (in disputes covered by the Directive) in cases where ADR is ongoing at the expiry of the 6 year period; and
- new statutory obligations on businesses to provide information to consumers regarding the availability of ADR schemes.

Member States were required to implement the requirements of the Directive into national law by 9 July 2015. The ODR Regulation took effect automatically six months later on 9 January 2016. Unlike the EU Directive on Cross-Border Mediation of 2008, the ODR Regulation was not abandoned on Brexit.

The Government has elected to proceed with establishing a 'residual' ADR scheme, which will be available where businesses are not obliged or committed to using another ADR scheme. The UK ODR contact point will not only be obliged to assist with cross-border EU disputes but will have the discretion to assist with purely domestic disputes if it considers appropriate in any particular case.

The UK response to the Directive on the implementation of domestic Online Dispute Resolution for Consumer Disputes was announced by Lord Dyson, then Master of the Rolls, in February 2015 following the report of the advisory group to the Civil Justice Council which was established to look at the wider potential for the use of ODR for resolving civil disputes of value less than £25,000 in England and Wales. The group explored its limitations and drawbacks, and the issues that need flagging up to protect consumers and businesses, but essentially the principal recommendations of the report were that HM Courts & Tribunals Service (HMCTS) should establish a new, Internet-based court service, known as HM Online Court (HMOC) to provide a three-tier service, the first being an online evaluation to categorize the disputants' problem, and to offer the options and remedies available. Secondly, to provide online facilitators: communicating via the Internet, these individuals will review papers and statements and help parties through mediation and negotiation. They will be supported where necessary, by telephone conferencing facilities. Additionally, there will be some automated negotiation, which are systems that help parties resolve their differences without the intervention of human experts. Finally, to provide Online Judges – full-time and part-time members of the Judiciary - who will decide suitable cases or parts of cases on an online basis, largely on the basis of papers submitted to them electronically as part of a structured process; again supported, where necessary, by telephone conferencing facilities.

It remains to be seen whether resources will be committed by government to meet these recommendations, involving the development of technical infrastructure and training. But on 25 July 2023[11] Lord Bellamy KC, Minister of Justice responsible for HMCTS announced that free mediation was to be part of 'the litigation journey' for thousands of civil claims, with the proposals expected to spare thousands of families from court and free up nearly 5,000 sitting days per year, boosting court capacity to help reduce waiting times for up to 92,000 of the most complex cases; that the government has committed to fully integrate mediation as a key step in the court process for small civil claims valued up to £10,000, starting with specified money claims which make up 80% of small claims. This could include claims such as a homeowner suing their builder for failure to deliver a service as promised or businesses recovering debts from a customer. Over 180,000 parties will be referred automatically to a free hour-long telephone session with a professional mediator provided by HM Courts and Tribunals Service (HMCTS) before their case can be progressed to a hearing. To support these changes coming into effect, HMCTS will be expanding the Small Claims Mediation Service (SCMS) by recruiting and training additional mediators and updating necessary technology. By integrating mediation for civil claims up to £10,000, the government is going further than the Civil Justice Council's recommendation for claims up to £500, supporting even more people to reach a resolution away from court.

11 See https://www.gov.uk/government/news/new-justice-reforms-to-free-up-vital-court-capacity

In the meantime, the 10th Biennial CEDR Mediation Audit (Feb 2023)[12] suggested that more than 17,000 claims in litigation had been resolved by mediation in 2022-3 with a settlement rate at or shortly after the day of the mediation of 92%.

The Adjudicative Model and the Historic Professional Psyche

The adjudicative or arbitral model, in all its forms, is seen historically as the core element of dispute processing, giving rise to both a cultural icon (the trial) and a social structure. The courts are seen as decision-makers, bureaucracies, instruments of state control, keepers of social norms and records, and a mechanism for applying uniform inherited patterns of authority, reflected in the acknowledgment of enforceable rights and obligations and the need for the enforcement and execution of awards and judgments. Academics[13] suggest it is also the primary source of legal scholarship in common-law systems.

The professional education of nearly all advocates focuses on the adjudication prototype as the primary form of processing disputes. Here the norm is for representatives to present proofs and arguments to an impartial, authoritative third-party decision-maker who gives a binding decision conferring a remedy or award on the basis of a pre-existing general rule.

Mediation (in all its forms) is a departure from the adjudication model. It offers party control and non-lawyerly or other professional language. Because it is not confined by a formal structure, except for the purpose of training mediators and having a consistent approach with which to educate disputants and their representatives, the dispute process has a wider relevance to parties; and the decision is not based on rulemaking since it is mediative and not arbitral, in the sense that an agreed outcome is fundamental. It impacts upon the parties as a therapeutic reintegration of their relationship based on compromise and the readjustment of their interests through shared gains. Mediators are trained to get the parties to focus more on their interests than their rights, although the two can be aligned, and are not mutually exclusive. Transformative mediation[14]

12 https://www.cedr.com/wp-content/uploads/2023/02/Tenth-CEDR-Mediation-Audit-2023.pdf

13 (Damaska 1978). Galanter. Marc, Adjudication, Litigation and Related Phenomena, ch 4 from *Law and the Social Sciences* Lipson L., and Wheeler S., editors 1986 Russell Sage Foundation; Galanter,Marc. *Compared to What? Assessing the Quality of Dispute Processing* (1989) 66:3 Denver University Law Review xi: Reports of the University of Wisconsin Dispute Processing Research Program Workshop on '*Identifying and Measuring the Quality of Dispute Resolution Processes and Outcomes',* Madison, July 13 and 14, 1987; Damaska, Mirjan R. *The Faces of Justice and State Authority* YUP 1986.

14 First articulated by Robert A. Baruch Bush and Joseph P. Folger in *The Promise of Mediation: Responding to Conflict Through Empowerment and Recognition* 2nd edn. 2006 Jossey-Bass, San Francisco, is an approach to conflict intervention that places the principles of empowerment and recognition at the core of helping people in conflict change how they

harnesses the energy generated by the dispute and transforms the process into a problem-solving exercise, rather than a fault-finding blame-attributing mechanism.

Unlike our court structure, as a process, informal mediation offers not only the promise of accessibility of language and form, but direct lay participation, privacy, no binding-outcome, and innovative solutions.

For the present and immediate past generation of lawyers, and particularly advocates, who have been programmed that their prime function is to prove their client's case and disprove that of their opponent, the mediation process comes as an enormous jolt to their professional psyche.

To them, disputes, even if referred to a mediation process, are still regarded as binary, i.e. a complaining party who claims an infringement of his rights based on social norms, seeks a remedy against a party the subject of complaint. Mobilisation of the complaint, or case, at the initiative of the parties requires a forum for the dispute to be processed. Participation is through expert intermediaries (lawyers with exclusive rights of audience) presenting evidence in support of requisite proofs and arguments. Disputants will expect there to be a forum that presides over a set of pre-existing forms to which it is committed – statutes and precedent. In arbitral form the repertoire of legal concepts has a narrow scope of relevance, and claims are assessed in the light of some bounded body of authoritative learning to which the forum is committed in advance.

Even more rigid than this is the element of state control: the prototypical adjudicative institution is an organ of government, located in a public building, staffed by state officers who apply public norms, and its sanctions are imposed by the compulsory powers of the state. Courts are coercive rather than voluntary since they impose outcomes regardless of the assent of the parties. This leads to a strong preponderance of claimant victories where the parties are content to have claims fought all the way to trial, since once the process is commenced, they are locked in and cannot leave without either the sanction of costs or their opponent continuing to judgment without them. Settlement tends to be as a result of the threat of the coercive powers of the court, often giving rise to capitulation by one party. In this jurisdiction the penalty and interim costs regime of the court plays no small part in party capitulation. The enormity of costs acts as a mechanism to lock parties in litigation, as settlement becomes more and more difficult, a problem that, I say

interact with each other. See also: Schwerin, Edward W. *Mediation, Citizen Empowerment and Transformational Politics* 1995 Praeger, Westport, Connecticut; Burgess, Heidi *Transformative Mediation* 1997 Conflict Research Consortium.

with great respect, Lord Justice Jackson's reforms failed to cure.

Lawyers create and defend *legal interests*, and *the perception of interests*, values and norms by the use of frames of reference; these crystallise into positions, supported by the factual and legal matrix; disputants use them to sustain beliefs, rationalise their self-interest, convince a broader audience of the rightness of their position and generate expectation of or have preference for specific outcomes.

Therefore, the ideological movement from adjudication to a flexible, client-empowered mediation process is particularly difficult for the lawyer. In facilitative mediation lawyers are generally drawn towards evaluation, since they cannot be unaffected by their underlying structures of beliefs, values and experiences, underpinned by their professional education, which characterise their initial approach to a disputant's rights and obligations under the law.

In simple terms we are discussing the difference between what is important to the law (as promoted by orthodox legal education and training) and what is important to the client. This can be shown in the simplest of forms (*see Fig. 1*):

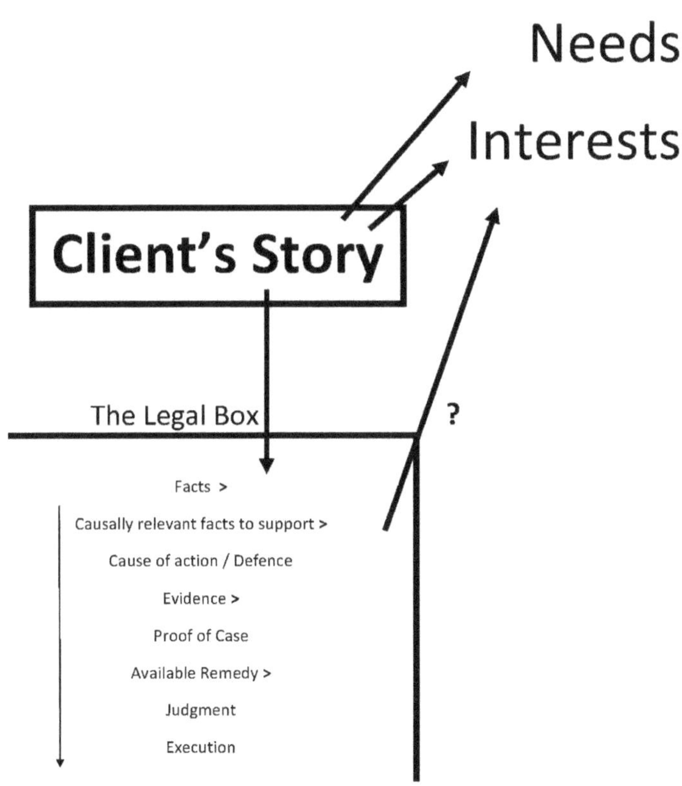

A client attends his solicitor's office. He has a problem which he presents in the form of his story. The story is sufficiently serious for him to be compelled to seek legal assistance. Applying the orthodoxy of his training the lawyer is obliged by the litigation process to distil from the facts presented only the material needed for the prosecution of a claim: causally relevant facts, i.e. those going to establish a legal cause of action or a defence. The lawyer is not concerned in terms of outcome, with anything other than what the court process can provide by way of a remedy, or what can be negotiated with an adversary. He or she then focuses on compiling the evidence needed to prove the case, or assess that of the other side, to manage the risk of running the case to trial, particularly in terms of cost effectiveness under the CPR regime, and the ultimate recoverability of any judgment. The client's wider interests, for example his need for all of his story to be heard, for recognition, empathy, validation, emotional release, catharsis and closure, may be addressed by a solicitor with a good bedside manner, and a modern outlook in client management, but these items are not usually catered for by the litigation process or the court hearing a disposal of the claim.

Even worse, the binary form in which the litigation process presents is designed to create a 'loser'. At least 50% of parties will be unhappy with the outcome by design. Applying risk to a cost benefit analysis the winner may also be a loser in terms of irrecoverable costs, wasted management time, opportunity cost, damage to reputation, stress and irreparable damage to relationships. Certainly, anecdotal evidence would suggest that a high proportion of 'winners' wish they had never entered into litigation at all.

For the purpose of Fig,1 the standard lawyer's role can be confined to the box entitled 'The Legal Case' to which I will refer as 'the Box'.

The contents of the Box leads inevitably to

- lawyer control of the claim or defence,
- the use of professional standards, language and jargon, unfamiliar to the lay client
- significant up-front costs irrespective of lawyers' fees
- an uncertain fee liability for the client: for the client a costs budget is only an indication.
- the giving away of management of the claim to the court
- the inability of the client to leave the process without either a costs

sanction or worse – the right of the other side to continue in his absence

- the uncertainty of outcome, both in terms of the eventual result, its true value to the client and its relevance to the client's true needs.

The potential for conflict between the client's true needs and the litigator's services tends to make lawyers defensive about their fees, about the procedure adopted, the litigation timetable, and the outcome. In so doing they embrace the client to the extent that he is locked into a system, or indeed captured within the Box. Most practitioners, even the most client-friendly and cost-conscious, are likely to recognise the existence of these problems.

The mediation process, by contrast, is interested in the whole of the client's story, and adopts a holistic approach to problem solving, rather than the bi-lateral polarisation which is concerned with 'winning' and 'losing' cases. The mediator is intent on uncovering the parties' true needs and interests, and any underlying difficulties which have impacted on their relationship should there be one to try and restore: see Fig 2 overleaf.

The mediator encourages parties to speak for themselves, to use non-professional language or technical jargon other than that concerned with the subject matter of the dispute, and to find and subscribe to their own solutions. Over and above that, mediation serves both lawyer and client where the concept of being found 'right' is not enough. The client needs a solution and the court cannot deliver a pragmatic remedy.

Lawyers who are inexperienced in this process find that it impacts directly on what they believe their function to be: to protect the client and advance his interests according to the strength of his legal case. In effect to lock him inside the Box which, in effect, becomes a fortress to defend – and in terms of negotiation, a 'position'.

They fail to understand that the legal case does not have to be proven in mediation and is there to be examined principally as a frame of reference to be considered, either if things go wrong and there is no acceptable settlement, or to measure any proposal against what might occur afterwards if the case has to go to court.

The advocate therefore has a very different role, which, as we shall see later in this book, is multi-faceted and not concerned merely to be the professional leading mouthpiece. Much of what those representing parties at mediation are concerned to do is to help the client evaluate his position outside the Box,

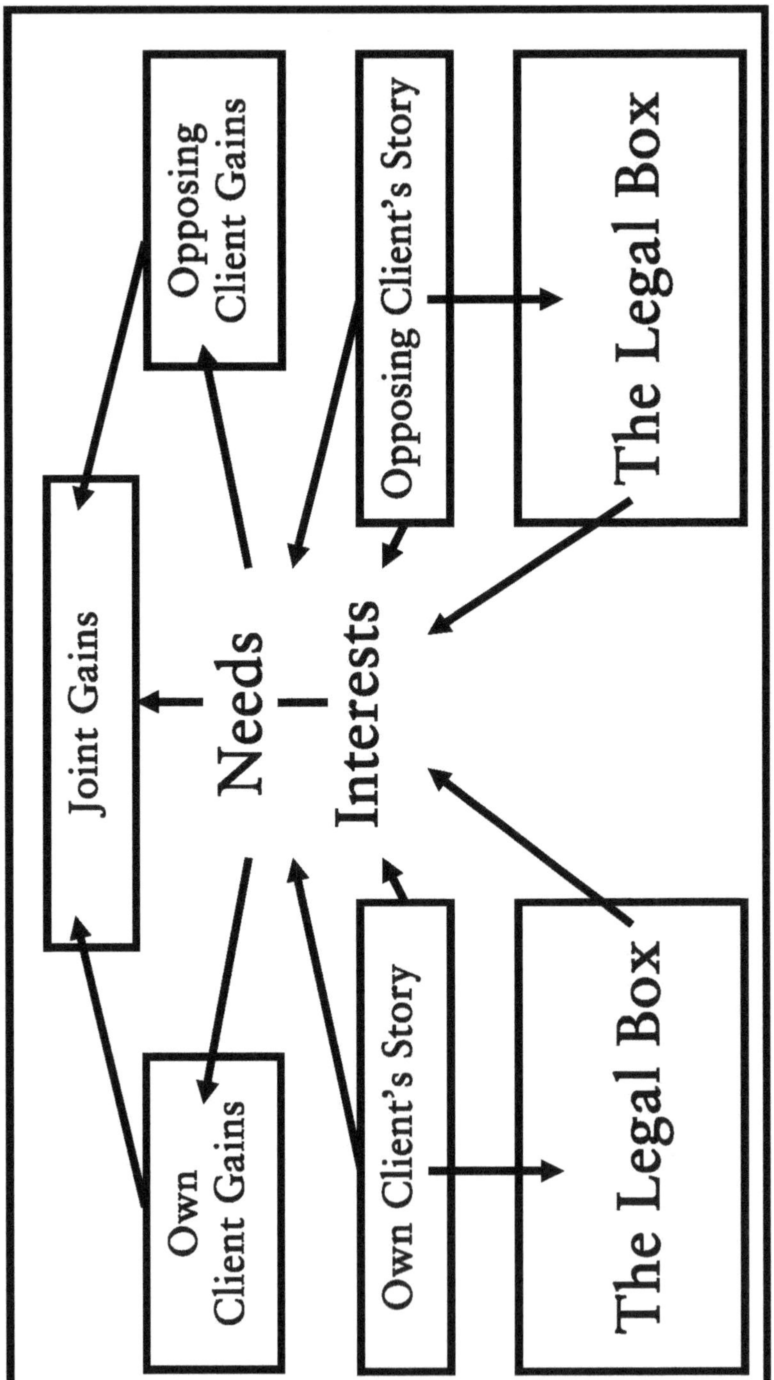

Fig 2: Mediator identifies needs and interests from both parties' stories and legal cases in order to promote individual gains and joint gains

comparing and contrasting the matters within to the client's wider interests and needs outside.

Why then, use a lawyer as an advocate in mediation?

The answer lies in (i) the skill set of the lawyer advocate; (ii) the diminishing reality of empowerment; and (iii) the shadow of the law, if not the annexing of private dispute resolution to the court process

(i) Lawyering skills

The 'handicap' of the lawyer's professional training and psyche is counterbalanced by his or her innate skills as an exponent of critical analysis, of problem solving and of communication in circumstances where dynamic change is part of the dispute process and has to be reacted to and catered for. The lawyer is trained at absorbing and processing information, seeing message patterns, finding linguistic cues and socially constructed meanings, and to these faculties trial advocates have the ability to meet and deal with dynamic change as the evidence emerges in its final form. His or her analysis of the cognitive frames people use in a given conflict provides insight and better understanding of the conflict dynamics, of finding new ways of reaching agreement by clarifying the perception of issues, sharpening the parties understanding of interests, and identifying the means of viewing the subject matter differently, or at least identifying those differences which cannot be bridged and which may have to be set aside.

(ii) The reality of empowerment

One of the central arguments put forward by the proponents of mediation is that it operates as a means of settling conflict that leaves responsibility for outcomes in the hands of the parties themselves, rather than have a decision imposed by a judge or reached by bargaining between partisan lawyers[15]. Ultimately authority belongs to parties and no-one else.

However the idea of client empowerment is undermined to some extent both by the activities of the mediator who uses reality testing to disguise evaluation (the facilitative mediator keeping the views he or she has nevertheless formed to him or herself) and the development of a more formal structure by private sector mediation service providers, state-sponsorship in court-annexed schemes, and the extension of state activity under government into areas previously outside its interest, particularly concerning social behaviour, and an opaque but increasingly coercive desire for disputes to be mediated in circumstances where the state retains some degree of control, but without concomitant expenditure[16].

15 Folberg (1983)

16 See Roberts (2006) and Damaksa (1978)

This has given rise to a creeping juridification of those forms of mediation which operate within the fringes of the mainstream civil jurisdiction in England and Wales: a corpus of procedural law is taking hold of mediation in areas which concern

- The validity of contractual clauses containing agreements to mediate[17]
- The enforceability of the mediation agreement[18]
- Confidentiality of the process[19]
- The existence or otherwise of a 'mediation privilege'[20]
- The enforceability of settlements obtained in mediation[21]
- Mediation under actual or implicit duress by the courts[22]

These are substantive legal issues for the advocate or party representative, and are not to be regarded as soft law, or merely matters for debate. In such areas the law actively embraces and regulates mediation practice as it would in considering its supervisory role in dealing with any other type of subordinate jurisdiction. It goes to the fundamental question of how courts view the legal nature of the mediation process, which is not presently regarded as, but soon may have to be, the delivery of a legal service. Lawyer mediation advocates will need to be able to address this issue when questioned by a judge during the case management process who wants to know about the suitability of the case for mediation.

Potentially mediation is seen by lawyers as no more than a type of procedural processing within a self-contained envelope or umbrella of confidentiality, but one which is no less affected by the law than any other form of without-prejudice negotiation. Increasingly the 'magic' attaching to mediation as a new force in dispute processing is wearing thin. The legal basis for mediation is

17 *Cable & Wireless Plc v IBM United Kingdom Ltd* [2002] EWHC 2059 (Comm); *Holloway v Chancery Mead* [2007] EWHC 2495 (TCC) [2008] 1 All ER (Comm) 653; *Balfour Beatty Construction Northern Ltd v Modus Corovest (Blackpool) Ltd* [2008] EWHC 3029 TCC; *Sul-merica CIA Nacional de Seguros SA v Ensa Engenharia SA* [2012] EWCA Civ 638.

18 *Vedatech Corpn v Crystal Decision UK Ltd and Crystal Decision (Japan) KK* [2003] EWCA Civ 1066; *Brown v Patel* [2007] EWHC 625 (Ch); see also Foskett QC, David *The Law and Practice of Compromise* Thomson Sweet & Maxwell 8th edn 2015 4-37/4-50

19 *Cumbria Waste Management v Baines Wilson* [2008] EWHC 786; *Farm Assist Ltd (in Liquidation) v DEFRA* (No.2) [2009] EWHC 1102 (TCC)

20 *Farm Assist Ltd (in Liquidation) v DEFRA (No.2)* [2009] EWHC 1102 (TCC)

21 *Brown v Patel* [2007] EWHC 625 (Ch);

22 *PGF II SA v OMFS Company 1 Ltd* [2013] EWCA Civ 1288 [2014] 1 WLR 1386; *Swain Mason & Others v Mills & Reeve* [2012] EWCA Civ 498; *Garritt-Critchley and Others v Ronnan and Solarpower PV Ltd* [2014] EWHC 1774 (Ch); *Laporte v Commissioner of Police for the Metropolis* [2015] EWHC 371 (QB); *Churchill v Merthyr Tydfil CBC op.cit.*

simply a contract (the mediation agreement) which transforms the dispute by party processing and is replaced by another contract (the settlement agreement). That it is within the envelope or umbrella of confidentiality and without prejudice doesn't make it any the less a contractual process - Fig 3.

Fig 3

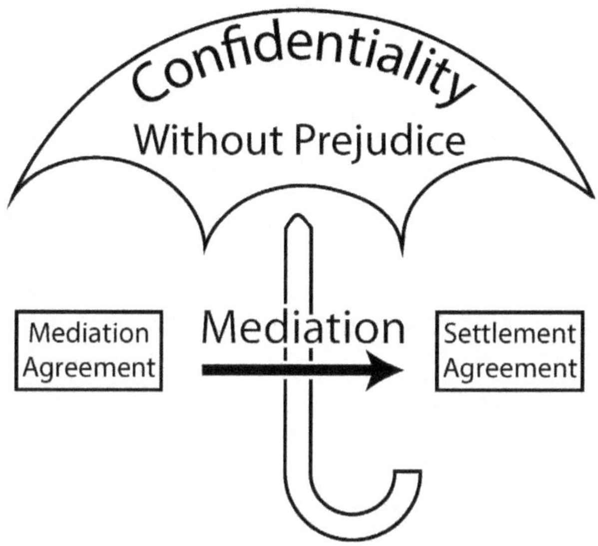

In reality there is no need to intellectualise about a process which for many lawyers can be regarded as simply a tool to be used when appropriate. Like any tool, its use improves with training and experience; with practice, it leads to sophistication, flexibility and expertise.

(iii) the shadow of the law and court-annexed procedure

Court agendas include large portions of routine administration and supervised bargaining. American academics[23] have suggested that courts provide a set of "counters" to be used in bargaining between disputants. For example, in divorce bargaining, which was in the past confined to maintenance, child support, child residency and matrimonial property, often one class would be used to offset another. Family mediation is increasingly being used to solve other types of family problems, such as

- Separation
- Parental contact
- Disputes between parent and child
- Disagreements over the care for an elderly or seriously ill relatives

23 Mnookin & Kornhauser (1979)

- Grandparents having contact with grandchildren
- Homelessness caused by family arguments

Some service providers offer Child Inclusive Mediation, which is offered to children involved in the relationship. This service is offered by trained mediators who work with children and is intended as a time for the child/ children to openly discuss their concerns.

This approach of 'mutual bargaining' is reflected in the 'Harvard model' of mediation where the concept of "bargaining endowment" is both widespread and can be seen in many complementary transactional or social relationships (husband/wife landlord/tenant purchaser/supplier) where each is based on the mutual dependence of activity.

Such counters exist within the court structure and its process – delay, costs, the uncertainty of outcome, imponderable factors such as the adequacy of proofs, exercise of the Court's discretion, the preparation of the lawyers, negotiating skills, an ability to respond to deadlines and emergencies, and an ability to recover or bear costs. These were considered by Professor Marc Galanter[24] who concluded that this bargaining between parties is a kind of "private ordering" that takes place in the shadow of the law. He suggested that the radiating effect of the courts leads to regulation within negotiation – the courts provide models (norms, procedures, structures, rationalisations) for an immense variety of regulatory settings, e.g. schools, trade unions, associations, clubs, and other host institutions which exercise regulatory authority in dispute processing to replace the expense and remoteness of the courts.

As courts have become more remote, more professional and, in England and Wales after 1999 and certainly now, almost prohibitively expensive, they are less places for individuals to air and resolve everyday disputes and more the province of professionals and a place for the extension of government concern into areas of life previously unregulated by the state, e.g. consumer affairs, environmental, health and safety, welfare and institutions dealing with state-dependent clients.

By the end of the 1970s shortcomings in the provision of justice were revealed, or at least perceived, in terms of cost, complexity, delay, and the separation of the law from ordinary citizens. From then onwards a jaundiced view gained ground that there was too much law and not enough justice. In England and Wales this was given credence by, among other things, the approach of Lord Denning as Master of the Rolls. This notion was, and remains fed, by the

24 (1981)

enormous growth of regulation by the state in most spheres of everyday existence. It is, however, just a popular notion since studies by Galanter (2006)[25] and Menkel-Meadow (2005)[26] show a continuation of the trend identified by Abel (1982)[27] of dispute settlement less by direct decisive resolution and more by mediation, distributing bargain-counters and pattern setting. A smaller proportion of the population are direct participants in contested adjudication, irrespective of the policy shift introduced by the Civil Procedure Rules in 1999.

This is exemplified by statistical evidence relating to the vanishing trial, which shows the number of trials in Western common law jurisdictions have been shrinking throughout the latter part of 20th century at a time when the rest of the law is growing substantially – the number of new laws, statutes, regulations, commentaries; the quantity of lawyers; the portion of GDP spent on law; and legal business, all appear to have grown at a tremendous rate *except* for trials and definitive pronouncements of law at the highest level, by domestic Supreme Courts. After 2016 HM Courts and Tribunals Service closed over 80 courts and support buildings across jurisdictions in England and Wales, reducing the Courts estate by very nearly 20%. Substantial increases in court fees in line with the Government's intention of making the justice system self-funding are simply driving litigants from the judgment seat. Online courts are not consistent with open justice.

The vanishing trial is disguised by the continuing media-driven myth of the litigious society: "blame/compensation culture" makes the serious decline in disputes coming to trial over the last 150 years invisible to public consciousness. In particular there has been a distinct fall in the last 20 years, dramatic in the UK since before the introduction of the CPR in absolute terms and noticeable beforehand over a longer term. The process of the "day in court" has been redeemed by bargaining and shut-off points due to a huge shift in politico-judicial philosophy, - the new primary role of court ('overriding objective' rule1.1 Part 1 CPR), - namely that settlement is good, judgment bad, a philosophy driven by intensive case management and supported by changes in institutional practice including the withdrawal of state funding, huge rises in court issue fees, the embracing of ADR and the outsourcing of dispute processing to other institutions.

---

25 Galanter, Marc. *The Privatisation of Justice and the Vanishing Trial* paper, IALS W G Hart Legal Workshop 2006: The Retreat of the State: Challenges to Law and Lawyers.

26 Menkel-Meadow, Carrie Is the Adversary System Really Dead? Dilemmas of Legal Ethics as Legal Institutions and Roles Involve (2004) 57 CLP 85.

27 Abel, Richard 'The Contradictions of Informal Justice' in *The Politics of Informal Justice* 1982 Academic Press, New York, ed. Abel R.

However as Galanter (2006) remarks[28], and to the detriment of the development of a culture of mediation, the trial holds a pivotal place in popular culture, with very little public or literary consciousness of mediation activity. What this means, for our purposes, is that at the outset of a conflict the disputant will seek the assistance and comfort of his lawyer as a hired gun, or champion, before the actual dispute procedure has been identified. Popular culture is not yet sufficiently sophisticated to recognise that mediation is not, or not necessarily, a legal process akin to a trial, and the mediation industry have done little to increase public awareness of the distinction in an attempt to create its own mystique. There will be no substantial extension of the market for mediation services until the industry demystifies and normalises its process.

The Changing Role of the Lawyer

At its heart mediation is a form of intervention in which the lawyer – or more particularly the litigator or dispute resolution specialist - acts as gatekeeper of the dispute.

Mediation ideologies are reflective of the classification of various roles through which people intervene as third parties in the conflicts of others, not in the nature of the intervention but its degree.

Black & Baumgartner (1983)[29] identified a typology of twelve third parties offering partisan support roles ranging from **informer, adviser, advocate** and **ally** to **surrogate**, and non-partisan roles involved in dispute processing as either a **facilitator** or having an arbitral function: from **friendly peacemaker, mediator**, **arbitrator** and **judge** to the **repressive peacemaker**. In therapeutic intervention the roles of **negotiator** and **healer** may be both partisan and non-partisan.

What is extraordinary is that a mediation advocate is likely during the various stages of his retainer, to play each of the twelve roles identified by this typology in his relationship with the client, from the creation of the retainer until the successful outcome of the mediation. Those who have received no training other than in their traditional roles will find themselves disadvantaged, their client potentially handicapped, and both lawyer and client may become uncomfortable with each other at some point during the process.

28 Galanter, Marc. *The Privatisation of Justice and the Vanishing Trial* paper, IALS Hart Workshop 2006

29 Black D. and Baumgartner M.P. 'Toward a Theory of the Third Party' in *Empirical Theories about Courts* 1983 Longman New York ed. Boyum K. and Mather L.

Lawyer or Non-Lawyer Advocate?

It follows from what I have said thus far, all litigators and at least those non-contentious lawyers who are involved in bargaining, must now have a basic understanding of the principles and law surrounding mediation to be able to act in an advisory role. They not only have a responsibility to identify cases, both pre-and mid-proceedings, for which mediation is appropriate, and to explain the mediation process to clients and other legal professionals. They have specific tasks within the process –

(1) Deciding to and persuading others to engage in the process

(2) Ascertaining the most appropriate time to mediate

(3) Choosing the mediator

(4) Controlling the pre-mediation element

(5) Team leading at the mediation itself

(6) Securing a working settlement which gives effect to an agreement with which the client is content

As advocates, they must be able to deal with all aspects of mediation within case management, something probably outside the remit or capability of non-lawyer mediation advocates. One such example concerns the enforceability of contractual mediation clauses. Most court schemes implicitly recognise a fairly formal facilitative model with a structured process, and consequently lawyer advocates will invariably use this model.

However, the courts do not necessarily regard mediation as a species of new procedure. In *Balfour Beatty Construction Northern Ltd v Modus Corovest (Blackpool) Ltd*[30] a number of disputes arose following the failure by Modus to honour an adjudication decision. First, Modus said that the application for enforcement should be stayed to mediation. Clause 39.1 of the contract stated:

> "Either party must identify to the other any dispute or difference ...that it considers to be capable of resolution by mediation and, upon being requested to do so, the other party shall within 7 days indicate whether or not it consents to participate in the mediation...The objective of mediation under clause 39 shall be to reach a binding agreement in resolution of the dispute..."

30 [2008] EWHC 3029 TCC

Mr Justice Coulson was not prepared to grant a stay. He said that the mediation agreement was nothing more than an agreement to agree. It was therefore too uncertain to be enforced by the court. Further, the Judge noted that even if there was a binding agreement to mediate, he would only stay the claim to mediation if the party making the claim was not entitled to summary judgment. If a party applies for summary judgment, it is because there is no defence to that claim. If that was right, it would be wrong to refer such a dispute to mediation.

This was contrary to the prior view of Mr Justice Colman in *Cable & Wireless Plc v IBM United Kingdom Ltd* [31] who decided that a mediation clause in a commercial contract which obliged the parties to attempt mediation before issuing proceedings was enforceable. However, there the contract expressly stated the mediation rules to be followed (CEDR Model Rules) and this factor was an important influence in the judge's decision that the clause should not be construed as an agreement to agree. The absence of specific mediation rules in the contractual agreement appeared to render a mediation clause unenforceable: see per Ramsey J. in *Holloway v Chancery Mead* [32].

This issue came before the Court of Appeal in *Sulmerica CIA Nacional de Seguros SA v Ensa Engenharia SA*[33]. There the court decided that an escalating dispute resolution clause in a contract which required mediation as a precursor to arbitration was invalid. The authority is of considerable importance since such clauses are used widely in many types of commercial contracts. It provided:-

> "11. Mediation
>
> If any dispute or difference of whatsoever nature arises out of or in connection with this Policy including any questions regarding its existence, validity or termination, hereafter termed as Dispute, the parties undertake that, prior to a reference to arbitration, they will seek to have the Dispute resolved amicably by mediation.
>
> All rights of the parties in respect of the Dispute are and shall remain fully reserved and the entire mediation including all documents produced or to which reference is made, discussion and oral presentation shall be strictly confidential to the parties and shall be conducted on the same basis as without prejudice negotiations, privileged, inadmissible, not subject to disclosure in any other proceedings whatsoever and shall not constitute any waiver of privilege whether between the parties or between either of them and a third party.

31 [2002] EWHC 2059 (Comm)
32 [2007] EWHC 2495 (TCC); [2008] 1 All ER (Comm) 653
33 [2012] EWCA Civ 638

> The mediation may be terminated should any party wish to do so by written notice to the appointed mediator and to the other party to that effect. Notice to terminate may be served at any time after the first meeting or discussion has taken place in mediation.
>
> If the Dispute has not been resolved to the satisfaction of either party within 90 days of the service of the notice initiating mediation, or if either party fails or refuses to participate in the mediation, or if either party serves written notice terminating the mediation under this clause, then either party may refer the Dispute to arbitration.
>
> Unless the parties otherwise agree, the fees and expenses of the mediator and all other costs of the mediation shall be born equally by the parties and each party shall bear their own respective costs incurred in the mediation regardless of the outcome of the mediation."

The court considered whether the clause imposed an enforceable obligation to mediate such that compliance with its terms was an essential precondition to arbitration. On analysis the clause contained no defined mediation process, nor made reference to a mediation service provider and the court distinguished *Cable & Wireless Plc v IBM* and *Holloway v Chancery Mead.* Lord Justice Moore-Bick said

> "The first paragraph contains merely an undertaking to seek to have the dispute resolved amicably through mediation. No provision is made for the process by which that is to be undertaken and none of the succeeding paragraphs touches on that question. I agree with the judge, therefore, that condition 11 is not apt to create an obligation to commence or participate in a mediation process. The most that might be said is that it imposes on any party who is contemplating referring a dispute to arbitration an invitation to join the other in an ad hoc mediation, but the content of even such a limited obligation is so uncertain as to render it impossible of enforcement in the absence of some defined mediation process. I think that the judge was right, therefore, to hold that condition 11 is incapable of giving rise to a binding obligation of any kind."

This suggests that there remains a degree of uncertainty as to what precisely makes a mediation clause binding. It appears that there needs at least to be reference to some procedural rules, if not a service provider whose established and recognised rules may be used.

In the present context this uncertainty underlines the view that there are some advisory and procedural aspects of working in mediation advocacy which will remain the preserve of the lawyers, particularly where the case starts in litigation and moves into mediation only after commencement of proceedings or when imminent proceedings are contemplated.

Part 2

The Decision to Mediate

Chapter 2
The Decision to Mediate

Occasionally the decision to mediate may be made for you, and you are presented with a mandatory contractual provision, a case management direction to that effect, or the prior agreement of the parties to the dispute before it arrives at your desk. More often than not you will be faced with making the decision yourself, either arising out of the curiosity of your lay client, a request from the other side or the court, or upon your own initiative. Don't wait to be asked. You should take the lead in a matter *so strategically and tactically important* in the context of the dispute, whether it is already within or remains outside the formal adversarial process of litigation or arbitration. Statistically most disputes settle anyway before trial – a mediated settlement is unlikely to be any more or any less favourable, although it could be considerably more inventive - but settlement should occur much earlier, therefore with concomitant time and costs benefits to your client.

One of the core decisions for the mediation advocate is when to mediate. Against a background of significant front-loaded legal costs, issue fees which are real significance to the ordinary litigant or businessmen and the uncertainty of precisely when the maximum cost benefit kicks in, this can become a tricky decision.

First, the question of whether to mediate at all.

To make the decision whether or not to have a case or dispute proceed to mediation requires:

- An understanding of the process: what mediation actually entails, and its different forms;
- An appreciation of possible – indeed, probable - outcomes to the dispute outside a negotiated agreement;
- Sufficient knowledge of the strength of the legal case or of your client's then position;

- An understanding of the true value of the case to the client in terms of

  (a) cost efficiency;

  (b) time efficiency;

  (c) what the client really wants to achieve if he can;

  (d) whether the remedy available from the court (even if achievable) can provide what is actually needed;

- Adequate knowledge of:

  (e) the client himself;

  (f) the client's wider business affairs;

  (g) any ongoing or intended ongoing relationship between the parties – whether commercial, social or personal.

Without this information you will not be able to assess whether the decision *to permit the client to mediate* is correct. I lay stress on the words in italics. You are the advocate. You are charged with the responsibility for tactical decisions in managing the claim or its defence. It is not merely a question of applying mediation theory, or of being seduced by the ADR industry or even worrying unduly about costs sanctions in the litigation at this stage, although later this should become an important concern.

You have to answer two basic questions:

1. Is the case suitable for mediation?

2. Is the case ripe for mediation?

2.1 Is the Case Suitable for Mediation?

It may well be so, but there can be inherent difficulties in persuading your client, your instructing solicitor or your principal, or the other side, that this is the case. For example, the benefits over cost may be marginal in the circumstances. Notwithstanding encouragement – even a mandatory approach - by the Court, the mediation process may be perceived as an additional rather than an alternative procedure, and come with an additional layer of cost.

The opening offer to mediate is still regarded in some quarters, mostly erroneously, as an indicator of weakness in a case that is being litigated. This stigma is based on the ignorance of the recipient, either of the process or the opportunity being presented, and such lack of knowledge takes time to eradicate. It does, however, lead to the second question and one that is of at least equal importance.

2.2 Is the Case Ripe for Mediation?

Mediation, yes (if the necessary parties can be persuaded), but if so, when? ADR may be utilised either before formal proceedings are issued or during the course of litigation or arbitration. To ascertain precisely when to call for ADR there are a number of questions you should consider.

- Have you enough information about the claim, its defence, any cross-claim or third party entanglement?
- Do the parties know and understand the issues being raised by each other?
- Does each party at least know its own version of the facts?
- Do you require full disclosure, or have you sufficient to proceed?
- Do you have a proper understanding of your own client's needs and interests?
- Are there non-parties to be brought in?
- Is the timing tactically astute to apply pressure to your opponent by using the CPR costs regime to afford you the maximum protection for your client's position, and cause the other side maximum prejudice?
- Conversely, is the potential cost saving such that mediation should be attempted as early as possible – even before proceedings have been issued?
- Is it a dispute that will turn on expert or other technical evidence?
- Is it possible to bring forward the time for ADR by obtaining early expert evidence or appointing a joint expert?

You really need to know the answer to each of these questions, not least to see if they are relevant to your client's situation.

Both of the key questions above should be placed in the context of meeting the client's best needs for resolving the dispute. That is why some distinguished commentators[1] and user organisations[2][17] now refer to 'ADR' not as *'alternative*

1 For example Professor Jane Gordon, University of Oregon.

2 Canadian National Energy Board; State of Oregon Department of Justice; United States Department of Education, Office of Special Education Programs National Centre on Dispute Resolution.

dispute resolution', but rather as '*appropriate* dispute resolution.' The International Chamber of Commerce in Paris ADR Rules refer to the acronym as '*amicable* dispute resolution'. I am also indebted to Grahame Aldous KC who proposed as a new definition '*accelerated* dispute resolution.'

As ADR processes become more sophisticated you must consider whether mediation is a better vehicle for settlement or determination of the issues than early neutral assessment, or expert determination, or the executive mini-trial, or concilio-arbitration, or a traditional arbitration procedure. To do so you need to be familiar with the different strengths and weaknesses of these variations on mediation processes in the context of what you know about your client's case. You must have an awareness of the fact that a reference to ADR by the court does not mean mediation or bust.

2.3 Getting the Client to Mediate

The first essential is to introduce your client to and familiarise him with the concept of mediation. Most clients are extremely nervous of the court environment, but there is an inherent respect, sometimes a sense of awe, about our judicial process. The average client will be even less familiar with mediation and might worry about being rushed into a strange procedure. He may well need convincing that a non-arbitral process will suit his need, particularly since he is likely to regard the mediator as a form of judge, which, of course, he is not. Your client will certainly want reassurance that his legal representatives are familiar with and can be tactically astute while using this process.

Mediators are trained to investigate the potential for joint gains in resolving disputes. That is one of their most important tools in unlocking the potential for settlement. Be aware that this investigation applies equally to the advocate at every stage of the process, from persuading his own client, his solicitor principal or his opponent to agree to mediate, through to analysing and proposing constructive settlement opportunities on the day itself.

From the very outset you will have to consider both 'own client gains' and 'joint gains' as the means by which you can demonstrate to your client that mediation will suit his desired outcome. The most obvious examples are cost and time savings, certainty of outcome and control over the process. To persuade either your own client or both parties to mediate you will need to consider and identify what value there is in avoiding arguments over the merits of the case. Look outside the immediate remedies that the court can provide:

- Your client may have a strong case – either actual or perceived - but he may be unaware of: the value of his wasted time; his irrecoverable costs; the time of any witnesses, employees or co-workers both in preparing for litigation and attending court; the impact of such loss of time, whether in management or production, on a business or employment; the impact of publicity; the destruction of party relationships by the operation of the litigation process; and the cost, effectiveness and time for execution of a judgment or recovery under an order.
- Your client may have a weak case: he may not wish to test it in court, or you may advise that it should not be tested on the merits so as to avoid an adverse precedent being set.
- There may be collateral or parallel disputes outside the strict ambit of the present cause of action – further disputes that strictly fall outside the rule in *Henderson v Henderson*[13] and CPR Part 3.4.3 which require that the parties should bring forward all matters between them in the same suit
- There may be a further or ongoing relationship between the parties either not in dispute, or one that the parties cannot change. This may be commercial, social or economic. It may extend to family relationships, that of neighbours living in close proximity, or co-employees or those with a social connection who occupy shared work or leisure facilities or social amenities.

Advancing mediation as a practical solution presupposes that your client is considering settlement at all. If he is determined to have his day in court at any cost, that position may well change once the true costs of present day litigation start to mount up, and to bite. Principles do not come cheap under the Civil Procedure Rules, and case management may drive your client inevitably towards mediation, whether as a willing participant or not. If the Court is indicating that mediation is regarded as appropriate, it is likely your client would be better off being seen to embrace the proposal than contest it.

3 (1843) 67 ER 313; [1843-1860] All ER Rep. 378.

2.4 Dealing with the Client's Questions

You have to be prepared to advise your client why mediation is right for him or her in the particular circumstances of this case. You can show him the advantages and disadvantages. Be ready to deal with his reaction, in particular his questions, which will be a fairly conventional response from litigants unfamiliar with the process.

Questions generally fall into four categories: first he will think that he is being deprived of his day in court when the judge can say both to the parties and to the wider world that he was right. This is a matter to be dealt with in terms of litigation risk and cost/benefit analysis. In addition you can explain that he will be able to express his viewpoint personally at the mediation, and seek vindication of his position, and that there may be considerable alternative 'own client gains.'

Your client may have a strong enough case to provide him with an open court personal vindication. However, in practical terms is 'being right' enough? Does it come with a practical solution to his problem which is worth the risk and cost?

Second he does not want the approach to the other side to mediate to be seen as a sign of weakness. This should be dealt with by reference to the requirements of the pre-action protocols and practice direction on pre-action conduct, the court rules on active case management, practice directions concerning mediation (CPR rr. 1.3, 1.4(2)(e), 3.1(4)), the penalty costs regime (CPR r.44.5 (3)) and the fact that any initial approach could be made by the mediation service provider or by the court rather than you or your firm or solicitor. Highlight the impact of *PGF II SA v OMFS and Bank of Scotland*[4] which severely impairs your ability to ignore a request for mediation from the other side.

Third, your client may ask how much the process of mediation will cost. His concern is that this represents a waste of money if no settlement is achieved. You will be able to explain the statistical success rate for satisfactory outcomes, and the fact that the mediation process creates a momentum towards settlement, even if no agreement is concluded on the day. You will ask him to consider the collateral benefits the mediation may bring within the litigation by reducing or clarifying issues, and enabling both you and him to have a good look at how the other side are likely to shape up at trial.

Finally he will want to know who is the right mediator. If he gets to that stage, he is already engaging in the process. At an early juncture you will either have

4 [2013] EWCA Civ 1288

a mediation service provider in mind, or if you are experienced in a particular field or have represented parties in successful mediations before, a list of appropriate individual mediators used by you or your chambers or firm.

2.5 Key Points to Explain

The client needs to be able to make an informed choice. Any explanation you give is likely to have regard to the following points:

(i) Your client's understanding of the role of the mediator is likely to be wrong. This process is not the imposition of a decision by a third party, but a consensual attempt to solve the problem in hand, and, where possible, any collateral or wider issues between the parties that exist or can be foreseen. Your client may be looking for goals to be achieved beyond the ambit of the existing dispute. Be that as it may, you must be able to rationalise the need for a mediator to add value rather than have an *inter-partes* negotiation. The mediator will be a confidential listener and a shuttle diplomat; he will filter parties communications with each other, absorb any emotional antagonism and push the parties to focus on underlying objectives rather than posturing or staking out a position; he will encourage joint problem solving, suggest appropriate compromises, possibly offer non-binding views on the merits (of a proposed settlement) (if pressed to do so) and also ask tough questions to discover and mirror to them the strengths and weaknesses of a party's case.[5]

(ii) The legal framework exists to protect your client's position; in particular it operates as a safety net. You will need to place emphasis on the "without prejudice" nature of the proceedings, the fact that they are confidential and that information exchanged or obtained in the course of a mediation may not ordinarily be used elsewhere afterwards[6], including in the litigation

(iii) The extent to which the process is consensual: your client may leave the mediation at any point (subject to the fact of his having done so potentially being prejudicial under CPR Part 44 should the dispute be determined in contentious litigation).

---

5 Mackie, Karl *The Effective Mediator* CEDR seminar paper February 2002.

6 *Venture Investment Placement Ltd v Hall* [2005] EWHC 1227 (Ch) ; *Reed Executive Plc v Reed Business Information* [2004] EWCA Civ 887; [2004] 1 WLR 3026 applying *Rush & Tompkins Ltd v GLC* [1989] AC 1290 HL; *Cumbria Waste Management v Baines Wilson* [2008] EWHC 786; *Farm Assist Ltd v DEFRA (No.2)* [2009] EWHC 1102 TTC.But cf Part 6 afterwards.

(iv) The fact that the mediation proposed may come under the ambit of a particular court-annexed scheme if the dispute is contained within a certain jurisdiction. If that is the case there may be an element of compulsion, particularly if voluntary take up under the scheme is low.

(v) Once a settlement has been agreed, it becomes enforceable as a matter of contract, and as long as it is workable and sufficiently certain, the courts will enforce it[7].

For commercial clients it should be stressed that the UK mediation industry has produced over the last three decades a very large number of well qualified, easily available and fairly priced mediators, including specialist practitioners and subject-matter experts. Most mediators entirely undervalue the gift they bring to clients. Although their functions are very different, you can make the point that a mediator can be chosen, unlike a judge.

Large corporate clients often present a problem at this stage, and sometimes later in the process. In a multi-layered or institutional concern, whether in the private or public sector, the question to mediate has to be placed before the appropriate decision-maker by his internal advisers. In organisations where there may be a blame culture there is a risk that people would rather not make a decision than make one and get it wrong. You may have to overcome this kind of culture and stand firm in advising that mediation should be tried, and at what stage in the management of the dispute.

Be sympathetic to a reluctant client. In many cases it is a hard decision for him to make not to fight a case in which he has belief, and he may be concerned reasonably about the 'blink first' mentality or what he perceives as an additional layer of costs. These perceptions can be overcome by demonstrating that entry into mediation is relatively risk-free: in a process which is non-adjudicative and non-binding you have the flexibility to act outside the constraints of the CPR and to exploit the dynamics of mediation procedure to the best advantage of your client. The court will give you credit for having engaged in the process even if it does not succeed. If it fails, although the costs may have been wasted, costs which are outside the scope of the mediation agreement itself will generally become costs in the case.[8] Unlike the strictures of litigation in mediation you have the opportunity to devise solutions to the

---

7 Sir David Foskett KC *The Law and Practice of Compromise* 9th edn 2024 Thomson Sweet & Maxwell ch.10,11 and 43.

8 See Part 7.3

problem, rather than present evidence and argument in an attempt to prove your client's position, and to address what the other side is saying, rather than score points from your opponent. It frees you to be creative.

2.6 Getting your Instructing Solicitor or Principal to Agree to Mediation

It should follow from what I have said thus far that mediation is not an arena for the unskilled or the naïve. However, the barrier to engaging in this process may not come from the lay client, but there may be resistance from your instructing solicitor, if you are counsel, or from your principal should you have one. It could come from counsel himself. Either way objection in the absence of a good arguable reason is now inconsistent with the CPR, most judicial thought and certainly case management, and indeed, commercial good sense.

Opposition may be due to the same problems of perception that accords with the initial reaction of the lay client. Although most major firms now embrace all forms of dispute resolution as part of their litigation departments, there is still a fairly widespread and genuine lack of enlightenment among senior lawyers, a prejudice to the effect that this process is somehow less lawyerly, and a worry about lowering of fee income in contentious business. For many 'ADR' is seen as *'Alarming Drop in Revenue.'* They haven't the foresight to recognise the marketing power, ultimately, of the truly satisfied client, repeat business and reputational enhancement.

You will need to argue that where mediation is entirely suited to the client's particular needs, and the court will, in applying active case management, regard it as suitable for the particular claim, your instructing solicitor or principal should take the credit for promoting it to the client. If the mediation is successful, even though there might be a diminution in the fee income that could otherwise have been achieved by litigating the particular case to trial, the firm will have achieved client satisfaction, leading to a strengthened relationship. The litigation may well have settled anyway - considerably over 90% of issued claim forms never get to trial. And if the mediation fails, the fee income is still available.

See whether there is or will be an impasse in any negotiations towards settlement; whether factors exist which suggest a compromise of the claim will be difficult, for example a serious power or economic imbalance between the parties, or a link between this dispute and other disputes (or present litigation). You may advise your instructing solicitor or principal that rather than pursue fruitless negotiations which may take months to lead nowhere, he should take the credit in the eyes of the court for moving the process along by proposing mediation.

At an early stage in the dispute you will be able to see if there is either a contractual trigger into mediation, or a court procedural directive – whether a local or jurisdictional-based court annexed or referred scheme, or an ad-hoc industry-based process.

2.7 Getting the Other Side to Mediate

Despite its many advantages, mediation is not a panacea, and there are cases where it is not appropriate; and as has been stressed, timing is equally, if not more, important. Therefore as a precursor I can not stress highly enough that you should not propose mediation to the other side unless and until you are satisfied that:

- it is appropriate for the dispute;
- your client understands what it is and why he should agree to it;
- it is the right tactic; and
- the time is right.[9]

The second obstacle you need to consider is the opposing party's expectation of the strength of its case and the likely outcome of a trial. Whatever view you take of the strength or otherwise of your own client's position you need to recognise that there may be serious and good faith differences between the parties' forecasts of the likely result. This operates to create a settlement gap that is difficult to bridge.

Thirdly, where relevant you should ponder the complexity of any situation in which you are instructed in a multi-party, multi-issue dispute. In most cases this should encourage mediation, but occasionally it can be a hurdle, and is likely to be perceived as such by any other party that is unfamiliar with mediation techniques for multi-party claims.

(1) If the subject matter of the dispute is contractual first see if there is an ADR/mediation clause, and, if so, whether it is mandatory and enforceable.[10] Whether mandatory or not, the existence of the clause should be drawn to the attention of the other side at the earliest opportunity. Let your opponent have the burden of explaining to a court why it should not be utilised.

9 See Dodson, Charles *Preparing for Mediation* (1997) 17 Resolutions, CEDR.

10 See e.g. *R G Carter Ltd v Edmund Nuttall Ltd* (2002) BLR 59; *O'Callaghan v Coral Racing Ltd* [1998] EWCA Civ 1801; *N v N* [1999] Fam. Div LTL Lawtel AC7800507.

(2) See if the other side's lawyers or professional advisors are members of either CEDR, ADR Group, SCMA, the CMC or one of the other widely recognised mediation service providers. Suggest that their opposition to mediation in your case is inconsistent with their membership of organisations promoting mediation.

(3) Point out that the Civil Procedure Rules require consideration of ADR anyway. Courts are serious about using CPR rr. 26.4, 1.3, 1.4(2)(e), 3.1(4), and the costs regime under r.44.5 (3). Where appropriate invite them to consider the practice directions provided for the specialist jurisdictions of the civil court: see, for example, Commercial Court Guide Part G

(4) If the other side have no prior experience of mediation and need an independent explanation of the process, provide them with some educational material.

(5) Show that the relevant business/social relationship can be preserved/ resumed.

(6) Underline that it is non-binding and therefore has little risk or downside.

(7) Where appropriate, suggest that information disclosed under pre-action protocols shows it is obvious that any creative commercial solution which the court cannot provide is the most desirable outcome for the parties.

(8) Reiterate that although mediation is no longer cheap in absolute terms, it remains a cheaper option than litigation taken to trial. High Court fees alone (that is costs excluding any other disbursements) amount to considerably over £18,000 per £100,000 claim from the issue of a claim form to the trial taking place. There are moves afoot to charge a daily rate for the use of the courtroom and judge, which you may think surprisingly mediaeval. (Perhaps in the future each different court will offer a discount to entice you to do business there!)

(9) A close analysis of the more recent cases[11] following *Halsey* suggests that judges will now generally consider imposing costs sanctions on parties who unreasonably decline mediation whether a judge recommends it or otherwise.

(10) Subject to the law as it develops after *Churchill*[12] there may be no choice anyway.

(11) For opponents who purport genuinely not to know the advantages of mediation they are these:

- It is desirable to be able to control the outcome of the dispute rather than have it imposed upon you, potentially leaving both

---

11 E.g. *Rolf v De Guerin* [2011] EWCA Civ 78; *Phillip Garritt-Critchley & Ors v Andrew Ronan and Solarpower PV Ltd* [2014] EWHC 1774 Ch; *Laporte v Commissioner of Police for the Metropolis* [2015] EWHC 371 (QB)

12 *Op.cit.*

parties dissatisfied by the experience. Many 'winners find that in real terms, taking into account time, irrecoverable costs and aggravation, they have not won anything at all.

- Where each side has some merit this may be reflected in a fairer outcome than the court is able to provide.
- The absence of a trial not necessarily wanted by both parties has its advantages: reduced costs, no full trial preparation, the litigation is not so protracted, and the absence of findings of fact that might subsequently be used by one of the parties.
- Generally there is a very speedy resolution.
- Those interests which are of real importance to either or both parties will not be obscured by technical or legal issues advanced by the lawyers within the framework of the litigation.
- There may be no real point in trying to fight against a legal principle where the determinative legal issues are already well settled.
- There may be a need to avoid an adverse precedent, and this consideration may attach itself to both sides.
- One or both parties may have good reasons to avoid the publicity which, potentially at least, is always thrown up by litigation whether at a local or even national level.
- One or both parties desires that, for commercial or other reasons, the existence of the dispute itself should not become known.
- One or both parties may have a desire to limit the disclosure they would otherwise have to provide in the course of the action.
- A party has disclosure which would be embarrassing, either in the context of the dispute, or generally.
- A party has trade or business secrets which it would prefer not to reveal but which might become public if the case went to trial.
- The case may settle before trial, and if so it is as well to try and stop it sooner rather than later. There may be no good reason why the case should not settle, but it requires the impetus of objective and outside thought.
- Perhaps neither side really wants to litigate, even though there are commercial or social reasons for doing so.
- A mediator will help diffuse the emotion or hostility that may otherwise bar any settlement.
- The uncertain outcome of a trial is generally a good reason to mediate.

If you cannot persuade your opponent to consider mediation, or if, for some good reason, you feel uncomfortable in doing so, one of the functions of a mediation service provider is to approach the other side at an early juncture to explore the desirability of mediation. Use an experienced neutral third party or a mediation service provider to break down the resistance to mediate. They will be better practised than you in dealing with the range of excuses made to evade the process because of its unsuitability for this case. They will be able to answer the typical assertions that mediation is not appropriate because the case is too complex, there are different legal opinions on the merits, the experts cannot agree, or there is too much or too little at stake.

Current judicial thought in the Court of Appeal after *Halsey,* namely in *Burchall v Bullard*[13], *Rolf v De Guerin,*[14] *Gaith v Indesit Company UK Ltd,*[15] *Faidi v Elliott Corporation,*[16] and *PGF*[17] is that there is only a limited range of cases where mediation is in fact unsuitable – the desire for a public law precedent, a clear case for summary judgment, and where urgent injunctive relief is required, although in both *PGF* and *Swain Mason & Ors v Mills & Reeve*[18] the Court emphasised that it was not contemplating a move towards mandatory or court directed mediation, even though the Court does have the power to do so. Even in claims for injunctive relief, the case can certainly proceed to mediation after an interim order is made; likewise after an attempt at summary judgment has been made.

The CPR and court annexed schemes should by now have overcome the 'don't blink first' mentality of litigants and their lawyers, and also ironed out any stance where a party insists on pre-conditions before entering the process. The strong support shown by the court for confidentiality[19], affording the contents of the mediation the same status as "without prejudice" negotiations, is designed to give confidence to the parties.

2.8 Arguing Against Mediation

As an advocate you must know equally how to argue in a case management hearing against your client being pushed into a mediation that you consider inappropriate to meet his or her needs. While the combined effect of *Halsey*[20], *Dunnett* v *Railtrack*[21] and *Hurst* v *Leeming*[22] and those cases referred to at part 2.7 above is that all members of the legal profession who conduct litigation

---

13 [2005] BLR 330

14 [2011] EWCA Civ 78

15 [2012] EWCA Civ 642

16 [2012] EWCA Civ 287

17 *Op.cit.*

18 [2012] EWCA Civ 498

19 *Venture Investment Placement Ltd v Hall* [2005] EWHC 1227 (Ch) and *Reed Executive Plc v Reed Business Information* [2004] EWCA Civ 887; see also Chapter 6.

20 *Op.cit.*

21 [2002] 1 WLR 2434

22 [2003] 1 Lloyds Rep 379

should now routinely consider with their clients whether their dispute is suitable for ADR, that most cases are to be regarded as suitable for mediation, and that (short of compulsion) a judge's encouragement for parties to go to ADR may be robust and he will not necessarily accept an unwillingness at face value, you have to be able to withstand such pressure if you genuinely believe it is wrong for your client on the facts as you know them to be.

We have touched upon the factors which will impede the court's charge towards mediation above. These concern situations where:

(a) At least one side requires a precedent.[23]

(b) There is in fact (or law) no bona fide dispute - one side's position is devoid of merit. It is not enough to be your subjective view, as a court will have to be persuaded there is no merit in trying to mediate.

(c) Your client needs a remedy which mediation cannot achieve, namely an injunction or other mandatory or prohibitory order of the court.

There are other arguments available to resist the drive towards mediation, or tactical considerations by reason of which your client should not engage the mediation process at this particular stage in the action. For example:

(a) The advantage of delay heavily favours one side.

(b) The case can be settled soon through unassisted negotiations, particularly where specialist lawyers or subject matter experts are involved.

(c) Conversely, there is no motivation to settle at all.

(d) One party requires a full open court personal vindication, with which position the court is likely to agree.

(e) The case concerns criminal activity, family relationships or requires the paramountcy of the court's jurisdiction.

(f) There are vital corporate interests involved.

(g) The amount in dispute is extremely large, or indeed so small that it cannot justify mediation costs.

(h) Taken together with any of the previous factors, more time is needed to properly evaluate each side's position and settlement possibilities.[24]

(i) In the context of the foregoing matter, expert evidence is needed before the decision to mediate can be taken.

(j) There has not been sufficient disclosure.

---

23 *McCook v Lobo* [2002] EWCA Civ 1760

24 *SITA v Wyatt* [2002] EWHC 2401 Ch; *Corenso v Burnden* [2003] EWHC 1805 (QB).

(k) In the particular circumstances of the case there should be an exchange of witness statements first.

(l) Where on any view the cost/benefit analysis suggests that the costs of the mediation will be disproportionate to the value of the claim.

Approach your argument against having a mediation with care and particularity. If the case proceeds to trial even if you win the court may wish to consider whether mediation was unreasonably refused at the behest of the losing party on any hearing to deal with costs, and will look at all of the pertinent circumstances including the nature of the dispute, the merits of the case, whether other settlement methods had been attempted, whether the costs of ADR might have been disproportionately high, whether the delay to accommodate some form of mediation would have delayed the trial significantly, and whether mediation had a reasonable prospect of success. Your or your client's belief in the strength of the case is not of itself a ground for refusing mediation,[25] and a judge may well deprive a winning party of his costs if he concludes that mediation would have been suitable, was likely to be fruitful and should at least have been tried.

25 Per Lightman J in *Hurst v Leeming* [2003] 1 Lloyds Rep 379

Part 3

Choosing a Mediator

Chapter 3
Choosing a Mediator

For an advocate the ability to choose the composition of your tribunal is an unusual and illuminating experience. Although it cannot be stressed too highly that a mediator has no arbitral powers and is not going to be a decision maker, the parties will undoubtedly respect him or her as a figure of authority as the chairman and convenor of the proceedings, and will rely upon his gravitas and experience. He will in fact assist in adjudicating on procedural matters, usually by providing direction and making positive suggestions with which the parties are expected to agree. Invariably your lay client is likely to regard him as a sort of judge, even though you must make it plain that he is not.

More often than not, as an advocate you may only be instructed after the mediator has been appointed. However, when available, the opportunity to select the appropriate mediator should never be wasted. Guidance over the selection is no less a function of the advocate than any other pre-hearing advisory work, and should be approached with care. If you are asked to advise at an early stage in the dispute there are two important practical questions to consider in choosing a mediator. First, should a mediation service provider be appointed? Second, should the mediator himself or herself be a lawyer; do you require an expert in the area of the dispute, or else an experienced layman (i.e. non-lawyer), remembering that in certain jurisdictions, for example Italy and Turkey, civil/commercial mediators have to be qualified lawyers.

You are looking for a mediator who has a number of qualities. Apart from having obtained an appropriate qualification from, and continuing professional education or current accreditation with, a recognised mediation training body or provider service, you need a person of reasonable experience having some knowledge of, if not expertise in, the area of the dispute. He or she needs to have a good bedside manner, with the common touch – hand holding is an integral part of the mediator's skill, since he also requires patience, and the ability to absorb a party's frustration, anger or anxiety. You will want as a candidate someone with innovative ideas or problem-solving skills who is a good communicator, and exudes a sense of authority without pomposity. He will himself need to be an advocate in the sense of being proficient in examining and testing a party's stated position and to deal readily with the consequences. Someone with energy and a sense of humour would be a useful bonus, as these can be important attributes.

3.1 Choosing the Right Mediator

Whether you opt for a mediation service provider or not, you still have to decide or agree who is the right mediator for your client. Presupposing that those institutions who train mediators provide accreditation and continuing education to a set quality threshold, and that the procedures, method and practice in which each train their own particular mediators are broadly similar, the question for you is how to match the most appropriate and desirable mediator to your dispute.

First, since you are an advocate, consider whether you want a mediator who is also a lawyer by professional background, if not actually in practice. The advantages are readily apparent: experienced litigators and counsel develop well-honed practical skills in critical analysis, problem solving and communication. They can be incisive in identifying key issues and focussing upon the factual and legal merits of a particular position. A mediator who is familiar with the area of law in question can, if called upon to do so, engage in debate on the law, know the key cases and recognise the legal merits of the parties' respective positions. A lawyer may also have practical experience of litigating disputes of the type being mediated.

Specialist lawyer mediators will readily understand the legal and commercial context in which the dispute sits; they will gain the respect of both advocates and their lay clients more quickly; there need be no time wasted in laboured explanation; the lay parties' suspicion, wariness or frustration may thus be minimised. They will be aware of procedural timetabling, case management and the impact of costs in the litigation.

Having said that, whilst you and your opposite number may be conscious of the legal parameters and merits of the dispute, a non-lawyer mediator may have a completely different overview of the settlement objectives of the parties. He or she will be far less likely to be concerned about legal practicalities or niceties, and will be less interested in whether or not you will be able to prove your case to a court on another occasion. In that sense a non-lawyer mediator may be of greater appeal to a party that has an obviously weaker case in law.

You should be aware that a non-lawyer mediator will not welcome being tied down to arguments concerning the legal aspects of the dispute. He may make you feel undue haste in getting to the horse-trading part of the process. He may be keener than a lawyer mediator to separate you from your client in the sense that he will regard you as the gatekeeper of your client's legal interests – he will not be terribly concerned about your client's legal interests – since his objective is to find a solution to the dispute using means that may well fall substantially outside of the legal constraints and procedures that you associate with the litigation. If such a mediator makes you feel uncomfortable please remember he is not a judge, and neither his task nor the process itself is intended to impose a settlement on your client.

Both advocates and lawyer mediators need to guard against a strictly legal analysis of the dispute. This may be difficult for all lawyers. The importance of analysing a dispute in the broadest terms and not confining it to its strictly legal nature is underlined by the approach of mediation training organisations when teaching new mediators to distinguish between facilitative and evaluative mediation. Evaluative mediation is essentially opinion forming, and lawyer mediators have great difficulty in refraining from making value judgments about the parties' positions. At least they can learn to restrain themselves from expressing an opinion unless expressly called upon to do so.

With a plethora of mediators now available the expertise and experience of your potential candidate is of real importance. You have the ability to select for your hearing a mediator who is an acknowledged authority in his specialist field, be it medical, technical, financial or legal. He will be able to identify most known solutions to common problems in that area and, hopefully, adapt them to fit the parties' particular circumstances.

In certain circumstances you may consider that a non-lawyer, non-specialist mediator happens to be the right person, particularly if he comes by recommendation to you or your party. Both you and your client need to feel confident that he will observe confidentiality; that he will exercise control over the proceedings, and certainly that he is able to control time; that he will keep all parties informed of what is going on; that he is seen to be neutral; that he has sufficient gravitas and authority – a particular advantage of using a former judge; that he has no personal agenda, is not a bully, will be even-handed, patient and an innovative problem solver, whether evaluative or facilitative.[1]

You may have to advise whether or not co-mediators are required. If there are a large number of parties or issues a single mediator may not be able to have sufficient creativity, or indeed time: mediator teams are useful in

1 The European Code of Conduct for Mediators has specific provisions about impartiality and confidentiality.

working with parties to build up trust and dealing with cultural or jurisdictional differences. A mediation team can be mixed between a lawyer and an expert, or mediators from or experienced in the separate cultures or jurisdictions. The appointment of a mediation team means that more than one activity can take place simultaneously at the hearing. Where a mediation team is involved, one solution that is sometimes adopted is to re-constitute as a form of arbitral hearing involving findings by a member of the mediation team who has not previously engaged in any confidential discussions. Whether or not a mediation team adopts such a solution, it is crucial that the members have complementary skills and work well together.

In the article *'Choose Carefully: All Mediators Are Not Created Equal* ' from his series *Mediation Strategies*[2] the well-known California mediator, Lee Jay Berman, advises if a mediation is going to have a chance at success, perhaps the most important decision is who will sit in the neutral chair at the head of the table. From case to case, that decision will vary. Advocates owe it to their clients to invest the time in investigating, strategising and selecting the right mediator for each case. He suggests that in a time when we have retired judges, litigators, transactional advocates, and professional mediators available, and when more mediators are specialising in particular areas of practice, the best way to select the right mediator requires a strategy.

He recommends, among others, the following considerations

- mediators need to be selected on a consensus basis, rather than a least objectionable or lowest-common-denominator basis. Mediation has a greater chance of settling the case if all parties believe in the mediator's reputation, personality and qualifications.
- Just because the other side has proposed a mediator that they have worked with before, that is no reason to object to that mediator. The mediator has no ability to make you agree to anything you don't want to, nor can they coerce or pressure you or your client. If the other advocate is proposing a mediator they are probably doing so because they feel that mediator at least can be trusted and has a client rapport, or has the ability to settle the case, which means finding mutually agreeable terms for settlement.
- Consider the level of actual mediation training your mediator has. After all, if settling the case was easy to do, you wouldn't need a third

2 See www.mediate.com archive material and the SCMA website newsletter archive at www.mediationadvocates.org.uk or www.scmastandards.com

party to assist you and your opposing number.

- Consider the mediator's record for tenacity to see the case through to resolution. A mediator can only keep going if they have the skills to keep trying different things, and if they have what some have called "an iron rear end" and are willing to sit and keep working for as long as it takes to get a case resolved. That tenacity, or resolve to settle a case, is one of the most important features to look for in evaluating a mediator, and in interviewing other counsel who have worked with that mediator in the past.

- Ask your opposite number about the type of mediator to which they would best respond. Some cases (and sometimes your opposite number) require an authoritative voice of a retired judge or litigator with decades of experience. Others may respond better to a persuasive, personable mediator who reaches people well and can see the big picture. Some cases require a macho authority figure, while others may do better with a more sensitive touch. It is important to consider variables such as these in each case. No case will be like any other, since the personalities at the table will be different and will respond to different types of mediators. You will also need to consider your relationship with your opposite number and whether you want your mediator to provide more of a facilitated negotiation or an evaluative appraisal of the case.

- Consider your client's state of mind. If they are highly emotional about the case, they will benefit (as will you) from a mediator who can handle emotional parties and help move them to a place where they can make a decision, gently guiding the case to a smooth settlement. If they are stubborn and intransigent, they may need logic and tenacious persuading. If they are weak decision-makers or are unsure about the fair value of their case, they may need the authority of a retired judge or seasoned litigator.

- Consider your own strengths and weaknesses. This may be the hardest part, but it is critical to know yourself with clarity. For example, if you have a strong, authoritative presence, you may benefit from a mediator who has a softer touch to complement you. If you tend to be more left-brained, or a more logical or linear thinker, you may want a mediator who is more right-brained, more emotionally attuned, and perhaps creative. If you have a client control problem, you may want a mediator whose style is more firm and directive.

- Consider the timing of the case. If your case is directed towards mediation by a date that you believe is too early in the case, and you are unable to persuade the judge of this, then you will want to select a tenacious mediator who is dedicated to following the case through the litigation process. Experienced mediators know that sometimes, the early mediation appointment is only the start of the mediation process, and that additional key disclosure may be required before a final settlement can be reached. You will want a mediator who is a real believer in peaceful resolutions and in not letting litigation get out of control unnecessarily. This could range from a no-nonsense retired judge to a former general counsel to a non-advocate mediator with business and economic sense.

- Consider the subject matter. It is not imperative, but it is helpful to have a mediator who understands the nature of the dispute. If the dispute is dissolution of a family business, it can be helpful to have a mediator who understands partnership, business and contract law. It could also be beneficial to have a mediator who is familiar with the workings of the particular industry in which the family operates their business. It may be even more beneficial to have a mediator who specialises in, or understands the unique dynamics of family businesses. The important thing to consider in selecting the mediator is that they are familiar with what it takes to discuss the issues and to reach a resolution. It is not enough for the mediator to understand the legal issues; he or she must understand how to relate enough to the parties and their legal team to bring the parties to a mutually agreeable resolution.

- Consider the difficulty level of the case. Many smaller cases can be less complex, such as a simple debt collection or personal injury case that most mediators might be able to resolve. Other cases are the type that only a small percentage of mediators can settle. For example, a wrongful death case may include legal issues, insurance coverage issues, medical issues, deep emotional loss issues, and structured settlement issues, and will require a very experienced mediator with lots of tools and skills. You will benefit by trying to match the skill level of the mediator to the difficulty level of the case. Some advocates will look at a very difficult case and assume that any mediation will fail, so they will pay little attention to the selection of mediator. Instead, try hiring a highly skilled mediator and give the mediation process a chance to settle the case.

- Ask colleagues for useful information as outlined above. Ask specific questions about each of these points, rather than simply asking if your colleague liked the mediator or thought he or she was competent. Even less informative is asking whether the case settled, since there are so many variables involved in whether a case settles or not, this may be the worst indicator of the mediator's skill and effectiveness.

3.2 The IMI Decision Tree

The International Mediation Institute publishes a number of tools to assist mediation advocates in running cases, of which one is a decision tree for finding the right mediator. It is included on page 80 and is part of the IMI 'Olé!' Concise Case Analysis & Evaluation Tool,[3] an important case management device for all serious practitioners of ADR. The decision tree invites you to pose a number of questions to assist in deciding what kind of mediator you need:

You may also need to consider the methodology of mediator selection:

- Should each side propose a list of potential mediators?
- Should the mediator(s) be selected from a common list?
- Should the mediator(s) be selected by an institution or court-annexed panel?
- Should you offer the other side to pick any neutral of their choice from a given list?
- What concerns may the other party have that need addressing?

Be aware whether mediator recommendations are coming from direct personal experience of working with that mediator before. Ask the other side whether and if so, how often the mediator has worked with them or their firm over the preceding, say, two years. Consider whether this is advantageous – a pre-existing relationship can make settlement proposals speedier and more likely, or disadvantageous – how it might look to your client. Even if there is no problem in reality, your client needs to feel comfortable with the process, and you need to raise this question with the other side in respect of all their recommendations. It will seem much worse if the facts come out during the mediation itself, with the client potentially distrusting the mediator, the other side for proposing him, and you for not finding out sooner and advising on the matter.

3 www.imi-mediation.com

ALTENBURGER

The IMI Decision Tree: http://www.imimediation.org/decision-tree.html

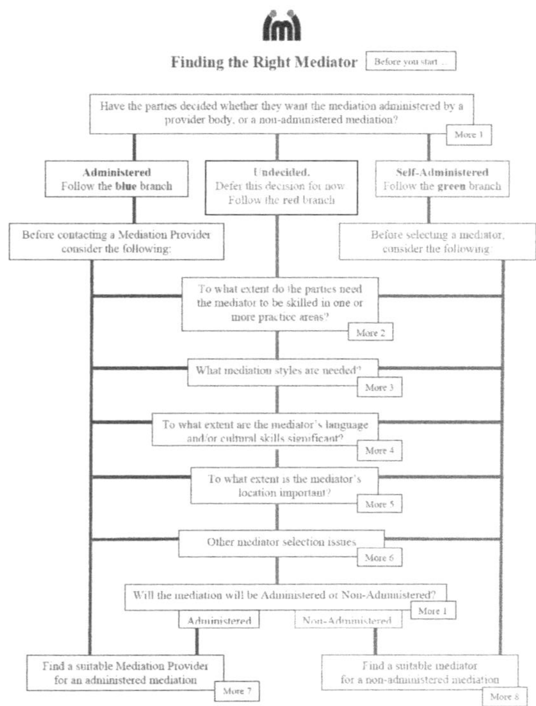

KEY QUESTIONS

1. Do the parties want an administered process or a self-administered mediation?
2. Do the parties want the mediator to be skilled in one or more practice areas?
3. What mediation style do the parties want?
   - Facilitative
   - Evaluative
   - Transformative
4. To what extent are the mediator's language or cultural skills significant?
5. To what extent is the mediator's location important?
6. Other key mediator selection issues
   - Availability
   - Costs
   - Use of Caucuses & Emotions
   - Code of Conduct
   - Mediator Profiles
   - References
   - Research/Feedback
   - Flexibility & hybrids (e.g., MEDALOA)

318 www.altenburger.ch

3.3 Mediation Service Providers

The great advantage of using a mediation service provider is the provision of administrative support, and a package which, for a global fee paid equally by both parties, will usually consist of:

- the supply of a recommended mediator on an approved list or accredited panel,
- his preparation and attendance,
- locating and hiring as necessary the venue,
- the management of the process from agreement to mediate until its conclusion.

Management of the process normally includes:

(i) providing explanatory material on the process itself;

(ii) identifying a shortlist of approved or accredited mediators experienced in such disputes, together with c.v. or résumé for each;

(iii) supplying an up to date standard form mediation agreement into which the parties will enter, together with the mediator;

(iv) agreeing and settling the mediator's instructions and remuneration;

(v) booking and dealing with the owners of the venue;

(vi) meeting any queries or problems raised by the parties, or the mediator;

(vii) co-ordinating the arrangements with the parties' lawyers;

(viii) conducting any post-mediation procedures.

There are now dozens of mediation service providers, ranging from training organisations, academic or professional institutions and trade bodies to private commercial firms. Absent using such a service most experienced mediators can be contacted directly.

You should choose a service provider with a substantial panel of mediators whose recommendations you can trust. You are looking for an organisation that will identify the right mediator for your dispute, and not merely nominate the same few, albeit highly experienced mediators, irrespective of the subject matter of the dispute, who are their trainers or faculty members. Its panel should have broad areas of expertise, and it must provide a fully administered service. This avoids contact directly with the mediator over minor but important details, which is likely to increase costs.

A fully administered service will:

- Help the parties agree the appropriate resolution process to use;
- Encourage reluctant parties to engage in the process;
- Advise on the appropriate mediator or neutral, or, where necessary and appropriate, the team of neutrals;
- Undertake and obtain a conflict check from the neutral;
- Provide as necessary a declaration of the neutral's independence;
- Negotiate the neutral's fee on behalf of parties and deal with his or her remuneration;
- Advise on the contents of the documents bundle;
- Advise on the contents of the case summaries;
- Seek to achieve balance between the parties attending the hearing;
- Secure from each party an agreement to the terms of the mediation or provide a standard form agreement for adoption, or as the basis for further discussion and amendment to suit the particular dispute;
- Secure and organise the venue, dealing with any problems that may arise;
- Provide the mediator with engrossed copies of the mediation agreement for signature by the parties on the day of the hearing;
- Deliver the appropriate papers to the mediator;
- Generally ensure that the process goes smoothly.

When selecting a service provider you should check precisely what the fee will include, and that the service provides all of the preceding matters.[4]

4 Fees may be negotiable.

Part 4

The Pre-Mediation Process

Chapter 4
The Pre-Mediation Process

4.1 Choosing The Venue

Unlike litigation, which is administered at fixed court sites depending upon their jurisdiction, you will have the opportunity to consider the most appropriate location for the mediation appointment, and should do so in geographical, physical, strategic and tactical terms. You may decide that the cost of the venue, party travel and accommodation makes it sensible for the mediation to be conducted online using a platform such as Zoom or Teams. If going digital, choose the platform with care for its stability, ease of use, sound and camera application and trouble shooting capability.

First discover whether the cost of the venue is included in any global fee. This should be the case if a mediation service provider is being used, otherwise there may be a separate hire charge raised. If an additional cost is being incurred consider whether it may be preferable to have the mediation cost free at the offices or chambers of one of the parties or their legal team. Identify where your clients, any attendees coming on their behalf, the other side and the mediator are located and propose the most central location where facilities are available. Mediators consider that reaching agreement on matters such as the venue and format of the mediation session is an important psychological step towards settlement; at least it moves the parties from areas of disagreement towards areas of agreement prior to the meeting.

In a two-party mediation a minimum of three rooms are usually required, one large enough for all participants, and two for private sessions. Where there are only two meeting rooms, one party will have private sessions in the plenary room. If there are insufficient rooms for the numbers attending, parties may have to make do with corridors, which is unsatisfactory. If the availability of rooms is generous the mediator may take the opportunity of having small parallel or simultaneous meetings between, for example, the experts, or the lawyers, while he pursues settlement avenues elsewhere. Whoever or whatever organisation hosts the mediation session, refreshments will have to be provided during the day and made available should the session go into the evening. The rooms should be accessible, comfortable, lit with natural light and heated, since parties may be occupying them for lengthy periods.

The parties' rooms need to have outside telephone lines if the wi-fi signal is unreliable, washrooms available both during and after business hours, and the host should make available wi-fi or broadband, fax or scanning and photocopying facilities, the first three to obtain additional information or documents, and the latter to ensure that any agreement is copied and distributed to all parties and the mediator prior to leaving the building, and afterwards to the mediation service provider. If at all possible, the venue needs to be staffed into the night, and information should be made available to the parties concerning local transport including taxis, last train times, parking availability after business hours, and local restaurants or takeaway services.

Strategic and tactical considerations often revolve around the question: should the mediation take place at your side's, their side's or a neutral venue? Occasionally parties to a dispute, particularly a defendant's solicitors or insurers believe that there is a tactical advantage in having control of the venue and require the claimant to attend their premises. If this is seen as a form of intimidation it will hardly be conducive to settlement. If having the mediation at one party's premises is genuinely, or can be portrayed as, a convenient cost-saving device, that is more acceptable. Invariably the mediator will prefer the parties to meet at a neutral location. For you the most important thing is that your client should feel comfortable and believe that the location, as in all other things, is a demonstration of the even-handedness of the process. He or she should not be put under pressure to accept a situation he does not want, nor feel he is being inconvenienced either by the other side or the mediator.

4.2 The Mediation Agreement

Despite the fact that mediation service providers, or indeed mediators working independently, will provide the parties with a current standard form mediation agreement which they have devised, a lawyer should review and, if necessary, revise the mediation documentation with input from the client. It may well be that someone with far more mediation experience than you has settled the agreement, but those appearing in mediation must take their clients through the document so that its terms are both comprehensive to the dispute and fully understood. These documents have developed organically with the growth of mediation practice and the response of the court to the mediation process over the last decade.

There are certain key points which must be found in every mediation agreement:

i. The entire proceedings are confidential and without prejudice.

ii. No party may call the mediator to give evidence in later proceedings of what he has learned in the course of the mediation[1]. This prohibition extends to costs proceedings.

iii. The process is voluntary: any party can call a halt to the proceedings without sanction.

iv. The mediator's role is to facilitate a settlement, not to pass any judgment or make any findings.

v. The terms of any agreed settlement are to be in writing.

In addition to these fundamental provisions, it is possible to agree the format or contents of the mediation by the insertion of agreed protocols into the agreement. Examples of such usual clauses as these are:

- The parties will have authority to settle on the day.
- The parties will observe the mediator's directions.
- The parties will remain at the mediation for a minimum of one private session each.
- The mediation may be terminated in the event of a specified circumstance.
- The parties will not record/tape the mediation sessions.

Some standard form mediation agreements now extend to fairly sizeable documents with explanatory notes and guidance as to the conduct of the mediator.

Good examples of two of these are to be found at Appendix II and III.

1 The question of the compellability of a mediator was one of the central features of *Farm Assist Ltd v DEFRA (No.2)* [2009] EWHC 1102 TCC in which the court concluded that a separate manifestation of 'mediation confidentiality' was vested in the mediator, but that this could be overridden in certain circumstances. See Part 6 for a further discussion. As a consequence the wording of the Mediation Agreement should extend the mediator's privilege, such as it is, beyond the pre-existing dispute to cover the entirety of the mediation process, including post-mediation appointment work of any kind performed by him or her, and any settlement agreement.

4.3 Document Preparation

It may be a broad generalisation but documents rarely play an important part in mediation, and the production of bundles comparable to a trial is certainly unnecessary on most occasions. That is because you are not trying to prove your case, although it may be vital to your negotiating stance that the mediator and the other side are made aware of how you see the strength of your position, which, presumably, you will wish or be able to support with objective documentary evidence. The strength of the legal case is ever-present as a frame of reference (see Fig. 1: 'the Box'). Bundles should be minimal however, perhaps the equivalent of a jointly agreed core bundle comprising only key documents and, if the dispute is in litigation, the salient court documents.

Remember that the mediator will need sufficient material to 'hit the ground running' since he is being asked to guide the parties in only a few hours to the resolution of a dispute which is likely to have been running for months if not years. He will need such time as you consider necessary for him to absorb the facts and key arguments, undertake some background research and consider possible strategies in advance of commencing the negotiation.

Having said that, the typical fee for the mediator will allow only for a relatively short period of preparation unless additional reading time is specifically agreed beforehand. Bear in mind what the role of the mediator is going to be. There is no point in running up a bill for preparing bundles of documents that the mediator will not use. Aim for a maximum of 100 pages unless the value of the dispute really justifies more.

For the advocate the task of identifying minimum key documents becomes very important. You will need to focus on those items vital to establish the background – limiting the statements of case or other case management material to only those needed to understand the issues - and those necessary for you to establish your case or undermine that of your opponent. All non-essential documents should be rejected. This means that *inter-partes* correspondence is seldom to be included unless you consider it absolutely crucial.[2]

The primary purpose of the documents is not to prove your case but to support the explanation of the issues that you are presenting to the other side. In considering what to include, see whether the issues appear to be clear to your opponent: parties sometimes surprise you at a very late stage of proceedings

2 If there are a large number of documents, consider whether a reading list will assist the mediator.

by their obvious misunderstanding of your client's position. This is particularly true of the way damages are calculated or argued. Documents that you wish to rely on in supporting your case on quantum should be furnished to the other side well in advance of the mediation hearing. Anything else can be brought with but is unlikely to be needed.

One *caveat* to the minimal documents rule applies, and that is the production and use of expert reports in the mediation. For cases turning on scientific or technical matters it may be essential for the mediator to develop a working understanding of the problem at hand and the issues dividing the parties, and it may not be possible for him to do so in the absence of such reports. You need to consider whether such reports concern peripheral matters and do not, in fact, go to the core of the dispute between the parties; or whether there are adequate paths to settlement without the mediator or the parties having to consider or resolve the issues for expert evidence which would otherwise have to be proven or disproven at a trial. If it is vital that the mediator deals with the issues being addressed by experts, decide whether a report which may have been prepared for trial is too long or complex, and whether a summary or abstract might suffice. If you adopt this course do not forget that there may be additional documents needed, which are necessary to support the expert opinion upon which you wish to rely.

There will be instances where you have to decide whether the mediator should be asked to read witness statements. You may be better off preparing short summaries of what, it is anticipated, each witness will deal with at the trial. Mediators are unlikely to see the need to read witness statements prepared for trial. However, you, as the advocate, must force the issue if you consider it sufficiently important, bearing in mind at all times that you have to prove nothing to the mediator other than that your client is prepared to negotiate a settlement from a position of strength. Ultimately it is for you to decide or agree what the mediator ought to have. He may require very little, but you must be confident in asserting what you feel he really needs to see in order to understand the dispute, whether statements of case, core submissions, core documents, an abstract of the witness evidence or full experts' reports.

There may be confidential documents that you wish the mediator to see but not your opponent. These may be sent separately to the mediator prior to the hearing or shown to him in private session.

It is in your client's interest for you to try to agree the minimum documents with your opposing number wherever possible. If you can reach an agreement on the contents of hearing bundles, a timetable, and the format and length of case summaries, this should create a momentum and general spirit of agreement in which the participants arrive at the mediation in the right frame of mind.

4.4 The Written Position / Participation / Interest Statement

It has generally come to be regarded as an essential feature of pre-mediation preparation that representatives for each party exchange with the others and send to the mediator in good time for the hearing a reasonably concise statement of their client's case and the submissions that they wish to make. Ironically, while the document has commonly come to be known as a position statement, the whole point of the mediation process is to get the parties to move away from positional to principled bargaining. To that end, some practitioners now call it the party's *participation* or *interest* statement.

The purpose of this document is really threefold: first, to inform the mediator and your opposing party of the live issues in dispute and your client's current position; second, to explain and justify the merits of your client's stance; and third, as a vehicle towards settlement, to indicate a willingness to make appropriate concessions and point up settlement options.[3]

In spite of the need for brevity you will wish to take advantage of the opportunity to make sufficient key points in the written position or interest statement to persuade the mediator and the other side of the strengths of the case as seen from your own viewpoint. Your opponent will read it and probably his client before the mediation, and, like any piece of effective written advocacy, it should aim to overwhelm the opposing party and deflate his expectation. Therefore, you should establish what the key evidence is in support of your client's case, explain why it has force, and why at trial your client is likely to succeed on the merits. You should identify his approach to settlement, rehearse the risks, and can even make an offer or indicate possible concessions.

It is therefore clear that some skill is needed in the preparation of this document. You are not settling a written opening as such, nor is it a statement of case, pleading or document with a formal structure, but it should contain a number of essential ingredients. Tactically (as we shall see in dealing with the opening statement at the mediation itself) it is more astute to direct it at the opposing lay party, since it may be the first time this information will have been received without the screening of their lawyers.

3 This document should contain as a header or footer: "Without Prejudice - For the Purposes of Mediation Only."

I suggest that your position statement should contain the following:

1. Identify the Parties *and* the Participants

The mediator does not necessarily know who everyone is, or his or her status. Provide a list of the key personalities he will need to know about and their involvement in the subject matter of the dispute. For ease of reference he may prefer this to be in alphabetical order. This should not be confined to the parties to litigation, or indeed the parties to the dispute. It should extend to anyone having an influence on the outcome, which may include spouses or relatives of individuals, and directors or managers of corporate or institutional parties. You may wish to identify insurers by institution.

2. The Relevant History

Set out in concise form the relevant history leading up to the dispute. Concise in this instance means what it says – tell the mediator only what he needs to know. This should include any court intervention, finding or relevant part-disposal of any contentious matter.

3. Outline the Dispute

This is a key part of the document. Identify the issues that comprise the whole dispute, or are contextually relevant. Set out those matters that are agreed, those not agreed and each party's views.

4. Your Client's Case

Set out your case both as to facts and law, and the nature and extent of the claims as to quantum. (If this is a personal injury claim you should attach an updated schedule of loss.) Identify, as required, those matters of fact and law in dispute between the parties. Where appropriate, explain your client's feelings about the conduct of the other side. Show why your client's case on the contested issues is likely to be preferred by a court were the matter to be tried.

Some modern commentators suggest that since the point of the mediation is to effect settlement there may be no point in elevating the case to be a focal feature, and therefore commencing the process by reminding parties of the ambit of the dispute. That is, with respect, a naïve view, and one which seeks to emasculate one of the principal roles of the legal or party representative – to found a legitimate basis for settlement set against the context of valuing a party's position, as well as their needs and interests. At the outset, one cannot simply discard the case, unless it is so weak as not to be worth pursuing.

5. The Gateway to Settlement

Identify those issues or claims that you believe are capable of being resolved. Explain why your client has agreed to mediation. Deal with any previous settlement history and prior or current offers. Indicate what your client hopes to achieve by the mediation – what are his legal, commercial and personal objectives. Do not close the door to settlement by setting at this stage any limits or pre-conditions. Be constructive and try to dispel any prior aggression between the party's representatives.

6. A Chronology

If the mediator requests one, or if you believe having one may assist the mediator, prepare a chronology. Such a document should be neutral and avoid positional statements, and if possible should be agreed. It should be short and concise providing the key dates and a succinct explanation of major events where necessary. It may help to reduce the number of factual disputes between the parties.

4.5 "Working" with the Mediator in the Pre-Mediation Phase

Advocates should now have enough experience of case management not to be disconcerted by being telephoned by the mediator in advance of the appointment. What is unusual by comparison with litigation is that a mediator, unlike a judge, can and frequently does contact each side separately beforehand, as he or she wishes. In training, mediators are encouraged to do so.

The mediation process does not start on the day of the mediation. Most substantial cases will benefit from a preliminary meeting between the mediator and the lawyers involved, or at least an exchange of telephone calls. It is perfectly possible for the mediator to see parties separately in advance should he choose to do so. This is particularly the case where he wants to get an early feel for the players involved, start building a rapport, particularly with the lawyers, or "pick up" on sticky issues or difficult people. Mostly a telephone or Zoom call will suffice. This is intended as the beginning of a constructive, co-operative process in which the mediator will outline the process and responsibilities of the participants, check the lawyers' mediation experience, confirm who will be in attendance, confirm that settlement authority exists, request such further information as may be necessary, ask how the claim might settle, explore any existing offers, and generate a broader discussion of any likely pitfalls or hindrances to settlement. This information, or the nuances contained in some aspects of it, cannot necessarily be picked up from documents.

The mediator is not restricted to speaking merely to the lawyers involved. He or she may wish to speak directly with those holding authority to settle in order to start an empathic relationship, or to explain the procedure. This illustrates the flexibility of the process in which you are engaged. It also demonstrates that your mindset as a mediation advocate must be different from that of an advocate dealing with a judge in litigation. Any direct approach to your client should also serve at this early stage as a warning about the possibility of your losing control over the client and his case, which is an essential feature of the lawyer/client relationship during litigation, particularly for an advocate.

Making early contact after the mediator is appointed is also your opportunity to demonstrate to him a co-operative attitude. You will need to deal with procedural matters with him or her, for example, the timetable for agreeing core documents, a list of issues, and the exchange of case summaries with the other side. Ask him whether you need to send him anything in advance. Make sure he has everything he needs. This begins a process of trust and confidence-building since you will have to trust him to treat all parties equally.

There are a number of common questions that a mediator might ask ahead of the mediation, the answers to which you will be expected to know. For example:

- Why has the dispute not settled so far?
- What concerns do either you or your client have about negotiating with the other side – i.e. why have you chosen to mediate rather than negotiate directly?
- What problems are likely to arise in mediation negotiations?
- What is required of the other side in order to bring about a satisfactory settlement at the mediation?
- What for your client are the consequences of success?
- And what for your client are the consequences of failure?

These are all matters that will assist the mediator to plan ahead, and to an extent force the parties each to reflect on their present position.

The ability to approach the mediator directly is a useful strategic tool. It enables you, on instructions, to provide confidential documents[4] and information to him or her; to explain issues the way your client sees them; to feed through ideas as to how you think the case might settle; or to indicate the attitude of your lay client or of his insurers. You can also tell the mediator of previous negotiations and offers.

4.6 Decisions as to Strategy

(1) Who Should Attend

At an early stage you will need to consider whether in fact the client needs legal representation at the mediation. There will be few occasions when you conclude that representation is unnecessary but they may occur, for example, if your client is an experienced professional or, if a company wishes to use its company secretary or legal or financial director. You may decide that for reasons of strategy and cost a client that you consider strong enough and competent enough to protect his own commercial interests should be permitted to attend himself, having guided him through the procedure, the likely course of the negotiations, and the arguments and methods of persuasion likely to be adopted by the mediator.

If representation is necessary you should decide what the legal team should comprise. A sizeable legal team can undermine the economy of the process, and the opposite party may find it intimidating. The plenary and caucus rooms may suffer undue overcrowding. You may even convey the wrong message: you may inadvertently overemphasise the importance to your client either of the dispute itself or his need to settle.

Undoubtedly there may be observers and support staff. City law firms are particularly gregarious and never seem to arrive without at least a small army of assistants. While the mediation process is a useful exercise for trainees and pupil barristers to observe, ideally attendance should be kept to a minimum. Always have the courtesy to ask in advance whether trainees or pupils may attend. Their presence may, at the least, have an impact on logistics. Where you are instructed to turn up with a large team you should agree this in advance with the mediator.

Counsel should be employed if he or she has had extensive contact with the dispute as prior litigation, or if it is likely that he will conduct the trial should the mediation fail: this will enable him to gain knowledge of the nuances of the

4 If you are sending a confidential briefing note to the mediator this should contain a header or footer stating in terms that it is confidential to and for the mediator's purposes only.

case he might not grasp from the papers, a feel for potential witnesses, and an insight into the lay client on the other side and his legal team. Counsel should also be engaged if he has particular specialist knowledge of the legal area of the dispute, experience as a mediation advocate or a particular relationship with any client involved (e.g. insurers). The flexibility of the process is such that counsel may be instructed without the attendance of a solicitor. In most smaller cases it will not be cost effective for counsel to attend.

There are rare occasions when the client himself does not have to attend. Such an instance may concern the defendant to a class action in the latter stages of a series of mediations dealing with similar subject matter but different claimants, by which time the defendant's negotiating position and range is already known. Usually, however, the client will attend either as an individual, or as a team that has the relevant knowledge, authority to settle, and includes the core personality involved in the dispute, and has directors or officers of equal importance to the other side.

The mediator will require the attendance of all parties necessary to effect a settlement of both the issue at hand and any relevant parallel or wider issues. The advocate must consider with care who needs to attend for his client. Despite your strong advice as to who should be present, not all parties will be able to send a representative with full authority to settle: for example, an innovative solution, which addresses a wider settlement arena than the immediate dispute, may require authority from a director or a board resolution. It may be that a company's finance director is not present and the need for his presence was not envisaged when the mediation commenced. A local authority may need the approval of its finance or treasury committee based on an advice that the settlement is appropriate. A common occurrence is where insurers may be involved and present at the mediation but the insured parties may wish to be discreet about the participation of insurers, or the level of their cover. Often if the proposed settlement is complex it may need to have underlying financial arrangements agreed between banks or guarantors. An advocate needs to be mindful of these possibilities well in advance of the day. It will not surprise the experienced mediator to learn at some point during the mediation that authority to settle is not infinite. However steps must be taken to ensure that authority for any reasonably envisaged settlement is present.

Those individuals who attend the mediation hearing because of their participation in the dispute (rather than its resolution) are not witnesses as such but tend to be regarded in much the same way. Many lawyers still regard mediation as a quasi-trial rather than a managed settlement negotiation and feel the need to invite the attendance of those who will be witnesses at the trial if the mediation does not succeed. Normally it is not necessary to have those involved with the facts in issue – indeed a resolution can be easier to achieve if they are not involved in mediation - unless they are the principal parties. It is better not to have too many people in attendance. Ideally those attending should be the parties themselves, and, where necessary, a senior representative of a company or entity with authority to settle and/or the insurer. The mediator should be told who will be in attendance and their respective status.

There are other factors to take into account. You must consider with care any personality conflicts of which you are aware. There may be managerial or other same side conflicts to bear in mind. A common example is the impact of the analysis of his decision-making on the person who made the decision being complained of. If he is likely to become aggressive or embarrassed if found wrong – will this impact upon the mediation, particularly his desire to settle or have his company settle? The advocate must find the means to remove any potential undercurrent of conflict in the same side before it occurs.

The use of experts at the hearing needs careful thought. There may be fundamental, technical, valuation, tax or accounting issues, the last three being common. Both you and the mediator will want to ensure parity in the use of experts in the sense that neither party should be disadvantaged by imbalance in the use of expert evidence. All expert evidence to be relied upon, even if incomplete or in draft form, should be exchanged before the date of the mediation. Surprises are not conducive to settlement – they will merely cause the other side to walk out. So both sides must know experts are to attend the mediation, their identity and field of expertise, why they are coming and what they will say. Agreement may need to be reached about whether experts or advisers should attend or be on standby to be called if necessary, or to attend by telephone or videoconference.

(2) Who should be Contactable?

Having a support team at the client's premises or solicitor's offices is very useful. Often during the course of the day, new information or documents can be required which may suddenly become vital during the latter stages of the mediation. These may relate to issues of liability or quantum, or to deal with the workability or impact of creative solutions. It may also be preferable to have interested third parties, for example the insurer, available to provide telephone instructions rather than be present at the mediation. Please remember that mediations may continue long after office hours and if a support team or third party contact is required out of hours arrangements must be made accordingly.

Common problems may only emerge during the settlement phase. Title to property may have to be searched to see if it is encumbered. Tax implications may have to be considered by the parties' respective accountants. Having the necessary professionals on call even after hours may save an adjournment. Foresight in these respects is a useful thing.

(3) The Role of Attendees

Before attending the mediation, lawyers must have a good understanding not only of their own role but that of everyone present and must ensure their client is equally aware. However strong the client's case appears to be, and however much you wish to protect your client's interests - to the extent of protecting him from what you consider being a bad deal in the context of his legal rights - it is your responsibility to recognise and support the philosophy and objectives of the mediation. Once you are instructed to attend as your client's advocate there is no room for personal cynicism about the process in which you are engaged. Nor will it assist for you to compare the progress of the mediation with that of a trial. If you are unprepared for what is to follow both your and your client's expectations will be seriously challenged and may be undermined.

As an advocate in mediation you must understand the central participatory role of clients in the process and be ready to:

- Allow the client to speak and to be heard in open and closed sessions. This is central to the dynamic of mediation, even though you may risk losing control of the client, and possibly the situation.
- Be a supporter, not just a mouthpiece. There is a considerable amount of hand-holding to be done, particularly where the client's expectation or optimism diminishes.
- Focus on interests as opposed to legal rights. Look at the wider picture for settlement options – the legal case should remain just a frame of reference, but settlement need not follow the legal case if the client's true interests are wider or his needs can be met elsewhere.
- Manage the client's expectations by acting as 'the agent of reality'.[5]
- Act as a constructive negotiator, promoting positive solutions.

5 Nesic, Miryana *Mediation advocacy: how to keep it on track for results* Paper delivered at CEDR First Mediators' Congress 20 November 2003.

- Keep open lines of communication in the face of challenging emotions and mistrust, strong feelings, grievances, and issues of credibility.
- Take responsibility for the client when his own feelings get the better of him.
- Ensure that the momentum is maintained during periods when your side is not in private session with the mediator as he deals with another party.

Your client's role should be equally well defined prior to arriving at the venue. You must work out in advance who is going to do what, and the effect of your client actively participating rather than just sitting and listening throughout the proceedings, as would be the case at a trial. Decide who will make the opening statement and do not assume that automatically it should be you as the advocate. Tactically you can use an emotional client to embarrass the other side or impress on them how sympathetically a judge might react at the trial to receiving this party's evidence. This can be an effective way of showing off a good witness or emphasising favourable facts. A personal injury case may in particular require a demonstration of the nature of the disability, and this can be of considerable impact if shown by someone who will clearly be a good witness.

In any event your client's active participation will bring home to him or her that this is the day in court, and this is the opportunity to give vent to his feelings about the matter in a controlled but otherwise unrestricted way.

The opening remarks can be split between advocate and client, or even advocate, client and expert. Whatever the decision, the division of active roles should be planned well in advance and the contents well prepared.

As to the role of experts who are asked to be present it is quite likely the mediator will have in mind how they should be used. He will probably ask experts to meet privately and separately, after any contribution they may have made in open session and produce some jointly agreed parameters which can be used on a without prejudice basis to assist settlement strategies.

Do not forget that some clients may wish just to sit and listen and take no active role until actively encouraged to do so by the mediator. Even then they may assume that representing their case is what you are being paid for. An experienced mediator will know how to draw the parties into active participation, and sometimes on a level that may make you feel superfluous, although you must do your best to stifle that feeling if progress is obviously being made towards a resolution of the dispute.

(4) Preparing the Attendees

It follows from these suggestions that it is essential that you arrange a pre-mediation conference with the lay client for him to understand precisely what mediation involves. The client should assemble all of the information necessary for his representatives to understand not only the dispute but also any commercial or wider interests that require protection or advancement. At the conference the client and his legal team can then begin to consider how he wishes to negotiate. To that end at least one decision maker must be involved at the earliest stages of preparation. It is important to establish the difference between 'wants' and 'needs'. The opportunity should also be taken to determine the difference between the client's best alternative to a negotiated agreement ('BATNA') and his worst alternative to a negotiated agreement ('WATNA')[6]. A detailed risk analysis is a good way to prepare for both negotiations and to reduce expectations, particularly those held by persons in a higher managerial, corporate or institutional tier than those personally involved with the facts in dispute, and to diffuse any previously held aggressive or other strong emotions. You as the lawyer should apply rigorous logic when comparing the litigation risk with any proposed commercial solution. If costs budgets for litigation have yet to be prepared, everyone needs to know likely costs of both sides in taking the dispute to trial, including the costs of any appeal or enforcement and the likely ratio of irrecoverable costs.

The advocate should also take the time to explain the tactics that a mediator might employ in relation to the parties, their lawyers and their experts. He must ascertain exactly what technical or legal assistance will be required.

Make all who are to attend aware that normally a mediation can be a very long day. Any movement towards settlement is initially very slow, and it may take a long time to start. The momentum tends to pick up as the day ends but there can be large obstructions over small issues near the end of a concluded settlement, and these may run well into the evening. In addition any agreement reached must be reduced to writing and signed by the parties before they leave. Everyone should know that it is quite common for this stage to be long after nightfall, including well after the last train or normal bus home.

To that end legal representatives should not undermine the process by announcing that they have tickets for an evening event and will be leaving at 5.00 pm. It is unprofessional, and potentially an act bringing their profession into disrepute. Experienced advocates should be aware that mediation

6 For a more detailed discussion see the chapter on ATNAs in *Advanced Mediation Advocacy*

appointments are usually not time limited and should certainly make no other professional or social arrangements following a mediation. If that is the client's choice, so be it, but it should not be yours.

Unlike litigation there are no strictures on formal rehearsal or the training of parties for what is in store. A useful exercise to conduct for your client is to bring together everyone involved in the dispute and divide them into two teams to rehearse the entire negotiation strategy, with one team arguing for your client and the other against. Be curious about the other side's bargaining position. Do not assume you know their view of the strengths and weaknesses of their case, or their underlying interests. You are unlikely to know anything of their personalities. But you can try and put yourself in their position to ascertain their client's needs and interests.

The client must be encouraged to keep an open mind about the process and its likely outcome, and therefore to be flexible about his expectations. These should not be absolute; he should have a negotiating range not a fixed position. The same can be said for each of the participants on your side, particularly insurers. Getting the participants into the right frame of mind is part of the mediation advocate's task. If there is travel involved in getting to the venue, suggest a relaxed dinner in the hotel the night before.

(5) Ethics and Other Matters

There are a number of other matters you should consider either yourself or together with your client in a pre-mediation conference, apart from dispute-specific items. These concern aspects of your professional relationship with your opponent, or the opposing party if he is unrepresented, and the mediator, namely how you intend to discharge your role during the mediation. At a trial an advocate's approach and conduct is governed by the Civil Procedure Rules,[7] specific case management directions, the law of evidence and his obligations to the Court[8] and to the governing or regulatory bodies of his profession. Subject to the disciplinary sanctions for conduct unbecoming a solicitor or barrister, the only rules governing an advocate's conduct at a mediation are those contained in the mediation agreement or otherwise agreed between the parties and the mediator as a matter of procedure. There are no rules of evidence. The advocate is engaged to protect or enhance the client's interests in settling the dispute by whatever means he may consider expedient, professional and proper. This freedom may conflict with the extent to which either he, on instructions, or his client is completely candid with the

7 And particularly the Overriding Objective under Part 1.

8 *Vernon v Bosely (No 2)* [1999] QB 18 CA.

mediator or with the other side in presenting his client's case or negotiating stance. The ethical dilemma for lawyers is still something of a grey area and the subject of some ongoing debate, however the bottom line is that conduct during a mediation, which brings the reputation of a profession into disrepute, is likely to attract a disciplinary sanction.

For practical purposes, when discussing in conference the tactical approach to adopt in the forthcoming negotiation, either with the opposite party or the mediator, it is as well to keep in mind the following:

(i) The mediator succeeds because he operates on the basis of a relationship of trust. Each party reposes their trust in him, and he for his part must assume that what he is told, particularly what he is told in confidence, or is told to advance to the other side, is truthful. A breakdown of trust in the mediator is likely to cause the mediation to fail. Should you break faith with him he will find it difficult to continue to represent your position to the other parties.

(ii) If the opposing party is unhappy or uncomfortable or aggrieved at your negotiating style or position, he may simply walk away at any time. This is very likely if your opponent believes you to be disingenuous.

(iii) Mediated agreements may be set aside by the courts for being induced by misrepresentation[9] in the same way as any other contract,[10] and with all the consequences that will necessarily flow from such an eventuality.

4.7 What Does the Client Want to Achieve?

The pre-mediation conference with a lay client should establish precisely what outcome is needed, not just in relation to the legal cause of action or defence, but taking into account the full range of wider commercial, relationship, personal and emotional interests where present. One effective way of doing this is to list out everything the client is interested in achieving and then prioritising these by dividing them into categories. I suggest that the categories be ranked 'needs' 'would like' 'nice to have' and the items within each category ranked with a value: see Figure 5. Once the list has been compiled with values attached, it is a useful exercise to anticipate the other side's list, attributing such values as you believe are appropriate. The differences in value will give rise to bargaining, with hopefully, each side having matters to which

9 *Vedatech Corpn v Crystal Decision UK Ltd and Crystal Decision (Japan) KK* [2003] EWCA Civ 1066.

10 Foskett, Sir David *The Law and Practice of Compromise* Thomson Sweet & Maxwell 8th edn 2015 4-37/4-50.

they attribute less value being available to trade, with the recipient attributing greater value in their hands.

Figure 5: Preparation of a Prioritised List of Needs and Interests

Own Client	*Client's Perception of Other Side's View of Us*	*Client's Perception of Other Side*	*Other Side Actual (Discover at Mediation)*
We Need *1.* *2.* *3.* *4.*	*They think we need* *1.* *2.* *3.* *4.*	*We think they need* *1.* *2.* *3.* *4.*	*They need* *1.* *2.* *3.* *4.*
We would like *5.* *6.* *7.* *8.*	*They think we would like* *5.* *6.* *7.* *8.*	*We think they would like* *5.* *6.* *7.* *8.*	*They Would Like* *5.* *6.* *7.* *8.*
Happy to have *9.* *10.* *11.* *12.*	*They think we might want* *9.* *10.* *11.* *12.*	*We think they might want* *9.* *10.* *11.* *12.*	*They're happy to have* *9.* *10.* *11.* *12.*

This notion of looking for 'differences' which may be traded is a common strategy of the mediator, and a task for the advocate is to try and use the mediator to ascertain the true values within the other side's list. An experienced mediator will use this process, but not reveal such information.

A similar approach may be to compile in advance matters/items/issues that might be given away: see Fig. 6 opposite.

Apparent single issue cases should be broken down into smaller items: a payment of money as the issue can be divided into several issues by the application of time, so that it includes having to consider and agree the amount, the nature of the payment i.e. a single transfer or tranches; if the latter, how many and over what period; any discounting; any interest; any provision for default; provision for costs; any confidentiality attaching to the settlement. Thus what appears to be a sole issue can be converted in to eight for the purpose of bargaining.

Fig 6 Preparation of a Bargaining Framework for Negotiation

Own Client	*Client's Perception of Other Side's View of Us*
We Will Give *1.* *2.* *3.* *4.*	*They think we will give* *1.* *2.* *3.* *4.*
We might give *5.* *6.* *7.* *8.*	*They think we might give* *5.* *6.* *7.* *8.*
We will not give *9.* *10.* *11.* *12.*	*They think we will not give* *9.* *10.* *11.* *12.*

4.8 Obtaining Authority to Settle

It is an essential requirement of the process that all sides come to the mediation with authority to settle, and the mediation agreement will usually specify that this is so. *All persons who have to approve the settlement* should ordinarily be present at the mediation session, and where the settlement is subject to approval by a higher authority, that higher authority must attend and see the process, otherwise he will not be affected by the dynamic which propels the parties towards the agreement: any party external to the mediation may need to be persuaded that the settlement figure is justified. Moreover this means the parties themselves have authority, and not just their legal advisers, unless the latter are fully authorised to settle.

The lawyer should be prepared for probing in advance about any limit of his or his client's authority to settle. The mediator may well wish to receive a formal acknowledgement from the lawyer that his authority extends to the full amount of the Claim. If in fact the settlement authority is limited, you should ensure that the limit extends at least beyond offers previously made and rejected. The mediator may also require specific information about settlement authority to be given from third parties, an obvious example being an insurer's reserve.

An advocate does not discharge his duty, will certainly ensure the mediation shall fail, and may well be guilty of professional misconduct, if:

> (1) he fails to come to mediation with appropriate authority e.g. the decision-maker does not attend, or his authority is wholly inadequate and he fails to advise the mediator about authority problems;
>
> (2) he misrepresents to the mediator the level of his authority; or
>
> (3) he represents at the mediation he has no authority as a tactic to buy time or to impose negotiation pressure on the other side.

A mediation advocate must never overlook authority issues. Even if he is confident about his client's authority to settle, towards the end of the mediation the considerable and perhaps unexpected movement that often takes place can be derailed by one side lacking necessary authority. The settlement itself may easily be jeopardised. Therefore if you cannot make sure that the client has the means to meet a settlement because the momentum of the process is running away and there may be some circumstance where it is not possible to obtain authority e.g. a board approval is required, at least indicate in good faith when the authority will be made available, come clean about the problem as early as possible, and have the courage to suspend the proceedings if you judge it necessary to do so.

4.9 Working up the Mediation 'Brief'

Preparing for the mediation itself is no less onerous a task for the advocate than getting up a brief for trial, although it will necessarily be different since the emphasis will be on establishing the client's wider needs and interests and investing time in creating a negotiating strategy for a positive outcome. He or she must know the legal case, including all the pertinent facts and witnesses involved or likely to be so; be fully conversant with all of the important and contested legal and factual issues, having identified and analysed them; and be able to list the strengths and weaknesses of both sides. This requirement is almost a constant since one of the principal roles of the mediation advocate is to be able to make comparison with the legal frame of reference ("The Box" in Figure 1[11]) and so keep a close eye on the offer on the table, and the client's best alternative to a negotiated agreement (BATNA)[12]. What you are being paid for is to guide your client upon the relative merits of any offer in mediation, and what is the most probable outcome if the mediation fails to obtain a settlement.

He or she will usually be asked to prepare and deliver a brief opening statement. This is not a repetition of the written position statement and the advocate should try to find something new to say.

Although the mediation advocate does not have to plan the examination and cross-examination of witnesses, he should formulate tough questions for the mediator to take to the other side in the caucus sessions to reality test during the exploration phase of the mediation, and to reduce the expectation of the party opposite. I shall say more about adversarial and collaborative strategies later.[13]

Unlike a trial brief the mediation advocate has to work out in some detail his settlement or negotiation strategy. He must have opening settlement positions on both liability and quantum. He should have identified those imponderable factors that might cause his starting point to come under pressure, for example new or clarified information, or the impact of the other side appearing more cogent or compelling than anticipated.

The mediation advocate should be aware of what his client will eventually be prepared to settle for. He must be primed with a negotiating strategy enabling him to know how to get to where he wants. In order to do this he will have considered where negotiations stand now, and have taken instructions or given advice on a realistic settlement range.

As a consequence, he should keep away from founding an offer or making a demand based on the age of the case or its current progress in litigation. If he can identify the best likely outcome for his client, the advocate should try to ascertain what offers or demands will get his client within range of that outcome, and then move in that direction.

At all times during his final preparation the advocate should know:

- What are the real prospects of success at trial.
- What is the real value of the claim.

11 See p39.

12 See page 99.

13 See pp110-111

- What, if any, are the particular needs of the client.
- What result would be in his best interest.

Other commentators[14] have suggested there is a benefit to be obtained from having a checklist for final preparation.

Any checklist should include the following steps:

(1) Review all the files and know what evidence supports the case: what are the witnesses, core documents, expert reports and real evidence? Ensure you have all the information necessary for a final evaluation of the case.

(2) Know what heads of damage are claimed: is quantum justified or supported for each?

(3) Prepare calculations of interest down to the mediation, and then to an expected trial date.

(4) Know what assertions of law are to be advanced on (i) liability and (ii) damages, with supporting relevant, recent authority. In evaluating the frame of reference which is the legal case the mediator may put the two lawyers together to thrash out the legal position, or may wish to challenge your own view of the law.

(5) List out the particular strengths and weaknesses in your case.

(6) List out the particular strengths and weaknesses in your opponent's case.

(7) Set out the costs to date of your own side, the expected costs of the other side, and the anticipated costs of both parties from here to the end of the trial. Make sure you go into the mediation hearing knowing your client's breakdown of costs to date and any revisions to costs budgets, and calculate the likely irrecoverable element. Get the other side to produce theirs, either by a direct request or through the mediator. It is vital he knows what they are.

8) Review the mediation procedure - know what to expect.

(9) Confirm the attendance of all necessary participants involved in the mediation, and that the necessary authority to settle is available – the dispute cannot settle otherwise

14 See in particular Nesic, Miryana *Mediation* Tottel 2001; Dodson, Charles *Preparing for Mediation* CEDR Resolutions issue 17 Summer 1997.

(10) Mull over your negotiation strategy and refine it: know what compensation or restitution is possible; what plans for future action are practicable; how emotional or psychological issues can be dealt with; and how to 'expand the pie' by identifying opportunities that will be of benefit to both sides, e.g. costs savings, tax savings, time and opportunity cost savings, restoration or preservation of commercial, social or family relationships.

(11) Consider whether the settlement aimed for has any necessary financial, tax or technical implications that might give rise either to authority problems or potentially cause a settlement agreement to be delayed.

(12) Settle the formal parts of a draft Tomlin Order or settlement agreement i.e. parties, recitals, anticipated settlement clauses.

(13) Prepare an optimum draft settlement agreement so that you have a structure and something to aim for.

(14) Ensure that you have available everything that you will need on the day of the mediation appointment:

(a) calculator

(b) lap-top computer

(c) mobile phone

(d) important contact numbers

(e) case summaries/position statements

(f) agreed documents bundle

(g) other documents to be made available if referred to

(h) schedule of damages

(i) interest calculation

(j) costs breakdown

(k) note of opening

(l) counsel's opinions

(m) draft *Tomlin* Order including, where appropriate, draft confidentiality clause.

4.10 Pre-Mediation Preparation

It will be plain by now from the tenor of this book that mediation is not merely a negotiating process that requires little or no preparation. Do not let a lawyer's natural cynicism assume that the mediation hearing will merely be a horse-trading session. It follows from the preceding section that your client's case must be mastered and prepared in the ordinary way: it may not be presented or run in a trial format in the sense that you are trying to prove your case before an impartial decision-making tribunal, but the intellectual considerations are just the same. Both lay and professional clients will not appreciate it if you are seen to have been casual in your preparation.

In proffering advice on the tactics and procedure you wish your client to use in the mediation you must be in a position to explain the process and the roles of each of the participants (Note – the 'participants', not merely the 'parties'). You must be able to advise your client where it is the case:

- Not to have absolute expectations – his case will be the subject of reality testing both by the mediator in private meetings, or caucuses, and by the other side in open or plenary sessions.
- To know what he wants to achieve in terms of priorities: he must be comfortable with what is essential and what is an ideal, whether a monetary settlement or otherwise (see Fig.2).
- To deal with the realities of the situation as it may change during the mediation, otherwise he may face winning a Pyrrhic victory.

And you should make it clear that:

- He is able to treat the mediation as his 'day in court', participating actively to make all the points about which he is concerned.
- The ambit of settlement options is not constrained by either strict legal merits or litigation procedure, and he can look elsewhere for goals he wants to achieve, including non-monetary goals, and matters outside the present dispute.
- Procedurally, there is a possibility that separate meetings may occur within the mediation, e.g. between the two lawyers only, or the experts, lay clients', accountants, or directors as the mediator considers appropriate and the parties agree.

4.11 The Advice on Mediation for the Client

If called upon to prepare written advice for your client dealing with the mediation, whether formal or informal, the contents will necessarily be different from an opinion on the legal or evidential merits of a case in litigation, or its potential outcome in terms of quantum.

At the legal level of the dispute, you will of course want to assess the cause of action or defence in terms of its merits and quantum. To that end you will summarise the facts of the case, the legal issues, and the evidence available; you will consider your client's prospects in terms of the quantum of damage likely to be recovered, and discuss any other relief required, including its enforceability, perhaps evaluating the best- and worst-case outcomes and what percentage chance of each is probable. You may wish to factor in any available choice of process or particular timescale. Certainly, costs liability will be an important consideration in view of the regime under CPR Part 44.

However, unlike an advice in litigation, your analysis of the client's position does not stop there. There are two further levels[157] of the dispute that need to be taken into account in providing an advice on mediation. Beyond the strictly legal analysis there is a commercial level to the dispute. You have to understand what commercial arrangement reflects the client's needs and interests, and see what, if any, commercial solutions are available and suitable that might take into account past and future business opportunities involving the parties.

There is also a personal level to the dispute that may be of great importance to your client. You need to contemplate and advise how the client can obtain personal closure and move on with his life. He is not able to secure one of the benefits of a litigated outcome – in court he may have the satisfaction of a judge telling him he was right, although conversely he risks the court's disapproval of his actions, or he may win or lose only on a legal technicality. To resolve any personal issues the client needs a process of catharsis, and experienced mediators will be alive to this and use it as a path to settlement.

To advise properly upon the conduct and potential outcome of the litigation you must have a clear view of what you want to achieve. Is a monetary settlement all your client wants? What are his priorities? What objectives are essential and what are an ideal? Your client will have to deal with the realities of the situation so you must know what these are, and in doing so you will come to see what range of proposals you can make.

15 See: *Mediation Advocacy – How to keep it on track for results* Miryana Nesic, Hammonds, seminar at the First CEDR Mediator's Congress, London, November 2003.

4.12 Fixing the Mediation Date

Once the decision to mediate has been taken and a mediator has been appointed the date for the mediation should be fixed as soon as reasonably practicable. The mediator will generally be chosen according to his or her diary commitments with a view to mediating within a relatively short time period. Since key benefits to the client are the intended savings in costs and time when compared to running the dispute in litigation, you need to take advantage of the momentum of the parties having agreed to mediate and having agreed the particular mediator's appointment. If litigation is running it is important to suspend the running of time in the action and to stop the costs clock by halting any wider investigatory, disclosure or other procedural work. In the meantime you can run the mediation as a limited, self-contained entity for the purpose of costs.

While there is certainly a strong element of pre-mediation preparation to be dealt with, and occasionally telephone calls, meetings or dealings with the mediator, generally you should aim at a delay of no longer than three to four weeks between the appointment of the mediator and the mediation itself. Often a factor in agreeing the mediator, or his services being procured by a mediation services provider, is his or her availability. Arguably getting an early date for the mediation is more important than worrying about preparation time. If you are aware that extensive preparation will be required, or the attendance of key personnel or experts, that is a different matter and the appointment will have to be delayed. But once the decision to mediate has been made, the process should be driven forward and not allowed to lapse by inactivity.

4.13 Getting it Wrong

There are undoubtedly lawyers who find themselves having to represent clients at mediations and who, while not openly hostile to the concept, are antipathetic and disapproving, certainly perhaps only paying lip-service to a case management proposal or seeing mediation as a means of protecting their costs position. They are either reluctant, or too lazy or ignorant about mediation procedures to commit to what is required of them. This ambivalence towards a process which most agree should succeed more often than fail, leads to bad personal lawyering habits which undermine the dynamic and will put the client at a real disadvantage. Either the mediation will fail when it may well have led to settlement, or the client will actually walk away with a smaller settlement or a greater feeling of dissatisfaction than should have been the case.

The most significant of these bad habits is poor preparation – not having an adequate grasp on the day of the facts, evidence, law, the party's true interests, the settlement options available, and sufficient knowledge of the costs. This undermines the possibility of making the client aware of his best and worst alternatives to a negotiated agreement.

By way of contrast, some advocates adopt entirely the wrong approach with their preparation by getting up the case as if it were for a trial, that is, by assuming they have to 'prove' to the mediator or persuade him their client's case is better than that of the other side. This leads to the inclusion of too much material, and either using documents for their probative value rather than as a vehicle for settlement, or being wary about which documents to disclose to the mediator for fear of waiver of privilege or their misuse.

As I have mentioned above, some advocates dismiss mediation as a simple 'horse trading' exercise, when in reality the process is much more sophisticated than they can see, and in this respect they fail to take advantage of what is now a highly developed and skilled exercise in meeting their client's true needs, or if particularly fortunate, gaining their client's desires.

Other practical problems created by inexperienced or ambivalent representation include:

(i) Failing to involve all of the relevant parties in the mediation, or all of the parties outside the litigation; had all relevant parties been involved this might have unlocked the settlement by assisting with the wider interests of the parties.

(ii) Failing to identify who should be present at the mediation itself, e.g. the insurer who will fund or the technician who might be needed to implement the solution – a person with relevant financial (e.g. tax) or technical (e.g. conveyancing) knowledge, peripheral to the main argument but important to any practical solution.

(iii) Bringing in inappropriate or difficult persons – persons close to the dispute who have too much self-interest to protect, either within hierarchical establishments or other employment contexts, to be useful.

(iv) Bringing in the wrong person – a manager without sufficient knowledge of the dispute, who can make no positive contribution to the proceedings.

A lawyer or other mediation representative who has a negative attitude about the process or about being there, will not be difficult to spot. He is likely to display unfamiliarity with the procedure and uncertainty over the lawyer's role or the behaviour of the mediator. He will monopolise the private sessions giving his client no chance to air private thoughts or grievances. He may well adopt the stance (or reveal his belief and advise) that to apologise or express regret is an admission of liability, express concern about having to compromise on a matter of principle, exaggerate the need to preserve face or avoid loss of face (including his own rather that that of his client), give wildly optimistic advice to his client and over rely on his initial advice.

Such a representative is a liability: he sees only what he wants to see; he finds it difficult to acknowledge or understand his client's loss, anger or frustration; he does not consider it his role to deal with the client's goals or non-legal risks, e.g. the impact of litigation bringing adverse publicity, irretrievable lost management time, and other hidden costs. Such a lawyer concentrates on legal questions and may miss entirely the important commercial interests, not only of his client, but those of the other side that might prompt an advantageous settlement. He is the sort of advocate who will use vague language and clichéd expressions in the mediation, such as, 'there are no guarantees,' or 'who knows what the judge will do'- when he should be specific and advise his client about the risks involved in litigation.

Equally dangerous is the lawyer who is too sure of himself. He neglects relevant information. He ridicules good suggestions because they have been made by the other side or by the mediator. He may consider that his client has already invested too much time and money in the conflict to settle in mediation; or he may have given bullish advice before and be fearful of challenging his own client in a private session to re-adjust the unrealistic expectations held by the client which are likely to be exposed by the process as it continues.

A lawyer may properly be fearful of giving advice because it is too early and he needs more facts and evidence before he can make an appropriate assessment. If so he should ensure that mediation only occurs when the time is right.

The ambivalent, uncertain or unprepared mediation advocate may become antagonistic or emotionally involved in the dispute. Or he may consider that settlement in mediation is a purely commercial matter for the client in which he does not need to participate as a lawyer. This is true of that breed of litigator who sees himself as a hired gun and finds it difficult to assume a conciliatory role even as a negotiator.

The answer seems to be whatever your personal thoughts about mediation, put the client's interests first. You can only do this by:

- Keeping an open mind;
- Forming an understanding of the process;
- Learning about the procedure;
- Being prepared in all aspects of your case;
- Understanding that the legal framework of the dispute may be only one aspect of the parties' interests;
- Being receptive to solutions which are outside the legal framework of the dispute;
- Using the mediator as a tool with which to obtain a benefit for your client, rather than seeing him as an obstacle.

If you adopt this approach you will not only engage properly with the process, your client will benefit from the holistic, healing approach with which mediation is concerned:- to give your client control of his problem, help him find a desirable solution to it, and enable him to draw a line and move on with his life.

Part 5

The Mediation Day

Chapter 5
The Mediation Day

5.1 Timetabling

In the UK civil/commercial mediation model most mediations last a single day. Complex or multi-party cases may last two or three days, but even in very high value claims it would be unusual for a mediation to last for much longer. This contrasts with the 'Harvard' model used by the ICC and others, most civil law jurisdictions, and by Family Mediators in this jurisdiction, which are based on a series of fixed appointments which may last a period of weeks, and in which there is very little if any private caucusing, that is private meetings between the mediator and one side only.

Time-limited mediations generally last for up to three hours depending on the mediator, and these may be a feature of court-annexed or other mediation appointments. Commercial time limited mediation schemes can last for four or five hours and be fixed by agreement. In such cases the time is usually only fixed in relation to the mediator's or mediation service provider's fee, which may be topped up at an hourly rate thereafter.

5.2 Practical Considerations

Do not expect the mediation will finish within the set time frame: it is notoriously difficult to concertina the time required for the process to succeed to the satisfaction of the parties into a mere three hours. Some exponents, such as a pioneer of mediation, Andrew Fraley, operate a very successful time-limited model, but they are a rarity.

Mediations commonly run well into the evening, and certainly after close of normal business hours. Mediators will sometimes take advantage of the 'locked-room syndrome' or the fear of missing last transport links to focus the parties' minds on settlement, or at least overcome the last hurdles. Being under pressure of time impacts on the settlement dynamics – either the client or his lawyer feels he must go or the pressure of time makes the settlement ultimately unsatisfactory when considered with hindsight. Therefore make sure you leave enough time in your schedule: do not fix afternoon meetings or conferences; do not expect to get away for social activities in the early evening. There is little more unprofessional than a representative sabotaging mediation by needing to leave. Mediators may well invite the lay party to continue in his or her absence. Warn your client of the possible length of the appointment and to come prepared for a very long day.

Even when agreement has been reached it may still take some time for a document incorporating the heads of agreement to be prepared. The mediator will not allow the lawyers to depart without having done so, since he will not risk the settlement becoming unravelled if the parties have second thoughts on the way home.

Allow for substantial periods of inactivity during the day when the mediator may be elsewhere and you have completed any tasks set for you and your client in his absence. You should constantly finesse your negotiating position, adapting to any additional information or change affecting your client. The client should be advised to bring something else to do, or to read. You should not, unless your client is absent.

Make sure of the due date, familiarise yourself with the location of the mediation, and ensure that you arrive on time. If you are visiting an unfamiliar venue allow time to park, and to unload and carry any necessary files and materials to the venue. Being late sends a wrong message. If possible arrive about 30 minutes early to meet the mediator and client and establish a base in the room in which your client's private sessions will be conducted.

Although you will have burdened the mediator beforehand with as little as possible, take with you to the mediation all files, copies of any documents intended for the other side, writing materials, a laptop, mobile telephone, and portable printer if you have one. Consider the use of visual aids pertinent to the issues, which may make it easier to carry your points to the mediator and the opposite party. If you are going to produce documents to the other side that they have not yet seen, hand them out after any explanation you need to give, not beforehand.

5.3 Procedure

Although a key feature of mediation is its flexibility, where the parties are free to choose their own procedure with the guidance of the mediator, a standard procedure has evolved. Sophisticated and experienced practitioners are free to modify this to suit themselves, their clients and the circumstances of their case, but the novice in both training and representation needs a framework. Irrespective of the venue, the mediator is, in effect, the host. He or she will meet and greet the parties, explain the facilities and give guidance on the day's proceedings. This introductory meeting is important as it will usually be the first opportunity most of the participants have to meet the mediator. Some mediators take their time over these preliminary meetings, seeking information or clarification, engaging with the parties to start to build a relationship of confidence and trust, exploring the format of the opening joint session, and where necessary, encouraging or even cajoling reluctant parties to join and participate in that meeting. Such meetings can commonly now take up to an hour per party.

The parties and their representatives will first be asked to read through and sign the mediation agreement, either in the privacy of their own rooms or at the commencement of the opening session. The mediator will then sign that document himself. This feature of private dispute processing is of itself unusual, since the mediator is likely to have been acting de facto under the terms of the mediation agreement for days, if not a few weeks, prior to its execution. It is generally presumed that each party has signed individually and now each can sign the copy of the other.

The Joint Session or 'Plenary'

At the beginning of the opening joint session, after everyone in the room has introduced themselves, the mediator will give a short introduction to the procedure and the approximate timetable in which he will explain his function. Most mediators will take this opportunity to explain a little of their own background and experience and make certain key points:

That the process is voluntary and the parties are free to leave if they choose;

- That the entire process is confidential and without prejudice to the extent the law permits,[1] and will remain so unless or until a settlement agreement is reached;
- That the contents of the private sessions are confidential and will not be disclosed to the other side unless the mediator is expressly permitted to do so;
- That the parties are expected to have settlement authority.

The mediator will also encourage the parties by acknowledging the progress they have made in merely agreeing to the process and attending; he or she will probably caution them not to read anything into his choice of the order in which he sees the parties privately or the relative length of any private sessions.

1 See Chapter 6.

Essentially the open meeting is client-centred. The seating should be the mediator, then a lay client either side of him, and then the lawyers and outside of them any experts, supporters and observers, including third party decision makers. This is intended to contrast with litigation where in all hearings the lawyer is placed between the judge and the opposing parties.

The mediator will invite an opening statement of about 5 - 10 minutes from the legal representatives of each party followed by a short statement from each lay client. He will stress that these statements must be uninterrupted, and should be listened to carefully. This is an important part of the process and one not to be waived lightly even if your client is reluctant to share a room with the other disputant. It also presents the lawyer with a unique opportunity to speak directly to the decision-maker on the other side without interruption. The statements may result in a discussion, but it flows from what I have said that this opportunity should be prepared for carefully. If you believe your client will make a good witness should the matter go to trial, show him or her off. If your client is angry or upset at the way he has been treated, or you think the other side do not yet comprehend the impact of their behaviour on your client, allow him to give vent to his feelings. This is the time to do so. The mediator will generally summarise the parties' respective positions, but should not allow the discussion to descend into direct questions, nor should you encourage that.

After the opening session the parties retire to separate rooms. The mediator will then move from room to room, speaking with the parties, until there is either resolution or deadlock. He seeks as much information as he needs, then explores with each party the strengths and weaknesses of its or their case and the quantum, risks, and costs implications. He will want to know each party's wider aspirations for a successful outcome, and try to assess what each regards as most important. Even if he is not evaluative the mediator is hardly passive. He will probe your contentions and expectations. At the end of each private session or caucus he will review what he has been told and clarify what he may reveal to the other side, including any offers. He will want to know about any previous settlement proposals and on what basis they were calculated and rejected.

The mediator may at some stage invite the parties to return to a joint open session, so that a direct explanation or presentation of a particular point can be made, or if there is some particular difficulty. He may fragment the parties' teams by having the experts, the lawyers, or the decision-makers meet entirely separately, either simultaneously or consecutively. On the other hand the mediator may decide for good reason to have no further joint meeting after the opening session.

The mediation will ordinarily be concluded in one of three ways: there will be a concluded agreement; there will be an insuperable difficulty causing one or both sides to withdraw; or the time available may expire with the parties adjourning the mediation to be continued on another occasion.

Where there is a settlement the lawyers will draft the necessary agreement in as much detail as then possible and those present with the requisite authority will sign it before leaving. If one or both of the parties withdraw the mediator may have to make a report to that effect to the mediation service provider or, where it is a court-annexed mediation, to the court. The mediator will only report the fact of failure and is not entitled to apportion blame or the court to investigate it[2]

If the time available for the appointment expires the parties may wish to assess whether there is sufficient momentum in the negotiations to continue without a mediator. It may take a little time for the client and his lawyers to assess the position. If the mediator is still required a further session should be arranged as soon as reasonably practicable after the first. In the family and Harvard mediation models a series of appointments are booked, against an agreed set agenda, rather than trying to conclude a settlement within a day.

5.4 The Opening Statement

Presenting the opening statement in mediation is unlike making opening submissions to a judge at trial. However strange it feels, the advocate should address the opposite party directly and not the mediator. At this early stage his aim is to provide information about his client's concerns, not to negotiate or altercate or to propose or accept solutions.

Unlike a trial there is no formal structure. The mediator decides who goes first. Invariably it will be the claimant, but not always. Most importantly you should be aware that there is usually no right of reply, although unlike a court hearing the mediator will now customarily invite the parties to speak personally after and in addition to the lawyers.

As I have said previously, do not waste the opportunity presented by the invitation to give an opening statement: the mediator will ask the other side to listen to you without interruption, and focus on what you are saying.[3] There are few opportunities in contentious work to be able to address directly a decision

2 See *Venture Investment Placement Ltd v Hall* [2005] EWHC 1227 (Ch). In subsequent costs proceedings the court may not investigate or make a finding why the mediation did not succeed.

3 Anecdotal evidence suggests that imaginative openings that grab the party's attention are often very effective.

maker on the other side without interruption, or his being overprotected by his own legal team. Make full use of it.

Prepare and, if you can, practice the opening statement before the session. This will aid conciseness and accuracy. Brevity is important. Be concise and business like. If you haven't done so before, introduce your team. Then provide an uncluttered, unemotional focus on the core issues, not minutiae, dealing with your client's current needs - not past obsessions or grievances. Do not include much history unless it is directly relevant to the present settlement process. Do not refer to documents unless you consider it absolutely vital to do so. On the other hand, a visual aid, such as a chart or diagram, might hold the attention of the opposing side and make it easier to explain either a complicated or a technical position. Either at the commencement or conclusion you should assert your client's desire to work towards a settlement or some such positive statement.

You will already have decided in advance who will be present at the first and any subsequent joint session. If it is tactically advantageous, divide the presentation between those who should deal with the law, the facts, and emotive or technical issues. You may wish to encourage your client to deal with his commercial imperatives or emotional concerns, and can expect the mediator to encourage personal exchanges. Letting the client give vent to his feelings is what the mediator wishes to happen. You, as the advocate, need to decide on their likely impact and potential importance. It may be the only time that your client can says precisely what he wants in the way he wants to say it. Of course it may not be, but your client should still be given the opportunity to express his version and understanding of events, unless you consider it would be disastrous to permit him to do so.

In preparing the contents of your opening statement consider each of the following items:

(i) How briefly to deal with the history of the matter: cut out all unnecessary detail; where possible focus on the present situation and the future rather than the past.

(ii) How to summarise the main points of the dispute between the parties as you see them, using broad themes: go over the facts of the case, indicating areas of agreement and disagreement and the available evidence. Explain your analysis of liability and damages based on the facts of the case; if you are responding, say why you disagree with your opponent's statement of case. Analyse any different levels at which the conflict operates, including substantive law and the risk to the respective parties in either commercial or personal terms against their desire to end the litigation.

(iii) How best to outline what you want to achieve in the mediation: avoid specific settlement figures at the outset and speak in general terms. Avoid emotive language but explain the impact of the dispute on your client. Suggest what decisions need to be made at the mediation.

You will need to be realistic. While emphasising your strengths and presenting your case in the most favourable way, do not ignore its weaknesses. Tell the other side if you have already factored weaknesses into a previous offer, or at least that you are conscious of the weaker points of your case for the purpose of negotiation.

Select language and a style of presentation that will engage the opposing party in what you are saying - tell them that which will keep their attention – and do not cause them to switch off by telling them what they do not want to hear. Be positive – explain that you wish to have a settlement that will satisfy both sides.

After you have concluded your own presentation, listen carefully and without interruption to what the other side are saying in their opening. Do not be dismissive. Get the client to listen carefully – he may well be hearing something for the first time or something he has not appreciated or realised before. It is such revelations that break the logjam of previously held entrenched positions. If he is cynical try to ensure that he does not express his cynicism with facial or other gestures that are likely to alienate or antagonise the other side.

On the other hand, be aware that the party opposite may not have a genuine interest in settlement, and may only be there to assess the strengths and weaknesses of your case, using the mediation as a tactical device within the litigation (at whatever risk to himself on costs). If you suspect this to be the case do not duck the issue, and raise it with the mediator in caucus early on. Ask for some tangible sign of goodwill and consider whether your client's best interests are served by remaining if you are not reassured.

5.5 Private and Open Sessions

We have already discussed the flexibility with which the mediator can manage the process, and the range of meetings he has open to him, particularly in a multi-party or multi-level dispute. There he may have a plenary meeting and then joint or group sessions, and deal with experts or lawyers or laymen in parallel or sequential meetings. Do not be a passive observer on the question of management. Make a constructive contribution as to how you think your client's interests will be best served. You can and should disagree with the mediator if you have a good reason for doing so.

Open Sessions

Having both conducted and heard the presentations in the initial open or plenary session you will be in a position to consider the tactical advantages and disadvantages of such open sessions. Invariably the mediator will move into caucus sessions and rarely have another open session until settlement is achieved. He may utilise an open session to try and overcome a particularly difficult topic within the dispute where otherwise there is a complete logjam, the issue needs to be dealt with by the parties on a face to face basis, and the alternative is that one party or the other will leave. Occasionally either the advocate or the mediator may consider that conveying an explanation of a position or argument on a second hand basis will not be as effective as direct dialogue.

Try and gauge the impact of the first open meeting from its outset. Often it will be the first time a client and his advisers have met for a while; sometimes they may not previously have met at all; certainly it will be the first occasion on which the client and his own team have an opportunity to hear what the other side is saying first hand, and see how they are likely to appear in court. This will enable you to form a view about the value of the open sessions. If you are acting for a client who, by reason of his manner or appearance, age, sex or disability, or by virtue of the subject matter of the dispute, is someone that naturally attracts sympathy, make as much use of personal contact as possible. This restores the conflict to the level of personal ownership, and may make institutional opponents, or insurers standing behind them, very uncomfortable. It also provides a vulnerable or emotional client with a sense of having his or her 'day in court'.

Closed Sessions

The private or closed session, or caucus as it is sometimes called, is a central feature of the mediation process in the model most frequently used in the United Kingdom. One can do away with open meetings, including the joint opening session, and some mediators do; but you cannot do without caucusing, since this is probably the most effective dynamic in mediation. Curiously the continental model, including that of the ICC, does not use caucusing and prefers the parties together all the time except for time-outs to seek advice.

In closed sessions the mediator holds a series of separate meetings with the parties in dispute. His or her aim is to bring the parties to a settlement by identifying hidden agendas and exploring problem solving proposals. The key is confidentiality. He will slowly build up trust, while at the same time offering the objective view of a neutral who is sympathetic to, but firm with, each party. But the mediator may only divulge what he has learned from one party in a closed session if express permission is given. You as the advocate must decide whether such permission should be given having first considered what, if any, impact such matters will have on the negotiation process. Sometimes the mediator will himself inform you that he would not advise disclosing a certain fact yet. On occasions he will hold the information ready to use when he thinks the time is right, which might be much later in the day, or may possibly remain unnecessary. There may be a conflict between you and your client about such disclosure, which should properly only be resolved in the absence of the mediator.

The caucus sessions are initially quite lengthy, particularly the first with each side, which is essentially an information-gathering exercise. These private meetings tend to speed up during the day, particularly once offers are made. Typically both parties will maintain in the initial open session and the early caucuses a legalistic position based on what they perceive as their rights (- they remain in 'the legal box' at Figure 1). As time passes and confidence in both the process and the mediator grows, solutions that are based on the best interest of the parties rather than strictly perceived legal rights become acceptable.

There are various forms of separate or private meetings in which the mediator will have different objectives. He may wish to speak to the client alone without the advice, influence or pressure from that party's lawyer. Both you and your client should be prepared in advance to deal with such a proposal. Equally the mediator may wish to see all client parties together, but without their lawyers, to focus on commercial settlement options which might not necessarily reflect their strict legal interests. Or he may wish to see the lawyers for the opposing parties together without clients, to explore realistic settlement options where the parties are themselves proving intransigent, unrealistic in their expectations or problematic. There may be an ethical difficulty which needs to be first exposed and dissected on the basis of professional fraternity. In this case you must be particularly wary of inadvertent breaches of client confidentiality.

There are some common matters that should concern the advocate in dealing with private sessions:

- Irrespective of which type of private meeting you become involved in check the confidentiality position with the mediator at the end of each session.
- Avoid becoming, or letting the client become over anxious at the length of another party's separate meeting with the mediator.
- Be careful not to fall into the trap of misreading empathy by the mediator as a lack of neutrality.
- Try to use the mediator to obtain information from the other side that you may need to construct a settlement which may meet their needs.
- Do not get frustrated, or let the client get frustrated, by what appears to be a lack of progress during private sessions, particularly in the early stages of the appointment.
- Make the best use of periods following a private session with the mediator to reflect on what has gone on during it to re-evaluate the case, your strategy, the options still open to your client, and to task the client appropriately.

5.6 The Role of the Advocate at the Mediation

Unlike the representative function of counsel at a trial, the mediation advocate is not present principally to convey his client's case to the mediator and the other side. He has an equally important role as his client's adviser. He must protect his client's best interests, as he sees them, while at the same time trying to make the process work. Occasionally these responsibilities conflict. The advocate must constantly evaluate the case and its progress in the mediation. He must stand up to an over-zealous mediator, when necessary. And while focusing on his client's legal interests, he must think laterally if a solution is to be found to overcome resistance while accommodating his client's legal position. To that extent the mediation advocate must release the client from the confines of the legal 'box' (see Fig 1) and allow the mediator to investigate any wider agenda or needs, while at the same time using the legal case as a frame of reference with which to ascertain realistically the client's best and worst alternatives to a negotiated agreement.

Mediation is a team game. The client must be included in the process from start to finish. This extends to preparing together during mediation and taking advantage of quiet time outside caucus sessions to adjust negotiating strategy throughout. Thus, you should explain right through the day what is happening and why. This will help your client relax and approach negotiations constructively. His goals may change as information flows during the course of the mediation. You have to keep analysing the perceived strengths and weaknesses of your case, and of his approach to settlement, as the position changes.

Unsurprisingly, the lawyer will wish to concentrate on issues of fact and law. The client, however, will have issues that may be of crucial importance to him but outside matters the lawyer sees as strictly relevant. When in joint session the advocate will usually either present the argument or support the decision-maker in presenting it. This will ensure that the joint meetings are concise, focused on real issues, and there is less risk of the mediation coming to an abrupt halt if a party reacts unfavourably to misgivings or emotions. You should avoid up-beat submissions, but express your confidence in the merits balanced with an emphasis on attending the mediation in good faith and with the intention of finding a solution that will suit both parties, not merely your client.

Advocacy during private sessions is equally different from trial work. A confrontational style is out of place. Consistent with defending your client's position, your mindset should be that the dispute is a problem to be solved not a conflict to be won. Therefore you need a constructive, problem solving approach, although the mediator must be persuaded of your points. You may need to overcome the mediator in caucus because he exerts a powerful influence. Allow him as a neutral to act instinctively. But be prepared to go back to the plenary session, to meet the lawyers on the other side, assist technical experts in a session confined to their discipline, and above all to view the process flexibly. This includes allowing discussions between clients and, where different, between principal decision-makers. For a lawyer to let go of his client in this way is difficult, but you must learn to let go at the right time.

You will need to support your client throughout the negotiation process: be a friend and supporter to the decision-maker when times get tough. This includes the position you should adopt outside sessions with the mediator or plenary sessions. This can be a rare and emotive situation for the lawyer, particularly if counsel is being instructed. Be active and use idle time creatively, advising on the strengths and weaknesses of both sides as they change. Consider inventive solutions as ways to overcome deadlock. Try to avoid entrenched positions; encourage your client to keep his temper under control, and as a last resort encourage him to stay when he talks of leaving.

The impact of your advocacy on the mediator, the other side and your own client, is likely to be dependent upon your preparation. It can be effective only if you are properly prepared and know your case throughout as much as for a trial, and you can analyse that of the other side for weaknesses. Without that knowledge it will be difficult to build a rapport with the client or provide good communication, and especially good listening. You also need to have an understanding as to why the client wants to take a certain course of action – his needs, motivations and desires. You will therefore have to cater for a non-legal approach, sometimes from the outset, and particularly where you have a weak case in law.

Know the documents. Even though there may only be a slim core bundle for the mediator, take all of your files. Know where to reach any document it transpires you must have, which the mediator has not seen. Often you may be required to answer a point raised by the other side and conveyed through the mediator. Finally you will be required to draft the settlement agreement.

This will be invariably as soon as the parties have come to terms, although you may start parts of it beforehand. The parties may not reach agreement at the hearing but only a little while afterwards, prompted by the momentum built up on the day.

Objectives

You should have some objectives in mind prior to arriving at the session. This is, after all, the parties' day in court. It can be cathartic – an opportunity to divest the client of his problem on terms acceptable to both sides. Therefore it is too important an occasion to waste due to inadequate preparation, inability to negotiate or unwillingness to listen closely to the other side. An advocate will only be of benefit in the process if he understands that the basis of the conflict has now become an object of discussion rather than a partisan contest, as the parties try to educate the mediator what needs to be done to satisfy each side simultaneously.

5.7 Working with the Mediator – Tactical Considerations

The mediator wishes to get a settlement. It is not his function to be an advocate, or to evaluate a position or advance what is fair. He is not concerned with whether the settlement is objectively fair, except for the purpose of durability. Having said that he is impartial, and must be trusted not to breach confidence. You must consider the issue of mutual trust and confidence between you and work at it to enable the mediator to do his job.

The mediator's training and technique is to get you to re-assess your client's position and risk, and to undermine your assessment of appropriate or effective settlement levels, and your client's expectation. He is likely to see you as resistant to the appropriate settlement level, at least at the outset of the mediation and perhaps for much of the day. As the day progresses he will look for the parties' underlying joint interests, and probe for the means to bring these closer and closer until, if possible, they overlap. This he will do by forcing each party to clarify its position. He keeps track of each party's changing stance; he directs the parties' attention from unproductive presentations, subtly analyses their line of reasoning and encourages them to broaden their perspective; he invents or helps new lines of progress towards workable solutions; he allows for the venting of emotional tensions and outbursts, and these he deflects or absorbs so as to encourage the parties to progress towards a settlement by generating an atmosphere of problem-solving enquiry. He will then have the lawyers assist him to draw together settlement options into a coherent package.

Although initially your client may regard the mediator as a quasi-judge and the process as some sort of quasi-trial, the advantages of the private session should dispel such notions. The client is here free from the stress of observation by the other side or by a judge. Both you and the mediator should promote the sense of privacy to make the client feel safe, and advance the dynamics of uninterrupted private communication. This is a three way process in which you have a relationship not only with your client but also with the mediator.

First, always be aware that the mediator will drive a wedge between you and your client if he thinks you are acting to impede a settlement. You should be able to overcome this if you are ready with innovative proposals, particularly those that add value to the process by solutions that are not available to a judge or arbitrator. You may work with the mediator to look for hidden agendas, and reveal the parties' true interests. If you have a difficult client you can use the mediator to deal with the situation known as reactive devaluation: this where your client will always place the worst interpretation on, or assume the worst intention of, an offer or statement coming from someone he regards as untrustworthy, whereas the same offer coming from someone seen as a friend or someone detached (i.e. the mediator) will either seem better or can at least be assessed more objectively. You should use the mediator to discuss proposals and options in front of your client, particularly where you yourself wonder whether the client is being frank with you or indeed himself about the real value of his position.

Although progress is driven by the ambit and momentum of the negotiations, you must remember that it is only the mediator who knows what both sides want. His aim will be to understand the parties' true interests and consequently obtain offers that overlap so that each party will obtain a settlement with which they are happy. This may not coincide with their strict legal rights, but if the client is in fact happy, do not let that concern you.

Throughout the hearing you should keep an eye on the mediator to ensure he is:

- including everyone in discussions;
- listening attentively to what has been said;
- demonstrating his understanding by responding and summarising; being neutral, open and non-judgmental;
- being approachable, open, friendly, and even-handed;
- observing and demonstrating confidentiality at all times.

5.8 Team Strategy

You must prepare and develop a settlement strategy, keeping the goal of mediation firmly in mind: you are there to settle, to stop the litigation costs clock running, and to stop your client's time being wasted by being engaged in the dispute, thus enabling him to get on with his business and his life. This means having an agenda that you may or may not want to disclose to the mediator. It may be in your client's interests to let the mediator know only part of his ambition, although generally as soon as you and your client feel confident in trusting the mediator he or she should be told all the client needs and wants. Among your client's agenda items will be those matters he wishes to prioritise: make sure you know what these are, and in due course, ensure the mediator is also aware of whatever is crucial. Work out with your client what he considers to be the value to him of each issue he wants to raise. Assess the realistic chances of success for each, bearing in mind that such an assessment is likely to change, and he will probably have to give way in a number of areas.

Work out how to apply your strategy according to the pace of the day. Negotiations usually start very slowly, with each side trying to justify its position to the mediator as a precursor to making any offer; the tempo picks up as offers are finally exchanged and the settlement begins to crystallise, and then slows down at the end when difficult concessions have to be made – with the final arguments often being raised over minutiae. Applying your tactics to the pace of what is going on will enable you to assess when to offer more and when to stand firm, particularly in dealing with optimism bias, that is, the over optimistic forecast of the opposing lawyer and his client, and indeed, your own client. Know when to move, how far and in what direction.

In formulating your strategy for the day:

(i) Determine the value of your client's settlement position in respect of each issue in dispute. Seek out those concessions that can be made at little cost.

(ii) Identify new factors that might cause you to change your mind about the viability of your case e.g. new or clarified information; the capabilities of the other side now that you have seen them.

(iii) Develop a structured negotiation plan. Work out the point at which you will settle and how to get there.

(iv) Avoid basing your offer or demand on the age of the case as it is being litigated or on its current position. The dynamics of mediation mean that cases can settle much earlier than in litigation, often before statements of case and generally well before disclosure or the exchange of witness statements.

(v) Plan to offer or demand at some point during the mediation what your client eventually will or hopes to settle for. There is no point in holding back and hoping for a better outcome post-mediation.

(vi) At the mediation don't see the mediator merely as a messenger, conveying offers with shuttle diplomacy. He or she will obtain information and use or re-frame it as they consider appropriate. Allow and expect him to have some leeway in developing possible outcomes.

(vii) Don't insist on monetary responses to your last offer. The mediator may get movement in principle in which each side tests offers without having to disclose, or yet disclose, a specific amount, for example 'we'll move if the other side moves'. You can test and make offers in general terms without having to disclose a specific amount.

(viii) Be candid with the mediator. Assist him to persuade the other side of the merits of your position, or how best to persuade them of it. He cannot act as a judge, but he can usefully identify and try to overcome misunderstandings and break down the problem of communication gaps leading to credibility issues, lack of trust between the parties and emotional or other grievances.

(ix) Determine whether there are, and if so identify, any facts you do not want the mediator to disclose to your opponent. But bear in mind if you have facts which will affect the outcome of the contest, not much is to be gained by concealing them if the only difference is whether you settle now or later. There may be facts you do not want to tell the other side, but which may be helpful for the mediator to know in confidence.

(x) Consider the position from the other side's perspective. How would your opposite number approach the debate?

(xi) Discuss your negotiating/settlement strategy with your client; tell him what you intend doing and why. Obtain regularly updated instructions on settlement during the course of the mediation when you are together privately.

(xii) Understand and apprehend the mediator's tactics, particularly how he will try to undermine your confidence in the strengths of your case even if he is a facilitative mediator.

A useful tool is to create a checklist for each stage of the negotiations. This will help clarify the current position and focus your thoughts on the next round:

1. Where do negotiations stand now?
2. Within what range will we settle?
3. Do we need to adjust the range to accommodate what we now know?
4. What do we need to learn from the other side which will impact on that range?
5. What offers/demands can we make to get within the range?

You should be conscious of the possibility of tension among your own party, for example between the ultimate decision maker and the person responsible for the dispute occurring. This may extend to friction between a principal and his representative – remember, agents have interests of their own which are rarely perfectly aligned with their client. A mediator may need to exploit this tension if he can identify it, and you will need a defensive strategy when that occurs.

Do not worry about being seen to be co-operative. A conciliatory approach does not mean folding. Your task is to conduct a principled and structured negotiation. Your client will appreciate progress more than your robustness. The mediator will appreciate assistance in reaching his goal, although assisting the mediator does not extend to abandoning the client. You must protect him, for example by the use of adjournments if your client is flagging or becoming drained.

Your tactics may in fact be dictated by express instructions from your client or his insurers. Some claims managers now have considerable experience of mediation and feel that they can exploit the process by being tough negotiators. For example they may make offers only open for acceptance on the day of the mediation or prejudicial information might be produced which has not been seen before, or a defendant's insurer may simply refuse to increase an offer. You need to be in a position to deal with such scenarios, to protect your client as necessary from such pressure and to ensure that his confidence is sustained.

5.9 Working Towards a Settlement

Perhaps the most difficult notion for the lawyer acting as a mediation advocate to grasp is that he does not need to obtain a legal solution to the problem. It is not necessary to build the settlement around rights and liabilities, just needs and interests. Rights and liabilities are only relevant in terms of projecting the likely outcome of a trial for the purpose of applying pressure to settle. The underlying interests may have nothing to do with rights or liabilities. If the mediator can expose these interests, practical and creative solutions may be available, at least as options. That is why lateral and creative thinking are so important to the process.

You must know your client's BATNA (best alternative to a negotiated agreement) and how to improve on it if possible. Equally you must know the WATNA (worst alternative to a negotiated agreement) and ensure that this includes recoverable/irrecoverable costs and interest. But more than this, you should anticipate the other side's equivalent position. "The more you can learn of their options the better prepared you are for negotiation. Knowing their alternatives, you can realistically estimate what you can expect from the negotiation. If they appear to overestimate their BATNA, you will want to lower their expectations."

Be curious about your opponent's position. Try to find the breakthrough or 'tipping point', which will cause movement and generate a sufficient momentum to bring about the settlement. You need to achieve a deal that suits everyone, since that is the desired outcome without which your client will not be able to get anything he wants: there is a balance to be struck between protecting your client's own interests by declining to offer concessions and failing to get any advantageous agreement at all.

You also need to discover what the client really wants. You have to be as much aware as the mediator of the difference between positions and interests, demands and needs, and claims and motivations.

5.10 Effective Mediation Management

The single most common reason for a dispute going to trial is that the client refuses to accept a reasonable offer of settlement, recommended as such by his own lawyer. Occasionally there are no offers made, but this is becoming increasingly unusual under the CPR costs regime where parties are obliged to protect their position at the earliest possible stage in the proceedings. The refusal to accept reasonable offers would suggest that lawyers need to keep in better communication with their clients about the true nature, risks and cost of litigation, the possibilities of settlement as a solution, and of all the important developments in the case. If this is true of litigation, it is certainly true of mediation.

A Harvard study of personal injury litigation in New York in the 1970s concluded that the more actively involved the client, the better the outcome for that client. The mediation advocate can thus better serve his client by keeping him actively engaged in the process. There are a number of strategies for this that can best be effected during the day in the privacy of the caucus room when the mediator is not present. These include:

(a) At the outset, before the opening plenary session, make clear if you have not already done so, or otherwise repeat the basic procedure to be expected during the day. Explain the probability that the dispute can be resolved by negotiation, rehearse the difficulties with litigation and discuss the kind of problems likely to be encountered. Make sure the client understands that he has a right to reject actions that both you and the mediator may recommend. Also get the client to confirm that the settlement being negotiated will compromise the whole of the present claim or dispute, and where specified, all disputes between the parties.

(b) Discuss with your client how his actions during the day might affect the negotiations. Advise him how he can help you. Caution him, if necessary, about his approach to the other side; conversely make sure he understands that he can say what he likes and express how he feels about the situation. You may in effect have to counsel him in areas relating to the claim, be they emotional, financial, or referable to his family, employment or health.

(c) Keep him informed throughout the day of how you see the mediation progressing. This will enable you to receive instant feedback from your client, and enable you to fine tune your strategy.

(d) Make sure he is informed about the relevant choices that are open to him at any one time. Identify what alternatives are available, and provide him with your professional experience in dealing with each alternative and their anticipated difficulties and benefits. If there are occasions, which require the client to provide informed consent to what you propose as the advocate, confirm his understanding of the position as the last task before resuming negotiations or seeing the mediator.

5.11 Negotiation Processes and Strategies within Mediation

Always be aware that ADR is concerned with the appropriateness to the client of the dispute resolution – you are meeting the client's best needs for resolving his dispute. Contrast this with litigation, where most of the court process is designed to compensate harm with an award of money. That is a pernicious doctrine because in many cases money is only a poor substitute for the loss suffered, [4] particularly a physical or psychological injury. Worse, the present state of civil justice in England and Wales offers high risk, high expense and disproportionate returns for anything other than high value claims.

Do not think that, while important, money is everything. The process of negotiation is not simply a process of bargaining where you are haggling to get nearer to your side of the middle of a monetary amount. It will enable you to evaluate the potential for joint gains and discover the interests and needs of both sides, including money but not exhaustively. Negotiation is interaction with a goal in mind.

Mediators recognise that fortunately, lawyers are reasonably predictable, due to their common training and shared or similar experiences in practice – they are basically co-operative since the professions lay great store in the concept of fraternity. Lawyers and other professionals perform and develop their positions over the duration of the mediation using information skills, and the process of lawyerly negotiation is structured with generally, a clear beginning, a middle and an end. The advocates know there must be movement in order

4 The themes in this section and 5.14 to 5.20 are developed from the investigatory work of Professor Gerald R. Williams, J Reuben Clark Law School, Brigham Young University, Utah, USA drawn from his Materials on Negotiation and Conflict Resolution for Lawyers used in the CEDR seminar *'Are You a Co-operative or Aggressive Negotiator and Does it Matter? Lawyers as Healers and Warriors.* September 1997 afterwards referred to as 'Williams'.

to compromise. They focus on when, why and how.

Competent and effective negotiation must be the subject of adequate preparation.

For the purpose of preparing this stage of the mediation:

- You must feel ready, otherwise do not negotiate.
- Your factual preparation must involve the client – this will provide him with a better understanding of the true nature of the case.
- Decide what your objectives are: money, or money plus other joint interests.
- You should have a clear strategy as to how you will reach your goals.
- Try to keep part of the process task orientated: make the other side work to prove their negotiating position by having them demonstrate where the numbers come from.
- Devise questions for the other side that can only be answered by the client, not his lawyer, to draw the opposite party directly into the process.
- Make sure you can bring your own client to settlement – if you have any doubt about this you must be prepared to negotiate with your own client.

Most people are conflict avoiders - they will absorb the harm done to them in order to get on with their lives - or at least they are conflict neutral. They are pushed into conflict by a straw that breaks the camel's back. They ascribe blame to the person or entity they perceive is doing them harm, and raise a claim. They need an avenue through which to channel conflict when their claim is rejected. That avenue leads to negotiation, mediation, arbitration and trial.[5] Mediation is assisted or managed negotiation. But in spite of its flexibility and its advantages over an arbitral system, mediation cannot escape from the necessary rituals embodied in negotiation.

First you must understand the difference between positional and principled negotiation. In litigation the lawyer who has to negotiate will generally engage in positional bargaining or haggling. Here each side takes up a position based on the outcome needed. The negotiator will focus on why he needs a particular outcome and what he can offer in return or demand as part of the process. He will haggle, threaten, or swap concessions and usually agree somewhere

5 Burgess, John Mediation Skills: What the Mediator Wants from Advocates 1 Serjeants Inn February 2005.

in the middle of the bargaining range. The difficulty with positional bargaining is that to improve the outcome, generally by extending the bargaining range at one end so as to accommodate a movement nearer your position than half way, subject to professional ethics, there is an incentive to misrepresent the position or your client's interests, to withhold sensitive information, make threats, bluff, dig your heels in or wait unreasonably, fail to listen to the other side, make only small and low concessions, make no concession without getting a return, and, occasionally, use walking out, or its threat, as a tactic. This approach is likely to produce only a limited outcome, and one that might give rise to future problems if there is an ongoing relationship.

Principled bargaining is a problem solving method in which you aim for a wise outcome produced in an efficient and amicable way, by negotiating on merits not merely advancing claims. Mediators are taught to work 'hard on the problem, soft on the people', to use objective criteria, to separate the personality issues from the problem, to focus on interests and invent options for mutual gain. Mediators therefore tend to move positional bargaining into principled bargaining. The dynamic works because the mediator has no stake in the dispute – a party is therefore less likely to adopt a positional negotiating stance with the mediator and is therefore more likely to reveal his real objectives and what he is prepared to concede.

The mediator introduces the element of 'objective criteria' into the parties' understanding of their own position. He can, if asked and he agrees, give an outside view on the validity of the case or the fairness of a proposal. He will exploit the differences between parties' perceptions of risk. He will seek to build up momentum towards a settlement by obtaining movement on a number of easy items. He may suggest non-party assistance in resolving difficult issues, by asking for further information, or provide tasks for the parties on each side to perform, such as number crunching. He will look for productive trade-offs, for example by suggesting that if the other side are willing to move on this, you should move on that.

The mediator will break up the formality or rhythm of the day if he thinks it will help. He may defer certain issues. He will certainly be a constructive force: he will emphasise positive progress and diffuse language with emotional content by channelling hostility between the parties into solving problems. An important role is to help parties save face in moving from previous strongly held positions.

Although the opening plenary session is intended normally only to establish your client's current position, it may turn into an open preliminary negotiating session, or subsequently you may find yourself in open negotiation. Persuasion at a joint meeting will require a balance between empathy and assertiveness – be neither aggressive nor submissive: assume your client's interests are legitimate and valid; explain to the other side in the presence of the mediator your own interests, needs and perspectives. Express an understanding of your opponent's argument, or at least a desire to understand. Be neither overtly sympathetic nor indicate agreement, but listen attentively and actively, looking for areas of potential mutual gain. Try, if you can, to lay the foundation for problem solving.

At the outset find a framework within which to negotiate as part of a reciprocal process that will allow both parties to emphasise their case and make the necessary assertions while at the same time avoid position-taking by identifying interests, needs, resources and capabilities. Do not evaluate what is said until later in private session. Try to brainstorm suggestions as a problem solving exercise, but without asserting ownership of any ideas that may be produced, and keep your client's ambitions realistic.

There are particular stresses to be encountered in open negotiating sessions, particularly where you are having to cope with running instructions, evaluate offers, look for potential problems, and understand and explain the risks to your client. The following guidance should be of practical assistance:

- Do not agree if you disagree.
- Always check with the client before making a concession.
- Explain the story – make sure the other side understands what you are saying.
- Make sure your client understands what the other side is saying.
- Establish within the specific context of the present negotiation what is important to your client, and why, and also establish whether there is anything else which is important to him.
- Do not lose any momentum - move on to the next objective once you have achieved all that you think you can achieve.
- Try to evaluate what is going on at all times – do not be confused by the negotiation dynamic.
- Be aware of the allocation of risk between the parties in any proposed solution to the dispute which is more creative than an award of money.

- Be aware of the allocation of risk between the parties should the mediation fail: at the point at which you stand, who will lose out more if one party decides to walk out?
- Look at the longer term.
- Anticipate problems.
- Don't take everything that is being said at face value. Read between the lines and try to decode messages.

It is far easier to negotiate in mediation if there are two or more issues to be resolved. If that is the case, negotiations involve integrating the interests of the parties. Where such interests may dovetail, there is genuine potential for joint gains, value can be created for both sides, and the 'pie' can be expanded before it is divided. By having subsidiary issues which can be resolved either by making concessions or giving away assets without injury to your client, you may be able to avoid inflicting needless harm on the opposing party and find it much easier getting to 'yes'. If, on the other hand, there is only a single issue being contested, there is only a limited distribution available, and aggressive negotiators tend to win. If there is no potential for joint gains it is difficult to argue for anything except to claim value for your own side and try to destroy the other's expectation or its investment in its own case. Therefore even single issue disputes should be deconstructed to look for potential mutual gains.

5.12 The Momentum to Expect

For the mediator the appointment will run in a series of phases with which he is familiar: introductory, exploration – to include information gathering and reality testing,- identifying solutions and problem solving, negotiation and bargaining, and settlement. The client's approach to the dynamics of negotiation in a successful mediation tends to pass through five different kinds of common stages or steps, all well known to behavioural psychologists:

(I) Denial

Your client will maintain he is not at fault, or he is not the one who needs to change. He has no conscious knowledge of the needs or desires of others, and no particular interest in meeting them unless they coincide with his own interests.

(Ii) Acceptance

He concedes that he may be part of the problem. This is a painful transition for the client. He moves to a position where he can accept that even if he is not part of the problem he may be able to find or move towards the solution.[6]

(Iii) Sacrifice

This stage is concerned with realisation and letting go. First comes a realisation by your client that there are two sides to the story in question, and the other side may have legitimate reasons for being so upset, or defensive, or vindictive; or worse, the possibility he might not win or those opposite not lose. Having moved from his original position there is something of a ritual mortification: he will have to sacrifice his pride, or greed, envy, arrogance, vanity, or conceit, and the belief in his own infallibility, his unwillingness to acknowledge another's point of view or needs, or his unwillingness to forgive another. It is at this point that the client is at his most vulnerable, although any cathartic experience will also commence here.

(Iv) Leap of Faith

Mediation is powerful because it facilitates leaps of faith in a way that litigation cannot. Even agreeing to mediation is a leap of faith since your client may worry that this alone may be perceived by the other side as a sign of weakness. That said, once your client recognises that winning is no longer a foregone conclusion, and that movement must come from him, using the mediator reduces the risk involved in leaps of faith. The progress towards settlement starts with small mutually reciprocal steps, apology, an acknowledgement of wrongdoing or wrong thinking, or concessions about the nature of his behaviour. This is answered by forgiveness, and that is replied to with contrition. Once the emotion has been broken with a leap of faith, negotiations to create a practical solution can follow.

(V) Renewal/Reconciliation

The final dynamic in the process is one of coming together, the healing of relations, or at least those positive feelings engendered by having reached a concluded agreement. Even if a fractured relationship is difficult to mend, the relief in having finalised the dispute gives a sense of renewal.

---

6 Williams p.44; Williams, Gerald R. *A Lawyer's Handbook for Effective Negotiation and Settlement* 5th ed. West 1995.

5.13 Traits of Effective and Ineffective Negotiators

Since the 1970s American academics have been studying the profiles of experienced negotiators,[7] categorising them broadly as 'co-operative' or 'aggressive' and attempting to establish whether those bearing such profiles were effective, ineffective or average negotiators. The results of such research have concluded that up to 87% of negotiators performed more effectively when they were co-operative. Of those who considered themselves aggressive negotiators (20% of the numbers studied) 85% were found to be ineffective or average in terms of results achieved, and only 15% effective. This suggests that the aggressive negotiator is likely to achieve the result he wishes in less than one in every six mediations in which he is the advocate. That is a sobering thought for those of you who believe that negotiation is about projecting strength in order to overcome your opponent. For every time such tactics work, there will most likely be five when they do not.

Professor Gerald Williams of Brigham Young University, Utah, USA analysed the objectives and traits of effective and ineffective negotiators in the following way.[8]

The effective cooperative negotiator is the embodiment of the idea of creating a win/win situation in which both sides get a fair settlement, while getting the best settlement available for his client. His conduct is trustworthy, ethical and fair; in negotiation he will be courteous, personable, tactful, sincere and fair-minded. He presents a realistic opening position, accurately evaluates the case and, in relative terms, does not make threats. He will engage in movement cooperatively (sometimes this is known as cooperative thrusts), but will use the strategy of tit-for-tat[9] both to protect his client's standpoint, probe his opponent's position and to secure the most gains available. He is willing to share information since cooperatives solve problems by reference to the merits rather than by shying away from their difficulties. He uses understatement and assumes that truth will out and speak for itself. The problem is that he is vulnerable to the aggressive negotiator who has no bounds of fairness, who will push him back if he can, and who assumes that if you back up you have no holding ground.

The effective aggressive negotiator has a zest for the well-fought contest. Although he wants to maximise the settlement for his client, he is unconcerned about establishing a win/win situation if he can win on a win/ lose situation, and if by outdoing or outmanoeuvring his opponent, he can be seen to be the winner.

7 Williams p.28, 29.

8 Williams p.30-32.

9 See p.150.

He is dominant, forceful and attacking; well prepared and uncooperative, he is a very good strategist and tactician who plans the timing and sequence of events and applies these rigidly. He will get to know his opponent but be entirely disinterested in the other side's needs. In his general approach there is a danger of overkill: he will usually begin with an unrealistic opening position; he will use threats freely in an attempt to intimidate; he reveals information only gradually, as if he was engaged in a game of deception, and he is willing to stretch the facts.

Both cooperative and aggressive negotiators who are effective share certain traits. They are equally well prepared, realistic, self-controlled, convincing, perceptive at reading clues and well versed in applying legal skills. In contrast both cooperative and aggressive negotiators may be ineffective due to certain traits.

The ineffective cooperative negotiator wants to maintain good relations with his opponent in order to get a deal that will meet his client's needs. This makes him obliging, patient and forgiving. He projects an image of being honest and trustful which may border on the gullible or naïve. He will be pressed to give away more and more without securing any advantage in return. His will is overborne since he feels the need to be nice to his opponent even when a normal person should be more aggressive. It is one thing to be obliging, but a successful negotiator needs to have the strength of will to be otherwise, and if he makes concessions, this should only be on the basis of a conscious choice.

The ineffective aggressive negotiator has some undesirable traits that make him fail. He is overtly hostile, arrogant, obnoxious and irritating. He is in fact unprepared on the facts and the law and he tends to bluff. He uses aggression as a substitute for preparation. In face-to-face negotiation he is quarrelsome, demanding and argumentative, often using a take-it-or-leave it approach. He is intolerant of and hostile to the needs of others, and his bullying approach leads the negotiations to collapse since he will inevitably drive the other side away from the negotiating table unless it is in an extremely weak position.

To an extent the lay client will expect his advocate to adopt the techniques of both the effective cooperative and aggressive negotiator as he sees the day progress. The experienced mediation advocate will understand that he is engaged in a ritual process and be patient with it, tolerating a less mature opponent. He will be vigilant and perceptive, allowing himself temporarily to suspend judgment, contain and channel energy, endure criticism, think quickly and act decisively.

5.14 Ten Rules for Effective Negotiation[10] within Mediation

1. DO NOT DEMAND AN OUTCOME THAT IS NOT FAIR TO BOTH SIDES

You want an outcome that is fair to your own client, and are unlikely to agree to anything less. But there is little to be gained from pushing your opponent to accept an outcome that his client will be unhappy with. If it is positively harmful to one party that is only creating a problem for the future.

2. GIVE CONTINUOUS FEEDBACK TO THE OTHER SIDE, IMMEDIATELY IF POSSIBLE

Keeping up the momentum is all-important in negotiation. Indicating agreement, disagreement or re-emphasising and explaining your own position can best achieve this. But it is essential to keep dialogue going. If you can, express positive agreement that takes issues out of consideration and promotes a feeling of progress, although there will be some circumstances where you should not appear to be too eager. Expressing disagreement is also imperative: do not let the other side build up its expectations without knowing you have a problem with a proposal – give negative feedback immediately, but be tactful and empathetic – and do not silently accept things that hurt your position. You can show that you are willing to be persuaded to change your mind and will make your concession at the appropriate time.

3. MAINTAIN YOUR FACTUAL POSITION EVERY TIME IT IS CHALLENGED

Both your opponent and the mediator will challenge your factual, and possibly your legal, position probing for weaknesses and uncertainties with the intention of undermining your commitment to your client's case. Re-emphasise your points every time they are challenged. Add new information where necessary, or restate the existing information in different ways, but do not let a challenge pass without comment.

4. OBSERVE BODY LANGUAGE

In any open session look closely at your opponent and his client. Become conscious of the strength of conviction in what they are saying by observing their use of body language. Remember that you will also be making signals, consciously or otherwise. Be conscious of your own body language and what messages you may be sending – some mediators are trained in assessing non-verbal communication.

10 Developed from Williams pp 62-5.

5. USE YOUR TEAM AS OBSERVERS

You cannot hope to see everything, particularly if you are immersed in advocacy. Use other members of your team – client, solicitor, insurer, expert or other witness – as observers, and question them as to how they perceive any open-session negotiations to be going. Let them either reinforce or contradict your own view. Do not waste the fact of their being present.

6. BE A CONTRARIAN

When in private play devil's advocate. Put yourself in your opponent's shoes and try to ascertain what tactics he must use to achieve his aims. This will not only enable you to see what should be coming, but also help you dispel misunderstanding or mistrust if you want to be a cooperative negotiator.

7. CONVEY AN IMPRESSION OF PROFESSIONALISM, INTEGRITY, CONFIDENCE AND EFFICIENCY

It goes almost without saying that a good impression will carry you forward, and a bad one will hamper your efforts from the outset.

8. LOOK APPROPRIATELY PREPARED

Visual impression, though worthy, is not enough. Have your law, facts, calculations and options ready for presentation. Never proceed until you are ready, since to do so will always work against your client's interests. Asking for more time should never prejudice you.

9. SUSTAIN A CLEAR, DISTINCT FACTUAL AND LEGAL THEME THROUGHOUT THE NEGOTIATION

Nothing is more persuasive than a clear theme supported by factual and legal points. It does not need to be complex nor the solutions offered complicated, but it should be organised and presented with confidence.

10. MINIMISE YOUR RELIANCE UPON NOTES

Know what you are going to say, whether to the mediator or to your opponent. Have your facts and argument ready so that you can concentrate on the other person, not your notes, during the negotiation. Constantly referring to notes makes you look unprepared, less confident of your case, and less sure of yourself. This should not stop you making notes when in negotiation, although this is a distraction which should be used sparingly. Make sure you understand what is being said before you write it down.

5.15 Negotiating Phases[11]

Just as psychologists have identified well-defined stages in the mediation process, so researchers have observed that most negotiation develops through certain phases. At the beginning negotiators establish a working relationship and adopt respectively their initial bargaining positions. Aggressive negotiators will try to convey the impression that they are irrevocably committed to their opening position. This, the opening phase of the negotiation, is actually quite lengthy with no perceptible movement by either side.

The middle stage of a negotiation commences when some outside factor gives impetus to the process, usually some sort of time deadline. At that point the negotiators commence working seriously on the question of whether an agreement is possible. This is when alternative solutions, compromise and concession making are sought.

The final stage is the most crucial. As the deadline approaches a crisis is often reached: the negotiators often feel trapped by the choice of whether to accept the last offer or let the mediation fail, unless another alternative can be devised. As a process either agreement is reached or the parties declare an impasse. If there is a settlement the parties will work out the details of the agreement; if an impasse is declared, the parties will have to make alternative arrangements, such as furthering the claim in litigation.

5.16 Opening Negotiating Positions

In negotiating psychology the first number is the most potent number in the negotiations since it must influence the second number. It must be selected with great care, balancing the fear that you cannot get what you don't ask for, with being so aggressive that the other side want to leave immediately. You must consider the likely impact on the other side of adopting a maximalist position, which is where you ask for considerably more than you expect to obtain by making a very high opening demand.

Contrast this with actually opening by asking for what you feel is fair to both sides (the 'equitable position'), either by giving your anticipated bottom line straight away, or by inflating your demand by a 'reasonable' amount which you will afterwards concede. A party that opens with his true bottom line has no room for manoeuvre except by offering alternative or additional nonmonetary solutions.

11 See Williams, Gerald R: *A Lawyer's Handbook for Effective Negotiation and Settlement* 5th edn West 1995.

Whether you start with a maximalist or equitable opening, the effective mediation negotiator will explore a variety of alternative solutions to the dispute in the hope of arriving at an optimum solution which provides the greatest possible benefit and the least possible damage to both sides, often looking at something the other side haven't considered.

Both sides may safely assume that the opening position is a product of posturing, and that both sides will be willing to move in order to obtain a settlement. The suggestion that one side or the other is unalterably committed to its opening position is illusory, although it may take a significant amount of time for the illusion to be dispelled since it will have been supported by reference to the legal and factual elements of the case.

5.17 Movement

The first impediment to securing movement in the negotiations is overcoming bluff and getting the other side to enter seriously into dialogue. It is a convention among lawyers to pretend that the lawyer who first suggests settlement has the weaker case; by the same token many lawyers believe that by holding out against settlement discussions they imply that theirs will be a winning case at trial. This is particularly true of insurer defendants and defence lawyers, for whom delay is normally advantageous. Both of these beliefs have led to cases proceeding to trial only to settle hurriedly at the last moment.

By electing to go to mediation, or having been nudged in that direction by the court, you have the benefit of the same context for negotiation, but the absence of pressure will pervade the opening part of the day unless there is strong independent motivation for the parties to start coming together. Movement comes only as the day wears on and it is apparent that there will be no point to the mediation without it: one party or the other will be asked by the mediator to put up or shut up – he will press both sides to say in terms whether they are here to obtain a settlement or not. At that point your predetermined scheme for subtly reducing your opening position should come into effect, either as the prime mover or in reply to a hint of movement from the other side. At the outset it need not be explicit or even a formulated cash offer, and can be based on principle – 'if you move, so will we'. Eventually the degrees of movement will crystallise into firm offers which usually also conform to a recognised pattern. This involves initially small movement followed by fairly large-scale movement, and then finally, very small-scale movement as you tentatively approach settlement. Invariably the last steps are the hardest.

5.18 Crisis and Deadlock

The point of crisis comes with the arrival of a deadline, or an impediment that prevents you from bridging a gap, and this can give rise to intense psychological pressure. Both a strong opponent and the mediator will use it. You may be faced with what you perceive to be the final offer from the other side; or the mediator may be relying upon a 'locked-door' syndrome to achieve a breakthrough. The pressure comes with the realisation by your party that should the last offer be refused the mediation will fail, and further litigation costs will be expended, and the trial perceived as inevitable; alternatively if the last offer is accepted your client will never know if you could have achieved more or paid less.

The way to break this psychological pressure is to remember that you are in fact not caught in a yes/no situation. The client always has three choices: (i) to accept your opponent's last offer, (ii) to reject your opponent's last offer, walk away and go to trial, or (iii) to come up with a new proposal. It is the third choice that is often the key to success. This third option prevents unnecessary deadlock, keeps the negotiation alive and puts pressure on your opponent to accept your revised offer. The closer you are to the deadline, the more seriously your opponent must consider your offer. Therefore always be in a position to modify your last offer as the best way to save face at the moment of deadlock, keep the process going and deflect the pressure of the crisis point to the other side.

Remember that the deadline may not be uniform and for reasons unknown to you the other side may have an entirely different time limit of their own. Deadlines can relate to the litigation, for example the imminence of the trial, the next case management conference or court direction, after the lifting of any automatic stay pending dispute resolution, or they can be fact related, for example the next delivery or payment due, the application of pressure from the bank on your client's credit, the next tranche of legal fees due, or pressure coming from other sources. The pre-arranged end of the mediation session is also a deadline that creates strong psychological pressure, although this is usually artificial since if the parties wish to continue and the mediator considers it worthwhile, either the mediation or bi-partisan negotiations can continue by agreement. If you or your client has a particular personal deadline – catching the last train, or flying out - it is unwise to reveal this as your opponent may use such a difficulty as a pressure point, even if he is the most cooperative of negotiators.

5.19 Dealing with Obnoxious Opponents[12]

What do you do when faced with an opponent who is irritating, rigid, hostile, arrogant, quarrelsome and egotistical? We have all come across professionals who serve their egos, not their clients, and who create a situation that is frustrating and considerably impedes the progress of the day. How do you negotiate with such a person? The key is self-control. You must not give way to your basic impulse to fight fire with fire – if you lose your own patience and goodwill the negotiations will be over before they start and your side will leave the mediation with a strong sense of wasted time and costs, which you may blame on the process itself. The fighting fire with fire approach will almost certainly lead to deadlock and failure.

Your aim is to outwit such negotiators by calling their bluff, putting maximum pressure on them to change their tactics and deal with you on a realistic and rational level. To do so you need to exercise enormous restraint to prevail successfully against an irritating opponent. Keep your temper. Don't quarrel. Give him a soft answer (at the risk of maddening him).

Remember that an opponent acting in this way is often unprepared on the facts and the law, unsure of the true value of his case and is therefore using bluff and bluster as a substitute. Adopt a position that you will not negotiate with this person so long as the irritating tactics continue: do not initiate negotiations while they do, and do not accede to your opponent's attempts to negotiate. Keep occasional or even frequent contact to educate him about the case, refer him to key facts and documents, or indicate key developments on your side. Make your communications non-threatening and invite cooperation. Express empathy and openly promise that you will commence your negotiation when the time is right. But all the time refuse to negotiate so long as the irritating tactics continue. Indicate your preparedness for the litigation to go on.

Be patient. Remember that if he is ineffective as a negotiator he is likely to be equally ineffective at trial. He should fold and either accept an invitation to negotiate on a reasonable and rational basis, or, if he chooses to have his side abandon the mediation, a wedge will usually have been driven between him and his client's confidence in his ability. You may well be negotiating with someone else shortly afterwards, with whom you can achieve a pre-trial settlement.

---

12 This and the following passage draw heavily from Williams's *Solving Particular Problems In Legal Negotiation* pp57-61.

5.20 Dealing with Overly Aggressive Opponents

When facing an effective aggressive opponent it is well to understand four basic defensive principles:[13]

(i) Know you are under attack.

(ii) Know what kind of attack you're facing. Learn to judge and recognise your opponent's weapons, his strength and his level of skill.

(iii) Know how to make your defence fit the attack – the response must match each aggressive move, it must be an appropriate response and at an appropriate level of intensity - proportionate and sufficient to secure your aim.[14]

(iv) Know how to follow through – you must be able to carry out your response once you have chosen it. Be prepared to feel and work through a certain amount of guilt, since healthy people don't enjoy causing other people pain even when it is well and thoroughly deserved.

When attempting to defuse the potency of an aggressive opponent, as a cooperative negotiator you will need to:

- Deal more effectively with the facts: accept the burden of demonstrating the credibility of your own facts. Prove you have something worth paying for. Recognise that your aggressive opponent will skilfully seek to discredit your facts. He and his client will have set their expectations by how far you are willing to let them go. Stay with your facts until your opponent recognises that there are strong points in your case and understands what they are.

- Present facts serially, not all together. Look for the reaction of your opponent on an item-by-item basis and decide what to do by reading the reaction.

- Present facts in their strategically most favourable light.

- Recognise that parties inevitably have a different view of the facts. Do not try to persuade your opponent to adopt your view of the facts, rather to take your view of them into account.

- Express willingness to change your view if he can demonstrate his position convincingly.

---

13 Four basic principles of verbal self defence - Elgin, Suzette Haden *The Gentle Art of Verbal Self-Defense* Prentice-Hall 1980 pp 3-5 Williams 58-61.

14 See Tit-for-tat p.[ ]

- Repeat the facts as often as they are challenged. Often the aggressive negotiator's strategy is to ignore or refute your facts. The solution is to show that your facts can sustain his attack.
- Adopt opening positions favourable to your client but clearly communicate that the position is temporary since the parties' interests and needs are not yet fully known, that some facts require more careful consideration, and that you invite and seek a creative solution for joint gains.
- Make few unilateral concessions, and never make a unilateral concession on the merits. Use the requirement of your client's approval as a device to stall on concessions. Make only concessions that do not hurt your position. Withhold any major concessions until a suitable package can be put together – make it at least a two-stage process. In order to preserve the negotiating climate you can acknowledge the other sides' interests and needs, and indicate that concessions will be made, but explain with good reasons why they are not available at present.
- Respond immediately and unambiguously to aggressive moves. Avoid mirroring aggressive behaviour but use a counter move: require an explanation, or a reference to the facts; cushion your response with empathy; express a recognition that a different point of view might be valid; admit your source of information may be wrong; use the need for consultation and instructions as a buffer, but never flatly refuse – give reasons, and consistently decline to make unwise or premature concessions; elaborate factors which weigh against granting requests, keep your client's options open, leave room to manoeuvre, and, like a proverbial boy scout, be prepared and look prepared.
- When dealing with this kind of an opponent, refuse to 'play the same game.' Disarm him by asking 'why' frequently – seek explanations for demands being made – and have him identify what are the interests sought to be met by the demands he is making. Look for objective criteria. And try to shame him – question his sense of fairness and whether his client really wants a settlement.

5.21 Using Tit-For-Tat as a Model Negotiating Strategy

There is a useful method for creating a balance between cooperative and aggressive negotiation, devised for use in game theory and usually referred to as the Anatole Rappaport model 'the Prisoner's Dilemma'.[15] It is the simple but

15 See Allman, William F *Nice Guys Finish First* Science (1984) vol 5 no 8 p25-31; Axelrod, Robert *The Evolution of Cooperation* Basic Books 1984.

effective strategy known as tit-for-tat, and it is this: always begin cooperatively then respond tit-for-tat to each cooperative or aggressive move by the other side.

As a tactical device it has six qualities that make it useful when negotiating in mediations:

1. It begins cooperatively, although cooperation is based on both anticipation of and the fact that cooperation will be mutual.

2. It retaliates perfectly in the sense that the response will be immediate, unambiguous, and appropriate – the cooperative negotiator will be vigilant of attack and will react, making it clear he is acting responsively to unacceptable aggression from the other side.

3. It is perfectly trustworthy – the negotiator never moves aggressively unless he is attacked.

4. It forgives perfectly – the response is immediate, unambiguous, and appropriate.

5. It is not greedy – the response doesn't object to gains made by the other side because they should be mutual.

6. It is perfectly patient: as a device it doesn't try to shortcut the negotiation process – it follows the ritual of negotiation.

Useful as tit-for-tat is in negotiation it does have one flaw of which to be wary: if one side mis-reads the other by interpreting a non-aggressive move as an attack, the misreading side will retaliate. The innocent side will respond in kind with both continuing to believe the other side started it. Such a situation can only be broken by a leap of faith by a cooperative negotiator, or by tracing the problem back to its source.

5.22 Forensic Skills of Mediation Advocates

Dealing with the Client

- Be with the client physically and psychologically.
- Make him feel trustful and important by your display of interest in his wider concerns – business, family, social – since the solution may come from within this wider sphere
- Do not interrupt him; do not ask him too many questions.
- Do not summarise what he is saying; acknowledge and empathise.

- Do not finish his sentences; don't use clichés in the way you speak to him, or be judgmental.
- Do not criticise his behaviour.
- If you need to question him, use open questions, rather than cross examine him or asking rhetorical questions.
- Once you have concluded a settlement, take the time and effort needed to justify and support the agreement: your client needs to feel happy about it so that he will not subsequently want to renounce or challenge it.

Dealing with the Mediator

- Avoid extreme opening offers and incremental concessions.
- He is likely to be able to see through artificial tactics – stonewalling, threatening, becoming angry, intimidating, ridiculing, or indeed, lying. In particular try not to lie to the mediator. Although he is not a judge and the mediation is not a court setting, it is not very becoming conduct or attractive in a lawyer or a professional man, and it is usually unproductive and potentially very damaging to the settlement dynamics if discovered by either mediator or the other side. It will lead to an immediate loss of the trust and confidence necessary to provide the momentum towards settlement; it might be impossible to recover.
- Be courteous.
- Do not talk over the mediator or your client or demonstrably fail to listen.
- Do not fake paying attention.
- Do not fail to disclose helpful information.
- Do not fix upon a single solution or run to the bottom line too quickly.
- Do not make allegations in bad faith as a negotiating tool, or fail to prioritise the client's needs.
- Do not assume the mediator will communicate with the other side as directed by you or your client – merely because he is given permission to carry some piece of information or even offer to the other side do not assume that he will do so, either when asked or at all.

You are more likely to succeed by being entirely cooperative towards the mediator, whether or not you agree with his approach. Promote interest-based negotiation and creative settlement options, engage in brainstorming, separate people issues from problem issues, and look for objective and independent or external criteria to justify settlement proposals; understand how to reciprocate; find ways to cross the last gap, justify splitting differences, and advance the last offer.

Dealing with Opposing Lawyers

- Keep your eyes on the ultimate objective of the process. It is to achieve a settlement.
- Clearly say what you really mean.
- Learn what your opponent really means.
- Do not assume either party (including your own) does not have ulterior motives for taking part in the mediation, the most obvious being to discover information.
- Do not assume any inequality of power can be rectified because the mediator is present.
- Do not assume the other side will accept either information given or a proposal when made.
- Do not assume everything said at the mediation will in fact remain confidential – a party might use it indirectly, and parties may breach or waive confidentiality.

Once you have reached a settlement do not indicate in any way that you feel you have gotten the better of your opponent: convey only that it was a good deal for both parties. Never suggest that you might have made more concessions or accepted a lower offer.

Dealing with Your Own Feelings

You will undoubtedly have to deal with situations that make you feel uncomfortable on a personal level. This is perfectly normal, particularly when you have started from a bullish position in the advice previously given to your client about the strength of his case. Strategies that help include:

- Finding ways to save face when you retreat from a previously held position or advice.
- Establishing the reason for a change in your negotiating position: you need to justify it to yourself as well as the client and the mediator.
- Taking 'time out' to reflect.

5.23 Control of the Client

You should anticipate that getting to settlement may require the mediator to drive a wedge between you and your client, at least to the extent of undermining the advice you are giving, which the mediator may feel is acting as a brake on the momentum. He may try to take over emotional control of the client who may become confused, nervous, bewildered, or angry. Your job is to prevent hurtful or unwise decisions or actions by the client, and to protect him from the harmful actions of the other side. The mediator will be aware of this and may use one of a number of techniques to try and neutralise you as an advocate if he feels that you are being over protective or defending either an overly legal interest or a position that he believes the client needs to release. As an extreme this may include asking you to meet in private session with your opponent thus giving the mediator access to your client in your absence.

This problem arises because to an extent you will feel the client needs to be protected from the mediator as well as the other side, particularly if you take a bullish view of the merits of his case. Your attitude is likely to stem from an inability to see outside the 'legal box' (See Fig. 1[16]). Look at his wider interests, and try to judge objectively whether the mediator is right – is the client better off with you taking more of a back seat role or is the mediator going for broke because that is his personal agenda? You may find yourself in personal conflict since you will feel that you are there to perform your job and should be seen to be doing what you are paid for. However there may come a point at which you have to let go.

Equally you may consider that the other side or the mediator is being reasonable and your client recalcitrant and irrational, and you are unable to make him see what is by any standards a good deal for him and one unlikely to be achieved as the outcome of litigation. It is then that you must use the mediator as a foil to prevent the likely conflict between your views and your instructions.

Neither of these scenarios are uncommon, and the novice mediation advocate should not worry unduly should they occur. The mediator will be aware of these dynamics. There is no reason why you should not be alert to them also.

Consider that part of the process, indeed part of the ritual, is that mediation will help the parties learn more about themselves and each other. The best way to settlement is if both parties have a change of heart – the mediator will be aiming for compromise plus reconciliation. Otherwise if parties maintain an 'all or nothing' approach they will head irrevocably towards trial.

16 See p39.

5.24 The Settlement Agreement

It is essential that the parties secure a concluded agreement that is workable, comprehensive, (both as to the dispute and any wider issues which have been introduced,) and enforceable. As your client's advocate it is vital that you get the form of the agreement right. As his lawyer it is part of your role to ensure that the settlement is enforceable. The terms must be certain, specific, effective, practical and complete, in particular dealing with who is to do what, when, and with what precise consequences. A provision will usually need to be inserted detailing what to do if one side or the other fails to adhere to the agreement or if it proves to be unworkable.

It is as well to take a draft containing the likely heads of agreement with you and, if litigation is running, a general form of Tomlin order. If the compromise contains terms found in a recognised standard form or precedent do not forget to bring it with you. Otherwise you will be forced to locate it, probably at a highly inconvenient time for doing so.

As you near settlement you should begin to draft the proposed agreement in your caucus room. Discuss the structure, form and contents with your client as early as possible, since you can formulate the structure as the mediation progresses. This will help focus on the details and will place the client's personal agenda in context.[17] At this point – prior to the actual agreement – your client must be clear about the practicalities of its implementation.

Be careful to strike a balance between too little, and too much detail. Do not be overly pedantic. Remember it is likely to be either quite late or very late, at the end of a long day. You may wish to keep the mediator informed of progress in drafting the agreement, and certainly where any problems arise.

While the document is being settled you should ask the decision maker in your party precisely who should be the signatory. Do not assume that you are signing it yourself, or do so without seeking express authority, irrespective of the fact that you are likely to have sufficient implied authority as a matter of law.

You may wish to consider the introduction of certain standard clauses irrespective of the nature of the settlement. These should deal with:

- confidentiality;
- any relevant choice of law or jurisdiction;

17 See York, Stephen D, *Preparing Your Client for Mediation* Resolutions issue 17 Summer 1997.

- the entire agreement between the parties;
- a default mechanism to deal with future disputes;
- whether, if there is a breach of this agreement, the original cause of action should be reinstated.

The settlement-specific clauses need to be certain as to:

- payment: who pays, to whom is payment made, and how much;
- the form in which payment is to be made;
- whether payment is to be immediate or in stages;
- the mechanism for default of payment;
- the provision of interest;
- the costs of the litigation;
- the costs of the mediation;
- any public statements;
- the discontinuance or withdrawal of proceedings;
- any special clauses dealing with enforceability;
- who is the signatory, his status or authority.

There will be occasions when the parties can do no more than agree outline heads of agreement, but this should be avoided wherever possible. Saving an hour at the end of the mediation by agreeing outline heads of agreement exposes the parties to the risk of further disputes in which the argument shifts from its original subject matter to contesting what has been agreed. It is essential that the intention of the parties is made plain, and there is at least sufficient detail to ensure that an impartial reader would have a clear idea of precisely what has been agreed. If there is no time to put in the complexity of the mechanics of the transaction, or, for example, the tax implications have not been advised upon or worked out, at least draw a distinction between the agreement itself and the mechanics for performing it.

5.25 Time-Limited Mediations

In a sense all mediations are governed by limits on time. However many litigants and their advocates may first be introduced to mediation by being asked to participate in court-annexed schemes in circumstances where the parties have not agreed to mediate beforehand. These include the outsourced National Mediation Helpline mediations.

It is possible for parties to agree that a mediation should be limited in time to three or four hours, or a half-day without using a court-annexed scheme. This may be intended as a cost-saving device because there is only a single or narrow issue to be negotiated, or the parties mistakenly assume that if agreement cannot be reached in that time, it is unlikely to be reached at all.

In either case, how is the advocate to deal with the curtailment or concentration of a process, which seemingly requires the time to pass through certain phases, including time for detailed negotiations? The answer depends to an extent on the approach of the mediator. Some will try to run the mediation in precisely the same way as if there were no time constraints. If he does he will try to compress the same events and process into shorter lengths of time, hoping to arrive at a satisfactory result. However more experienced and more confident mediators will probably jettison less important parts of the procedure and concentrate on the more important ones. For example he may either get rid of or limit the opening plenary session. In addition it may be that a guillotine is put on private caucusing. Certainly the preliminary posturing by both sides will be reduced, and offers expected far sooner than in a full day mediation. In other words the mediator will adopt a more focused approach to the management of the process and will discourage exhaustive discussion of the issues.

As you might expect, time limited mediations have a higher failure rate, particularly where the court has bounced an otherwise unwilling participant into trying them. However, in the hands of an experienced mediator, who is capable of successful time management, this process offers the client real value for money, in that there are no venue costs and none relating to the administration of a mediation service provider. In addition both court-annexed schemes and practising time-limited mediators will charge fees that are fixed.

As in all mediations the key to success is in the amount of pre-mediation preparation that can be completed. The fact that time is limited does not mean that a representative can avoid doing the necessary preparation. Quite the contrary is true. Before you attend you should have a thorough knowledge of the strengths and weaknesses of your own case, including arguments on liability and quantum, interest and causation; you need to know much the same about the case of your opponent; you need detailed information on the costs position of both sides, both historic and projected. Thus you will want to know the costs to date, the likely time to trial, and the likely duration and costs of the trial.

There will be an extremely limited bundle of core documents made available to the mediator, often consisting of nothing more than the statements of case. If there is time in advance the mediator may contact you beforehand, but again, that is unlikely. Under court-annexed schemes he will be paid extremely low rates. Fixed price fees in the private sector also allow for very little pre-mediation reading in by the mediator.

Before arriving you should be well aware of what to bring and how you are going to proceed. Your tactics will be far less sophisticated. But in each phase of the mediation the other side has to be persuaded that there is something in it for them.

Make a list of objective criteria: establish what it is you want by 7 p.m. (or 2 p.m.) that you haven't got now. Then consider the process: how to get what you want in a way that is most effective. Take a view of the most efficient use of your time, and that of any other attendees. Put short time fragments into a framework. Know what high figure and what low figure to request when the mediator asks for your position. That will be your negotiation range. Be able to explain to the mediator why there is a gap between the figures. Know how much it will cost to fight the gap, particularly whether the gap is less than the cost of going to trial. That may be the determinative factor in accepting the last offer or walking away.

If you are acting for insurers, ask them to provide their risk cost analysis. The mediator may well ask for this. He will certainly ask the defendants what sort of a settlement they are looking for, and hope to move it into the claimant's negotiating range.

Remember that short as it is, it is still the client's day in court. Help negotiate a settlement with which he can be comfortable at the end of the session. Do not allow him to be bullied into an agreement simply because of the shortage of time. Ensure that he understands and is happy, albeit reluctantly, with any offer by the other side, which you believe cannot be improved upon.

Part 6

Mediation Privilege and Confidentiality

Chapter 6
Mediation Privilege And Confidentiality[1]

6.1 The Existence of Mediation Privilege

One of the clearest views we have of the creeping juridification of mediation by the courts is the examination of privilege and confidentiality attaching to the mediation process, and, in doing so, consideration of the future compellability of the mediator. Mediation trainers and mediator service providers have long proceeded on the basis that the mediator is not compellable at trial as a witness of the contents of a previous mediation of the dispute, whether the outcome was a settlement or otherwise. This sense of security for mediators is borne out of the contractual protection usually given by the parties in the mediation agreement. For the industry, the very essence of mediation depends upon the participants in the process being confident they can be as frank at all times and open with each other and the mediator as they would wish without fear that anything they said, or any document they produced solely for the purposes of the mediation, or any concession they may choose to make in the course of exploring a settlement, might subsequently be admitted into evidence in later court proceedings.

The common law countries are divided in their approach as to what protection the courts will give to mediation in this respect. According to the analysis of Michel Kallipetis KC, one of the leading UK commercial mediators, there are two distinct views: some jurisdictions consider that mediation is 'no more than assisted without prejudice negotiations' while others consider that mediation has an entirely separate privilege of its own[2]. In the first, the courts have regarded meditation privilege or confidentiality as subject to all the usual challenges with which we are familiar, and which for convenience, are listed below. In the second, some jurisdictions regard mediation privilege as absolute and will not admit any evidence at all of what transpired in a mediation, while others, though recognising the existence of such a privilege, permit the courts to admit evidence 'in the interests of justice'.

1 For this chapter I am greatly indebted to Michel Kallipetis KC FCIArb, a leading mediator and past Chairman of the Bar ADR Committee, for permission to draw upon a note on this subject provided to the Hong Kong Bar Association in November, 2009.

2 For example Nigeria, and Civil Law countries such as Turkey, Greece, Brazil and Thailand

Given the increasingly widespread use of mediation, and the greater judicial encouragement to mediate rather then litigate, the whole question of mediation confidentiality and privilege needs seriously to be reviewed and some form of consensus achieved.

In England and Wales the courts have intervened to consider this aspect of mediation on a number of occasions. At the date of writing the courts still proceed on a case-by-case basis.

A slightly wider starting point may usefully be found in the analysis of the law on 'without prejudice' negotiations contained in *Unilever plc v Proctor and Gamble*[3], on the court's approach to the admission of statements made in without prejudice negotiations in subsequent litigation. There, the plaintiff wished to use statements made in a without prejudice meeting to support an action to restrain a threatened infringement of a patent on the basis of alleged threats made in that meeting. Laddie J's decision to strike out the proceedings as an abuse was upheld by the Court of Appeal. Walker LJ reviewed all the modern authorities and summarised the major principles [page 2444 D to 2445 G] as follows:

> (1) When the issue is whether without prejudice communications have resulted in a concluded compromise agreement, those communications are admissible: *Tomlin v Standard Telephones and Cables Ltd*[4]
>
> (2) Evidence of negotiations is also admissible to show that an agreement apparently concluded between the parties during the negotiations should be set aside on the ground of misrepresentation, fraud or undue influence: *Underwood v Cox*[5]
>
> (3) Even if there is no concluded compromise, a clear statement made by one party to negotiations on which the other party is intended to act and does in fact act may be admissible as giving rise to an estoppel: See Neuberger J in *Hodgkinson & Corby Ltd v Wards Mobility Services Ltd*[6]
>
> 4) Apart from any concluded contract or estoppel, one party may be allowed to give evidence of what the other said or wrote in without prejudice negotiations if the exclusion of the evidence would act as a cloak for perjury, blackmail or other 'unambiguous impropriety'. However, the court would only allow the exception to be applied in the clearest cases of abuse of a privileged situation: *Forster v Friedland*[7]
>
> (5) Evidence of negotiations may be given (for instance on an application to strike out proceedings for want of prosecution) in order to explain delay or apparent acquiescence, albeit that the exception is limited to the

3 [2000] 1 WLR 2436

4 [1969] 1 W.L.R. 1378

5 (1912) 4 D.L.R. 66

6 [1997] F.S.R. 178

7 C.A. (Civil Division) Transcript No. 205 of 1993

fact that such letters had been written and the dates at which they were written. *Walker v Walker*[8]

(6) The exception for an offer made expressly "without prejudice save as to costs" is clearly recognised as an express or implied agreement between the parties to vary the public policy rule: *Rush & Tompkins v GLC*[9]

Kallipetis believes the observations of Robert Walker LJ (at page 2448H to 2449B), where that judge reiterated that the without prejudice rule is founded partly in public policy and partly in the agreement of the parties, are of particular importance to the question of mediation privilege. The modern approach is to protect admissions against interest made in without prejudice negotiations –

> "*to dissect out identifiable admissions and withhold protection from the rest of without prejudice communications (except for a special reason) would not only create huge practical difficulties but would be contrary to the underlying objective of giving protection to the parties "to speak freely about all the issues in litigation both factual and legal when seeking a compromise and, for the purpose of establishing a compromise, admitting certain facts"* (quoting Lord Griffiths in *Rush v Tomkins*[10])

As has been said earlier in this work, *Halsey v. Milton Keynes General NHS Trust*[11] was a seminal decision of the Court of Appeal giving encouragement to parties to use mediation to resolve their disputes. While principally concerned with the costs sanction on parties who refuse unreasonably to mediate, Dyson LJ made wider observations on the use of mediation at [14] (which, presumably, are to be regarded as *obiter dicta* after *Churchill*[12] but may nonetheless be useful in presenting argument):

> "*We make it clear that it was common ground at the outset (and we accept) that parties are entitled in an ADR to adopt whatever position they wish, and if as a result the dispute is not settled, that is not a matter for the court. As is submitted by the Law Society, if the integrity and confidentiality of the mediation process is to be respected, the court should not know, and therefore should not investigate, why the process did not result in agreement.*"

Subsequently, in *Reed Executive plc v. Reed Business Information Ltd,*[13] that court was asked to look at without prejudice correspondence to establish a claim for costs alleging one party had unreasonably refused to mediate. The Court of Appeal rejected any suggestion that *Halsey* had changed the substantive law, namely that protection given to without prejudice negotiations will not be removed by the court save in exceptional circumstances.[14]

8 23 Q.B.D. 335
9 [1989] AC 1280
10 [1989] A.C. 1280 at 1300
11 [2004]1 WLR 3002
12 [2023] EWCA Civ 1416
13 [2004] 1 WLR 3026 per Jacob LJ @ [14]
14 Law as set out in *Walker v Wilsher* (1889) 23 QBD 335.

In *Venture Investment Placement Ltd v. Hal*[15] the court granted an injunction to prevent disclosure of the contents of a without prejudice discussion. Judge Reid QC rightly observed

[at paragraph 11]:-

> " *Mediation proceedings do have to be guarded with great care. The whole point of mediation proceedings is that parties can be frank and open with each other, and that what is revealed in the course of mediation proceedings is not to be used for or against either party in the litigation, if mediation proceedings fail*".

6.2 Challenges to Mediation Privilege

However there have been some decisions where the courts have allowed a party to introduce in subsequent litigation evidence of what transpired in a mediation. The trend has been to follow the 'without prejudice' line and admit the evidence either where the parties have themselves waived their privilege, or where the court has been persuaded that the evidence was admissible under one of the exceptions set out by Walker LJ in *Unilever plc v Proctor and Gamble.*

In *Brown v Patel*[16] a Mrs Rice purported to sell a property to Mrs Patel. Mrs Rice's trustee in bankruptcy, Mr Brown, brought proceedings under s.339 of the Insolvency Act against Mrs Patel alleging that the sale to her was at an undervalue. Mrs Patel denied this, and a three-day trial was set. A mediation took place shortly before trial, for which the parties signed a standard form ADR Group mediation agreement which provided (among other things) that:

(a) confidentiality would apply to statements and documents prepared for the mediation save those already disclosed in the litigation, and

(b) no settlement would be legally binding unless reduced to writing and signed by each party.

The mediation failed to give rise to a written settlement signed by each party. A preliminary issue at the trial was whether there has been an enforceable concluded settlement, and the judge decided to hear evidence about what happened at the later stages of the mediation, even though he recognised that he might later rule that such evidence was inadmissible. He turned first to the without prejudice rule and exceptions to its effect. He described mediation as "*assisted without prejudice negotiation*", with no special privileged status. Although it was argued that some kind of special mediation privilege exists

15 [2005] EWHC 1227 (Ch)
16 [2007] EWHC 625 (Ch)

or is beginning to emerge, he found no extant authority for this, even though he saw that the need for such a privilege might arise for consideration in the future. On the basis that he regarded mediation as a without prejudice negotiation, he held that the exceptions to the without prejudice rule which allowed evidence to be admitted, also apply to mediation.

Applying the decisions in *Muller v Linsley & Mortimer*[17] and *Tomlin v Standard Telephones and Cables*[18], the judge held that a court can find and enforce a binding contract reached by means of without prejudice negotiations and concluded that he was required to consider events, documents and offers, otherwise without prejudice, in order to make such a ruling.

Among the many arguments which the judge rejected as reasons why he should not hear the evidence of what transpired in the mediation were the following:

> (a) Clause 1.4 of the mediation agreement expressly stated that no settlement was legally binding unless reduced to writing and signed by the parties. As this had not occurred, it followed that there had been no settlement, and it was thus otiose to receive evidence as to whether any agreement had been reached, as, unless it complied with the self-imposed formalities of the mediation process, no court could find there to be an (otherwise) enforceable contract of settlement.
>
> (b) The confidentiality provisions of the mediation agreement prevented the parties from giving evidence about what happened. However, as the court had rejected the first argument, the second ground for seeking to exclude enquiry into what had transpired, was effectively undermined, and it was conceded that this provision could not prevent an enquiry into whether a concluded agreement had been reached within what the judge regarded as simply without prejudice negotiations.

The judge decided that although an offer had been 'left on the table' which had been accepted by the trustee, the offer was not certain enough in its terms; also, the provisions of clause 1.4 of the mediation agreement were not met. He therefore concluded that the parties had agreed terms 'subject to contract'. He rejected the argument that, by agreeing to leave an offer open for acceptance, Mrs Patel had varied or waived the terms of clause 1.4. Vitally, he accepted that offers were frequently left open at this stage, so that a valid offer and acceptance the next day would still be bound by the mediation agreement as a settlement reached in the mediation.

During 2007 and 2008 the trend seemed to be leaning against protecting the existence of mediation confidentiality. In *Cattley v Pollard*[19] a party to a

17 [1996] PNLR 74
18 [1969] 1 Lloyd's Rep. 309 CA
19 [2007] Ch 353

mediation was ordered to give disclosure of mediation documents which were relevant to the issue of issues in subsequent proceedings. In *Earl of Malmesbury v Strutt and Parker*[20] the judge made a ruling on costs after considering, among other things, evidence led by both parties as to the offers each had made at a prior mediation. For a reason best known to them, counsel agreed that the contents of the mediation should be disclosed, it being assumed that only the parties had a right of confidentiality and this could be waived by consent.

However a different result occurred in *Cumbria Waste Management v Baines Wilson*[21]. There the Department for the Environment, Food and Rural Affairs (DEFRA) were facing a series of claims arising out of the foot and mouth epidemic in the spring and summer of 2001 which caused a crisis in British agriculture and tourism. They settled an early claim by Cumbria at mediation. Dissatisfied with the amount of the DEFRA payment, Cumbria sued the solicitors who had drafted their original contract. Those solicitors sought disclosure of the mediation papers in order to explore the reasonableness of the settlement reached. Inevitably they relied on *Muller* to overcome DEFRA's assertion of without prejudice privilege. But the Judge was able to find that the truth or falsity of statements made in the mediation *would* be at issue in the claim against the solicitors. DEFRA successfully objected that statements made at the mediation could, once revealed, effectively be used as admissions in the upcoming claims by other similar companies. The solicitors could not bring themselves within the *Muller* exception to the without prejudice rule and disclosure was declined.

The widest debate in this area has been prompted by the decision of Mr Justice Ramsey in *Farm Assist Ltd v DEFRA (No.2)* [22]. In that case the judge refused to set aside on her application, a witness summons issued against leading mediator, Jane Andrewartha, to give evidence of the circumstances in which a settlement had come about in a mediation in which she was engaged, where the liquidator of Farm Assist was challenging its enforceability some four years after the event on the ground of the settlement at the mediation having been procured by DEFRA through economic duress.

DEFRA reacted to the allegation by seeking disclosure of all documents in Farm Assist's possession which contained the legal and expert advice it had received leading to the decision to settle with DEFRA at the mediation; this to include advice given during and after the mediation, whether or not

20 [2008] EWHC 424 (QB)
21 [2008] EWHC 786
22 [2009] EWHC1102 TCC

the mediator was present. Farm Assist objected on the ground that legal professional privilege protected it from disclosure. DEFRA argued that Farm Assist had waived such privilege by bringing proceedings against them which made material Farm Assist's thinking at the mediation.

In *Farm Assist Ltd v DEFRA (No.1)*[23] Ramsey J. had earlier held that such advice was not disclosable by virtue of legal professional privilege and the issue of proceedings did not of itself amount to an implied waiver by the liquidators of Farm Assist. The Judge also declined to strike out the claim, and accordingly the focus of the parties' attention turned to whether the mediator could herself be called as a material witness to any alleged pressure brought to bear by DEFRA on Farm Assist by way of economic duress. She would have been present at any joint meetings in which relevant remarks may have been made; she would have carried offers and information between the parties, and discussed terms of settlement privately with them

Since there had been no reported case in the UK of a mediator actually having been compelled to give evidence, whether a witness summons should stand is an important question, particularly here where both parties consented to the mediator being called (the liquidators agreed as the mediator had already indicated that she had neither notes nor any independent recollection of the contents of the mediation).

The relevant signed mediation agreement (of 2003) expressly provided for confidentiality as to the existence of the mediation and in relation to all information arising in relation to it including any settlement terms, documents covered by specific "without prejudice" privilege, and that the mediator should not to be called "*as a witness, consultant, arbitrator or expert in any litigation or arbitration in relation to the Dispute, and the Mediator will not act voluntarily in any such capacity without the written agreement of all the parties*".

The judge found as a matter of interpretation that the restriction on calling the mediator as witness as drafted was confined to 'the Dispute' – and not wide enough to cover a different dispute, namely whether economic duress had been deployed by one of the parties to procure settlement during the mediation. *Practitioners are accordingly advised to check with care the wording in drafts of standard form mediation agreements for the ambit of restrictions imposed on party use of the mediator after the event.* Most mediation service providers immediately amended their standard form agreements to deal with Ramsey J.'s remarks. In addition trainee mediators

23 [2008] EWHC 3079 TCC; [2008] All ER (D)124

have since been trained expressly to destroy all of the papers and to discipline themselves to forget what occurred, should they not have been doing so previously.

On broad considerations of the existence of confidentiality and privilege in mediations the judge concluded by reference to existing authorities as follows:

> (1) Confidentiality: The proceedings are confidential both as between the parties and as between the parties and the mediator. As a result, even if the parties agree that matters can be referred to outside the mediation, the mediator can enforce the confidentiality provision. The court will generally uphold that confidentiality but where it is necessary in the interests of justice for evidence to be given of confidential matters, the Courts will order or permit that evidence to be given or produced.
>
> (2) Without Prejudice Privilege: The proceedings are covered. This is a privilege which exists between the parties, who can waive it. It is not a privilege of the mediator.
>
> (3) Other Privileges: If another privilege attached to documents which are produced by a party and shown to a mediator, that party retains that privilege and it is not waived by disclosure to the mediator or by waiver of the without prejudice privilege.

Applying the present situation to his findings the judge found the parties had agreed to waive "without prejudice" privilege and that the mediator had disclosed her limited documentation; that an allegation of wrongdoing at the mediation was at the core of the claim; the clause in the relevant mediation agreement purporting to prevent the mediator from being called was not effective to prevent her from being called on this issue; the mediator has said that she had no helpful recollection of what happened at the mediation; the mediator had an enforceable right to confidentiality unless she should be called as a witness "in the interests of justice".

Having decided the central allegation of economic duress inevitably involved consideration of what the mediator said and did, and that her absence of recollection did not of itself justify not calling her for this to be tested out, he found "*as an exception" to* the mediator's right to confidentiality that "*the interests of justice lie strongly in favour of evidence being given of what was said and done".*

While practitioners will appreciate the importance of the mediator having been found to have an independent right to enforce confidentiality, the decision on the facts whether to find the existence of an exception is questionable, if not wrong. Given that on any occasion where a party is dissatisfied with the outcome of a mediation - either where there are grounds to impeach a settlement he or she no longer wishes to be bound by, or the conduct of the opposing party is complained of, or there is merely an argument on liability for costs – he or she would wish to compel the mediator to provide evidence in support, it is difficult to see on what basis the judge found this situation an exception to the general rule he himself had established.

The judge sought comfort for the existence of an exception to the mediator's right of confidentiality from the judgment of Sir Thomas Bingham MR in *Re D (Minors) (Conciliation: Disclosure of Information)*[24]. *In re D.* was a case concerning a statement made by a conciliator (a mediator) about meetings held with the mother and father in proceedings under the Children Act 1989. The judge at first instance decided that the statement should be excluded from evidence and the mother appealed. The Court of Appeal upheld the decision of the judge. Sir Thomas Bingham MR at p.239 emphasised the strong public policy imperative that lies behind the exclusion of such evidence when parties are negotiating arrangements for their children, "*unless parties can speak freely and uninhibitedly, without worries about weakening their position in contested litigation if that becomes necessary, the conciliation will be doomed to fail*".

He went on to say at p.241

> "In our judgment, the law is that evidence may not be given in proceedings under the Children Act 1989 of statements made by one or other of the parties in the course of meetings held or communications made for the purpose of conciliation save in the very unusual case where a statement is made clearly indicating that the maker has in the past caused or is likely in the future to cause serious harm to the well-being of a child."
>
> "....Even in the rare case which falls within the narrow exception we have defined, the trial judge will still have to exercise a discretion whether or not to admit the evidence. He will admit it only if, in his judgment, the public interest in protecting the interests of the child outweighs the public interest in preserving the confidentiality of attempted conciliation."

However, as Kallipetis commented afterwards in the *Mediator Magazine*[25],

> "While acknowledging that in *Re D* the court was clearly dealing with a different position, Ramsey J does appear to have ignored the three express reservations which the Master of the Rolls made, namely: 1. The decision was solely concerned with the welfare of children; 2. The decision was only concerned with privilege "properly so called...and has

24 [1993] Fam 231

25 *Mediators Awake: the Ongoing Debate over Mediation Privilege* Michel Kallipetis KC Mediator Magazine July 2009

> nothing to do with duties of confidence and does not seek to define the circumstances in which a duty of confidence may be superseded by other public interest considerations" 3. The Court of Appeal "deliberately stated the law in terms appropriate to cover this case and no other. We have not thought it desirable to attempt any more general statement. If and when cases arise not covered by this ruling, they will have to be decided in the light of their own special circumstances".
>
> Ramsey J also referred at length to the decision of HH Judge Frances Kirkham (also another trained mediator) in *Cumbria Waste Management v. Baines Wilson* [2008] EWHC 786, which the mediation community hailed as a welcome recognition that mediation privilege was to be upheld by the Courts. Curiously he did not refer to her unequivocal decision that the mediator should not be required to give evidence of what transpired in a mediation."

Thus even 15 years after *Farm Assist (No 2)* the debate on mediation privilege remains open. This decision attracted wide interest[26] at the time. Commentators generally agree that it is also likely to be incompatible with the then binding European Directive on Mediation in relation to cross-border disputes. However it will not be clarified in the Court of Appeal, at least not in the *Farm Assist* case, since the parties had come to terms even prior to Ramsey J handing down his decision, which makes the value of the authority itself questionable.

The England and Wales Civil Mediation Council issued a Guidance Note for mediators (Mediation Confidentiality - 8th July 2009) which suggests that mediation agreements should continue to specify that the mediation proceedings are conducted on a "without prejudice" basis; should continue to make it clear that what is said during mediation proceedings will be confidential; and should not restrict the circumstances in which a mediator cannot be compelled to give evidence in court *(sic)*.

An article by Heather Allen for the CEDR website in January, 2013 discusses the then position at length: http://www.cedr.com/articles/?item=Confidentiality-a-guide-for-mediators. The compellability of mediators has not changed in the jurisdiction of England and Wales since *Farm Assist*. Outside this jurisdiction as she says,

> 'Mediator compellability is the only aspect of mediation confidentiality that has found its way into the EU Mediation Directive (*currently not applicable in the UK to mediations of cross-border disputes involving parties from EU States*), and even then it has done so in a deficient way. The Directive provides that mediators shall not be called to give evidence in litigation or arbitration except where necessary for public policy reasons, instancing

26 *Calling all Mediators: a review of Farm Assist v DEFRA* Tony Allen, *CEDR Resolutions Magazine* July, 2009 (www.cedr.com); *Farm Assist: Mediators Get Another Dose of Disclosure* Bill Woods QC *Mediator Magazine* July 2009; *Mediation Privilege?* The Hon. Mr Justice Briggs, *New Law Journal*, 3rd and 10th April 2009

child protection and prevention of physical or psychological harm as possible grounds; or where disclosure is necessary in order to implement or enforce a mediated settlement. However, there is an overriding exception, which is when the parties agree that the mediator is to be called, apparently about any aspect of what happened at the mediation and not limited to the above exceptions. Stricter rules may be introduced by EU States, but the problem in England & Wales is that it is not clear whether our rules are stricter or not, as there is a dearth of senior court authority on this topic.'

Within the arena of Family Conciliation subsequent authorities followed *Re D*. In *Re E (A Child) (Mediation Privilege)*[27], Mr L Samuels QC (sitting as a High Court Judge) granted an application to prevent a party relying on matters that took place in a mediation concerning disputed childcare arrangements. He relied upon the obiter observations of Williams J in *Re D (A Child) (Hague Convention: Mediation)*[28] which he found fitted neatly with his analysis. At paragraph 8 of his judgment Williams J said:

> "I would say that I consider there is a strong argument for holding that mediation in the context of 1980 Hague Convention proceedings, with the international dimension that it contains, with the peculiar intensity of the post-abduction environment, and where the cloak of confidentiality arises not simply from inference but from express terms, will not necessarily attract the *Unilever plc v The Procter & Gamble Co* [2000] 1 WLR 2436 exceptions but rather would be immune from disclosure in all circumstances, save for those identified in *In re D (Minors) (Conciliation: Disclosure of Information)* [1993] Fam 231 and accepted within the mediation framework itself, namely disclosure might be justified where there was a risk of significant harm to a child. In so far as I can, in this limited context, I would want to reassure mediators that the cloak of confidentiality remains as securely fastened as ever it was."
>
> 'Further support for this analysis is to be found in PD12B FPR 2010 para 5.11, under the heading 'Non-court resolution of disputed arrangements for children' where it is said that:
>
> > "Mediation is a confidential process; none of the parties to the mediation may provide information to the court as to the content of any discussions held in mediation and/or the reasons why agreement was not reached. Similarly, the mediator may not provide such information, unless the mediator considers that a safeguarding issue arises."
>
> Such an analysis also fits entirely with the terms of the written agreement signed by these parties on entering into mediation....
>
> The public interest in promoting and supporting mediation to enable parents to resolve disputes about their children, without recourse to the court and contested litigation, is at least as strong today as it was when

27 [2020] EWHC 3379 (Fam)

28 [2017] EWHC 3363 (Fam) [2018] 4 WLR 45

> In *Re D* was determined in 1993. That public interest was reinforced by Williams J in the 2017 *Re D*, specifically in the context of a dispute under the Hague Convention.
>
> The father does not seek to argue that disclosure of discussions between these parties within mediation is justified by reason of a significant risk of harm to E. Nor does he suggest that one of the other Unilever exceptions does or should apply. Instead, he proposes that mediation privilege or the 'without prejudice rule' should give way to the wider interests of justice, his right to a fair trial and a simple test of relevance.
>
> In my judgment, the authorities relied upon by Ms Gilmore in support of that proposition are not really on point. There is undoubtedly a public interest in the court being able to "get at the truth" in the words of Baroness Hale in Re A. However, the pathway to the truth is unlikely to lie through disclosure of the otherwise privileged discussions within mediation. Parties must be free to discuss candidly all options for settlement and 'think the unthinkable' without fearing that their words will be used against them in any subsequent litigation. Mediators must be free to perform their valuable role without fearing they will be dragged into that litigation either by court orders for provision of their notes or to be called to give evidence for one parent and against the other. Otherwise, to paraphrase Lord Bingham MR, the mediation process is likely to fail.'

In *Interactive Technology Corporation Ltd v Ferster & Ors.*[29] Mrs Justice Rose again considered the issue of "mediation privilege" and reaffirmed that no such separate and distinct privilege exists in English law. This was in the context of deciding whether existing rules concerning without prejudice correspondence being disclosable if it served an improper purpose could be overridden. Here, in a minority shareholder's petition under s.994 of the Companies Act 2006 against his two brothers, co-shareholders in a limited company, the applicant sought a winding-up of the company on the grounds of unfairly prejudicial conduct on the part of the respondents. A mediation took place and the respondents offered to sell their shares to the applicant. After the mediation the mediator wrote a letter to the applicant's solicitor. There was no dispute that the letter from the mediator was an accurate statement of the respondents' stance, which contained an express threat to issue contempt proceedings against him unless he agreed a higher price. Despite being marked 'without prejudice' the judge allowed the applicant to amend the petition to specifically plead its contents since it was being used for unambiguous impropriety and could not therefore be cloaked using without prejudice protection, even though emerging from their mediation.

It appears therefore, that no mediation privilege currently exists. Without prejudice correspondence is subject to the *Unilever* rules and exceptions, and in any event may be waived by the parties. And the parties may also waive

29 [2015] EWHC 3895 (Ch)

confidentiality to the extent that the Court can compel the attendance of the mediator in circumstances where it is in the interests of justice to do so, in respect of which each case will turn on its own facts. At the time of writing the law is ripe for further guidance from the Court of Appeal.

Part 7

Costs

Chapter 7
COSTS ISSUES

A number of costs issues arise in the context of mediation, which are considered under the following topics:

- Mediation Costs
- Litigation Costs and ADR
- Mediation Costs and Funding Arrangements
- Adverse costs awards in litigation for a party's unreasonable failure to mediate

Although these issues are rooted in the particular approach of the CPR and the Courts in costs matters in England and Wales, some of the applied learning is relevant to any jurisdiction where costs operate on a one-way costs shifting basis, i.e. the loser pays the costs of the winner, and the courts exercise a supervisory jurisdiction to determine the reasonableness of a bill, and a discretion over the amount recoverable by the winning party in terms of proportionality.

7.1 Mediation Costs

Mediation does not operate in a vacuum. As a process it is entirely contractual, even if directed by the Court, and hopefully, it succeeds in producing a further enforceable contract which settles the dispute between the parties. That being so it is for the parties to contract between themselves who will be responsible for the costs of the mediation. These include the costs of the mediator, any separate charge by a service provider for administration or for room hire and refreshments, and the costs of party representatives and experts or other professional participants, for example accountants.

Most standard form mediation agreements provide for the costs of the mediation to be met by the parties equally, and usually provide for payment in advance. There is nothing to prevent parties negotiating something different, and this occasionally happens where there is substantial inequality of arms, or a party is trying to induce the other side to come to mediation at all. During the course of the mediation a party may make it a term of the settlement that the agreement be varied to the extent that the mediation costs are provided for.

It is unwise that the parties leave the position as silent. The costs of the mediation should properly be defined in the mediation agreement to avoid confusion. It may be the case that parties will return their own contribution to the cost of the mediator and the room hire, but if the dispute proceeds to litigation afterwards, they may try to recover their legal costs of the mediation as costs in the litigation.

7.2 Litigation Costs and ADR

When deciding whether to mediate, the issue of costs, particularly what costs a client is likely to recover, is usually a crucial consideration. Before considering this issue, it is important to remember that mediations are not cheap per se: they are an attractive alternative to litigation which either proceeds to trial or at least has a substantial amount of costs expended upon it in the stages leading up to trial. Having said that HM Small Claims Mediation Service is intended to be free to users. Many service providers now offer fixed cost schemes depending on the value of the dispute, and care should be taken in understanding what is meant by value.

It is noteworthy the assertion by the mediation industry that mediation presents substantial cost savings by comparison with full-scale litigation is based on the assumption that the mediation will succeed. Should the mediation fail, or merely create a momentum towards settlement but which requires further steps to be taken in the litigation, the costs of the mediation will have to be aggregated with the litigation costs. If that occurs the costs of a failed mediation may be significant.

There are a number of reasons why mediations can be costly. These might include the following:

- Over the last few years the mediation process has been getting far more sophisticated in the hands of the lawyer representatives. Thus representatives approach (and should approach) the preparation for a mediation in the same way as a preparation for a trial, albeit with different procedures and using different advocacy techniques; they must allot adequate preparation time, including a pre-mediation conference with the client as necessary to identify the true negotiating parameters.
- Fees must take into account pre-appointment preparation, to include settling a case summary for the mediator and possibly a reply to that of

the other side and having personal communications with the mediator in advance of the appointment.

- In assessing 'hearing' fees the litigator should be conscious of the fact that even mediations starting early in the morning may not conclude until well into the evening. It may be necessary to have a fee for the day with an additional hourly rate for after-business hours, alternatively a fee for a day and a half. It is quite common for the mediator to charge on this basis and is surprisingly successful in bringing the parties to settlement just before the hourly-rate basis of extra charges comes in.
- In addition, it will have to be decided whether expert evidence will be necessary for the mediation, and if so the form it should take, and the directions if any, for pre-appointment exchange of reports or summaries. This may extend to property, tax or other accountancy advice on the nature and operation of the proposed settlement.
- Witness statements or at least summaries of evidence may be necessary.
- As with arbitration, the parties are directly contributing to the costs of the mediator and the venue.
- There may be ancillary costs (hidden or open) which are payable to the mediation service provider (e.g. cost of catering, photocopying etc). An MSP is likely to build in a profit element into its administration fee.

On the other hand, mediations can be cheaper than litigation, and the flexibility of the mediation process is a reason why costs savings can be achieved. For example:

- The speed of the process restricts the amount of chargeable time likely to be incurred.
- The absence of formal structure means that the parties are free to choose the procedure, including the degree of formality or otherwise. They will certainly wish to dispense with matters that can result in a significant cost saving.
- There is no formality about CPR Part 20 or counterclaims or those by or involving third or other additional parties. The procedure is thus far less expensive than a multi-party claim in litigation.
- The mediation is not a trial or tribunal: since the process is non-adjudicatory no findings need be made. Evidence, disclosure and documentation are substantially reduced and may be dispensed with altogether.

- There are no costs associated with the delivery of a judgment or consideration of an appeal.
- Moreover, the litigation may (and under CPR case management invariably will) be suspended by agreement during the mediation process to prevent further litigation costs accruing outside the mediation.

7.3 The Recoverability of Costs

Any analysis of what costs might be recoverable has to take into account all the situations in which a client might have incurred costs, including the costs of the mediation and of the litigation.

Costs of the Mediation in the Litigation

Parties have the freedom to choose how costs flow in mediation. The conventional principle in litigation that the loser pays the winner's costs is often alien to a resolution process whose fundamental approach is that both parties feel that they have achieved a benefit from participation. As has been suggested above, ordinarily each party will pay an equal share of the costs of the mediation to the service provider in advance, unless agreed otherwise, and a clause acknowledging liability for a share of the mediation costs will be contained in the mediation agreement. This avoids the cost of the mediation becoming an issue within the mediation. Parties can make it an issue if they wish but this will be an extra and unnecessary sticking point, which may impede settlement. Thus, unless otherwise agreed, parties to a mediation should expect to pay in advance for half the costs of the mediator, the room hire and any service fee to the mediation service provider, and pay their own costs of legal representation.

Should the mediation fail to bring about a settlement and the matter proceeds to trial, the Court does have jurisdiction to award the costs of the mediation: *Chantrey Vellacott -v- The Convergence Group PLC and Others.*[1] In that case Rimer J was invited to award costs by reference to the conduct of the parties in a failed mediation. Surprisingly counsel for both parties waived confidentiality to enable the judge to consider contentious allegations. The context was his consideration of much wider costs issues, including applications for non-party costs under s.51 Senior Courts Act 1981. In the exercise of his discretion the judge followed the then paragraph 17.3 of the Chancery Guide 2005 and the Court of Appeal in *Eagleson v. Liddell* [2] both of which make provision for the costs of following an ADR procedure.

1 [2007] EWHC 1774 (Ch)
2 [2001] EWCA Civ 155

Litigation Costs in the Mediation

Liability for litigation costs forms part of the claim being mediated. It is an issue that party representatives *must* confront before the mediation. Thus, parties to a mediation are not properly prepared unless they attend knowing:

- The amount of costs they have incurred to date (including the costs of the mediation) - this needs to be as specific as possible.
- A good estimate of the likely costs that will be incurred to the end of the trial if necessary.
- A reasonable estimate of the recoverable/irrecoverable element of their total costs on detailed assessment (on the standard and indemnity bases of assessment respectively).
- The impact of any own client funding arrangement, e,g. damages based agreement, after the event insurance, third party funding agreement.

In addition, either before, or during, the mediation each party ought to obtain from any other party details of that other party's costs, including an estimate of their costs to date, of their likely future costs, and of the recoverable/ irrecoverable element of their total bill.

This information is essential in being able to calculate the BATNA.

Should the mediation fail or the litigation not be settled until after the mediation process has concluded, the legal costs of the mediation will usually be claimed by the successful party as part of his litigation costs (see above). This remains something of a grey area, particularly where the mediation is not court-directed. However, two frequently deployed arguments, with which representatives should be familiar, are as follows:

- The mediation agreement is a complete collateral contract which stands outside the litigation and accordingly self-regulates the costs. To the extent that the mediation agreement does not specify the parties' liability for costs, they are borne by the party incurring them. If this argument succeeds, then the costs provided for within the agreement e.g. that each party pay a specified proportion of the costs of the mediator, the room hire and any service fee to the mediation service provider would be provided for but that all other costs would be irrecoverable.

- The mediation has narrowed down the issues in dispute which should be reflected in appropriate costs' order having regard to the court's discretion under CPR Pt 44.[3]

Ordinarily the court cannot open up what occurred within the mediation for the purpose of exercising its discretion as to costs in the litigation. As was discussed in Part 6, the starting point remains that the contents of the mediation process are wholly without prejudice and confidential. However, absent waiver of the kind which occurred in *Chantrey Vellacott,* a number of costs decisions (e.g. *Shirayama Shokusan v Danovo*[4] and *Halsey v Milton Keynes General NHS Trust*[5]) suggest that the court is entitled to make an assumption of what may have occurred had a mediation taken place when it did not do so.

Mediation Costs and Public Funding

The Legal Services Commission ("LSC") favours the use of mediation to reduce publicly funded litigation. The Court of Appeal has said in the strongest terms that publicly funded claims must be mediated where possible: see *R (Cowl and others) v Plymouth City Council.*[6] Although the availability of public funding has become more and more remote to litigants, in principle there seems to be no reason why litigators acting for a party having the benefit of an unqualified public funding certificate should not recover their fees in a mediation. However, solicitors should always confirm with the LSC that fees for mediation work are recoverable.

7.4 Mediation Costs and Funding Agreements

Conditional Fee Agreements grew in popularity as a means of funding litigation after they were originally permitted in 1995. However the CFA system come under the sharp focus of criticism in the Jackson Review of Costs in Civil Cases[7] and the changes that Sir Rupert Jackson recommended came into fruition after April, 2013 as a result of which any "success fee" to which lawyers were entitled to in addition to their base costs fee was no longer to be borne by the losing defendant, but would come out of the recoverable damages awarded to the claimant, subject to a cap of 25%. This made the scheme far less attractive to claimant lawyers operating on a 'no win no fee' basis.

3 See Part 44.3(4)(a) and (b) and (5)(b),(c) and (d)
4 [2003] EWHC 390 (Ch); [2004] 1 WLR 2985
5 *Op.cit* [2004] 1 WLR 3002
6 [2001] EWCA Civ 1935; [2002] 1 WLR 803
7 Published January, 2010

In addition, Jackson introduced a damages-based agreement where clients may engage their lawyers on the basis that professional fees will be taken out of any award, again with fees for personal injury and clinical negligence claimants being capped at 25% of the damages.

Since litigation costs are usually part of the claim being mediated, as part of mediation preparation the parties' representatives ought to obtain detailed information about their own and each other's litigation costs.

Where the successful party is funded by a CFA, DBA or some other form of third party funding, representatives have also to be aware of its possible impact on any settlement. For example:

- Where the settlement provides for payment of a sum in respect of damages and for payment of the CFA-funded party's costs, to be subject to detailed assessment, the parties must be clear whether it is intended that these costs include a success fee.
- If the settlement distinguishes between monies paid in respect of damages and in respect of costs to the CFA-funded party, there is likely to be much discussion about the precise amount of recoverable costs. Where a success fee is payable, this has the effect of substantially increasing the total costs, and ordinarily it is this element that proves to be one of the biggest stumbling blocks in negotiating a satisfactory outcome in the mediation.
- Where the settlement provides for payment of one inclusive sum representing damages and the CFA-funded party's costs, the CFA-funded representative and his client have to be clear how much each is going to recover. It is suggested that such costs-inclusive offers have the potential to create considerable friction between client and representative, particularly where it has been calculated on the basis that the base costs and success fee of the other side are over-stated. The CFA-funded representative should anticipate the problem and work out a solution with the client in advance of the mediation. Otherwise, the mediator may find himself having to assist in negotiations between the solicitor and his own client.

7.5 The Relevance of Court-Directed Mediation

On various occasions the courts have directed the parties to undertake mediation, often as part of their case management powers, although prior to *Churchill* now clarifying the position, *Halsey* had the effect of stopping at more than a strong suggestion. For example in *Kinstreet Ltd v Balmargo Corporation Ltd*[8] Arden J directed that the parties use ADR despite the objection of one party, on the basis that the costs of going to trial would exceed the amount claimed. Later in *Muman v Nagasena*,[9] the Court of Appeal stayed proceedings issued by charitable trustees against the claimant's wishes until the parties had made an attempt to resolve the dispute through mediation. Another example is provided by *Cable & Wireless Plc v IBM UK Ltd*[10] where Colman J enforced a mediation clause in a commercial agreement by staying proceedings, although this was not followed in the subsequent case of *Sulmerica CIA Nacional de Seguros SA v Ensa Engenharia SA*[11] where the Court of Appeal set out constraints on the enforceability of contractual mediation clauses[12].

In *R (Cowl and others) v Plymouth City Council*[13] the Court of Appeal provided express support for earlier judicial attempts to require parties to mediate. In that case, the court stated that it was of paramount importance that litigation should be avoided whenever possible, and that in order to achieve this, judges could question the parties as to the steps taken to avoid litigation, including requiring them to justify their decision not to embark on ADR.

The facts of *Cowl* were as follows: the claimants lived in a residential care home owned and run by the defendant, which wanted to close it. The claimants sought judicial review of the closure decision. The defendant offered to treat the claimant's application for judicial review as a complaint for consideration by an independent panel that would make a non-binding decision albeit one to which the defendant would have regard. Permission to apply for judicial review was granted by Harrison J but at the substantive hearing Scott Baker J found against the claimants and indicated that the complaints procedure should have been adopted. In dismissing the appeal, the Court of Appeal considered that ADR in the form of the complaints procedure was a viable option. The claimants had not provided any reasonable basis for objecting to the complaints procedure and accordingly the parties should have come to a resolution without resorting to publicly funded litigation. The failure to adopt ADR where public money was involved was indefensible.

8 [2000] CP Rep 62
9 [1999] EWCA Civ 764 [2000] 1 WLR 299
10 [2002] EWHC 2059 Comm; [2002] All ER (D) 277
11 [2012] EWCA Civ 638
12 See page 50 above.
13 [2001] EWCA Civ 1935; [2002] 1 WLR 803

One feature of these cases was the Courts' apparent zeal in driving parties into mediation, particularly where public funds are involved. By so doing, they arguably risked undermining the consensual process of mediation.

Perhaps recognising this danger, the courts have in a number of cases since 2004 made clear that a party could not be ordered to submit to mediation as this would be contrary to Art 6 of the European Convention on Human Rights, most prominently the *Halsey* decision itself. With the finding in *Churchill*[14] that *Halsey* was obiter on the point, the Article 6 argument falls away. However there remains a tension between two principles, namely the courts' desire to achieve higher levels of settlement by mediation and its recognition of a party's right to have "his day in court". The principal mechanism under which both principles are observed is by the use of adverse costs orders in appropriate circumstances for a party's unreasonable failure to mediate (or engage in any other appropriate form of ADR). Representatives in every case have to be astute to ensure that their client's conduct does not expose it to adverse costs orders.

7.6 Adverse Costs Awards for a Party's Failure to Mediate

The mechanism for forcing parties to evaluate their position on ADR/ mediation is the impact of the costs regime at CPR Part 44.4. Under Part 44.4(3) "in deciding what order (if any) to make about costs the court must have regard to all the circumstances, including - (a) the conduct of all the parties." Thus it is a mandatory requirement of the CPR that judges have regard to the conduct of the parties in deciding costs issues.

Under Part 44.4(3)(a)(ii) "the conduct of all the parties includes – (a) conduct before, as well as during, the proceedings, and in particular the efforts made, if any, before and during the proceedings in order to try to resolve the dispute; ... (c) the manner in which a party has pursued or defended his case or a particular allegation or issue".

Following the decision of the Court of Appeal in *Dyson v Leeds City Council (No. 1)*[15] in which reference was made to the overriding objective, and to the court's duty to manage cases, including "taking a strong view about the rejection of encouraging noises we are making" by imposing adverse costs orders, the case law developed quickly and in favour of ADR. A particular feature of the subsequent cases was that the courts took the opportunity of encouraging the disposal of cases by ADR in every field of law and indicated their readiness

14 [2023] EWCA Civ 1416 @[20-21]

15 [2000] CP Rep 42

to reduce a successful party's costs if they had, without justification, rejected offers of mediation from their opponents. *Dyson* was followed by *R (Cowl and others) v Plymouth City Council* (see above).

The trend in adverse costs orders in the Court of Appeal really started with *Dunnett v Railtrack*[16] (Brooke, Robert Walker and Sedley LJJ). Here the claimant had rented a farm adjacent to the defendant's railway lines. An accommodation gate crossing the lines was left open and three of the claimant's horses were killed when they strayed onto the track. The claimant sought damages for negligence. The claim failed both at first instance and in the Court of Appeal. When granting permission to appeal, Schiemann LJ had strongly recommended the possibility of ADR, and in particular a mediated settlement. The claimant sought ADR but the defendant, which argued that it was confident of success and that it would derive no benefit from mediation, rejected this. Despite succeeding in the Court of Appeal, the defendant was deprived of its appeal costs. The court held that often in cases a claimant might be satisfied with an apology and an explanation of what had occurred, something which could be explored using ADR. It was emphasised that it was a lawyer's duty to further the overriding objective under CPR Part 1.1; if parties rejected ADR out of hand they would suffer the consequences when costs came to be decided.

In giving the leading judgment, Brooke LJ appears to have been influenced by policy considerations, as indicated by the following passage:

> "It is to be hoped that any publicity given to this part of the judgment of the court will draw the attention of lawyers to their duties to further the overriding objective in the way that is set out in CPR Pt 1 and to the possibility that, if they turn down out of hand the chance of alternative dispute resolution when suggested by the court, as happened on this occasion, they may have to face uncomfortable costs consequence."

It is also perhaps significant that there is no suggestion in the judgment that the claimant would have necessarily been satisfied with an apology or explanation. Moreover the court expressly declined to look at such settlement offers as had been made notwithstanding the refusal to mediate.

The approach of the Court of Appeal in Dunnett was then applied in a number of later cases, including:

- *Neal v Jones Motors*[17] where a successful party's recoverable costs were reduced by £5,000 for failure to follow the court's recommendation to mediate.

16 [2002] EWCA Civ 302 [2002] 1 WLR 2434
17 [2002] EWCA Civ 1730

- *Royal Bank of Canada v Secretary of State for Defence*[18] where Lewison J had to decide whether a break notice had been served by the defendant in a landlord and tenant case. The defendant won on the merits. However the claimant had expressed, on a number of occasions, its willingness to mediate the claim. Although the Lord Chancellor's Department had made a formal pledge committing government departments and agencies to settle cases through ADR, the court noted that the defendant had not abided by that pledge. The judge held that a willingness to mediate was something which was significant in deciding where costs were to lie. Accordingly he made no order as to costs, thus penalising the winning government department.
- *Virani v Manuel Revert Y CIA SA*[19] where the Court of Appeal was required to decide in what currency the claimant's damages ought to be awarded. On the application for permission to appeal, the defendant appellant had been offered the Court of Appeal's mediation service by the single Lord Justice. Notwithstanding such offer, the appellant declined to enter into any form of mediation. This refusal attracted the penalty of the successful respondent's costs being assessed on the indemnity, as opposed to the standard, basis of assessment.

However not all courts slavishly followed *Dunnett*: in *Hurst v Leeming*[20] Lightman J stated that where an unsuccessful litigant sought to argue that his opponent should be penalised in costs for refusing an offer to mediate, such rejection had to be considered on its own merits; any such refusal would only escape sanction by the court if it could be shown that mediation in the particular circumstances had no real prospects of success. Despite Lightman J's obvious enthusiasm for ADR, he concluded that mediation in the present case had no real prospect of success by reason of the character and attitude of the party offering mediation and he therefore refused to penalise the successful party in costs. Although the judge's approach is more nuanced, one drawback is that it requires the court to consider what would have happened had there been a mediation. Given that many judges have very limited training in the mediation process, there is a risk that this exercise will be speculative.

A little later in *Societe Internationale de Telecommunications Aeronuatiques SC ("SITA") v Watson Wyatt; Maxwell Batley (Part 20 Defs)*[21] Park J was required to consider a costs application by an unsuccessful litigant, based on the

18 [2003] EWHC 1841 (ChD)

19 [2003] EWCA Civ. 1651; [2004] Lloyd's Rep 4

20 [2001] EWHC (Ch) 1051 [2003] 1 Lloyds Rep 379

21 [2002] EWHC Ch 2401

successful party's refusal of three offers of mediation during the proceedings. The judge did not (in terms) use as his starting point the question of whether mediation would have had a real prospect of success. In fact he expressly distinguished both *Dunnett* and *Hurst v Leeming*. He found against the unsuccessful litigant on the issue. In reaching his conclusion that the refusal of offers to mediate was reasonable, he took account of the length of time allowed in the offer of mediation for preparation of the mediation by the offeree party, the offeror's objective, namely that the other party should make a contribution in a settlement involving a third party (rather than to dispose of the dispute between offeror and offeree), and the robust terms in which the offer of mediation was made.

In *Valentine v Allen, Nash & Nash*[22] the Court of Appeal determined the issue of costs on an unsuccessful appeal brought by the claimant in proceedings to restrain an alleged trespass to land. The court concluded that the fact that the claimant's offer of mediation was refused by the respondents did not detract from the usual order that an unsuccessful appellant was to pay the respondent's costs in resisting the appeal since it was clear that the respondents had made real efforts to settle the dispute.

This is a clear contrast on the facts to *Dunnett* where, it will be remembered, the court declined to look at alternative attempts to settle.

Matters were then clarified by the Court of Appeal in *Halsey v Milton Keynes General NHS Trust.*[23] In the first case (*Halsey*), a claim by a Fatal Accidents Act claimant was dismissed and the judge awarded costs to the defendant despite the fact that it had refused the claimant's invitation to mediate. The claimant then appealed on costs. In the second case (*Steel v Joy & another*) the first defendant was unsuccessful in contribution proceedings against the second defendant. The second defendant was awarded its costs although it had refused the first defendant's invitation to mediate. The first defendant appealed on liability and costs. The Court of Appeal dismissed the appeals on costs by the claimant in *Halsey* and the first defendant in *Steel v Joy*. In reaching its decision the court articulated the following principles:

- To oblige truly unwilling parties to refer their disputes to mediation would be to impose an unacceptable obstruction on their right of access to the courts.
- In deciding whether to deprive a successful party of all or some of its costs for refusing to go to ADR it had to be borne in mind that this was an

22 [2003] EWCA Civ 1274

23 Op cit. [2004] EWCA Civ 576 [2004] 1 WLR 3002

exception to the general rule in CPR Part 44.3(2) and the burden was on the unsuccessful party to show why the general rule should be departed from.

- Such a departure was not justified unless it could be shown that the successful litigant acted unreasonably having regard to all the circumstances of the case.

However, the court considered the following as important but non-exhaustive factors to be taken into account:

- The nature of the dispute: some matters were intrinsically unsuitable for ADR.
- The merits of the case: a party's reasonable belief that he has a strong case would be relevant to reasonableness of his refusal of ADR, for otherwise the fear of costs sanctions might be used to extract unmerited settlements. If his declared belief was in fact spurious or not reasonably held, the court would be astute to this point. Where a case was evenly balanced, a party's belief that he would win ought to be given little or no weight when considering a refusal was reasonable save that his belief must not be unreasonable.
- Whether other settlement methods had been attempted but rejected.
- Where the costs of the mediation would be disproportionately high.
- Delay: this might be relevant if mediation was suggested late in the day and the effect of accepting it at that stage would be to delay the trial.
- Whether the mediation had a reasonable prospect of success: this was a relevant but not determinative factor. The burden would normally be on the unsuccessful party to show that there was a reasonable prospect of success (cf. *Hurst v Leeming*).
- Whether the court had encouraged mediation: the more that the court had encouraged mediation, the more likely it was that the unsuccessful party would discharge the burden of showing the successful party's refusal was unreasonable.
- Public bodies were not in any special position.

One point left unresolved by *Halsey* was whether the courts could in future receive in evidence any "without prejudice" documents or negotiations passing between the parties when considering the reasonableness of a party's refusal to mediate.

In *Reed Executive v Reed Business Information*[24] the Court of Appeal decided that judges could not. Halsey did not change the law that "without prejudice" material remained inadmissible (unless both parties agreed). However, on the issue of costs, any "Calderbank" material could be looked at by the court. As Jacob LJ indicated, the inability of the court to look at "without prejudice" material means that in some instances, the court cannot decide whether a party's refusal to mediate was reasonable.

In the instant case, the Court of Appeal did not think that the refusal of Reed Business Information ("RBI"), the successful appellants, to mediate before the appeal hearing was unreasonable. Since RBI had lost at first instance, they would have been negotiating from a position of weakness; moreover the proposal was made at a late stage; in addition it was satisfied that RBI had a reasonable (and as it turned out justified) belief in their prospects of success. In those circumstances the court concluded that the possibility of ADR was not a relevant factor to take into account on the question of costs.[25]

In *Daniels v Commissioner of Police For The Metropolis*[26] the Court of Appeal relied upon the guidance found in *Halsey* when dismissing a claimant's costs appeal. At first instance, the claimant, a police officer, had lost her personal injury claim against the defendant and was ordered to pay its costs. As part of her appeal, she contended that the defendant's refusal to negotiate, as evinced by its rejection of her Pt 36 offers to settle, was unreasonable and that accordingly it should be deprived of part of its costs. In dismissing the appeal, the Court of Appeal adopted the approach set out in *Halsey*. Recognising that not all of the principles identified in the earlier decision would be relevant where (as here) the issue was unreasonableness in refusing to negotiate, Dyson LJ found two that were germane, namely the merits of the case and whether the mediation would have had a reasonable prospect of success. He observed that it might be entirely reasonable for a public body to take the view that it would contest (what it considered to be) unfounded claims to deter others. He continued: "If defendants, who routinely face what they consider to be unfounded claims, wish to take a stand and contest them rather than make payments (even nuisance value payments) to buy them off, then the court

24 [2004] EWCA Civ 887 [2004] 1 WLR 3026

25 Cf. *Burchell v Bollard* [2005] EWCA Civ 358; [2005] BLR 330. Where the Court of Appeal stated that a party should not ignore a reasonable request to negotiate before proceedings started.

26 [2005] EWCA Civ 1312

should be slow to characterise such conduct as unreasonable so as to deprive defendants of their costs, if they are ultimately successful."

In *Hickman v Blake Lapthorn*[27] Jack J was required to consider Halsey in the context of a costs argument between unsuccessful defendants to a lawyers' negligence claim. The judge had already found the first and second defendants, the solicitor and barrister respectively, liable for negligence in the conduct of personal injury litigation. The solicitor contended that he had been prepared to mediate the claim before substantial costs were incurred but nothing had come of it because the barrister had refused to enter into negotiations or mediate. In those circumstances it was argued, the claimant's costs from that date should be paid by the barrister defendant only and not by both defendants. In rejecting that submission, the judge accepted that there was a strong possibility that a settlement could be achieved close to the sum eventually awarded. However, the solicitor defendant had not satisfied him that the barrister's refusal to mediate was unreasonable, particularly having regard to the large difference between the defendants in valuing the claim. Refusing to take a "commercial" view of litigation was not, Jack J observed, necessarily unreasonable.

The trend towards making adverse awards continues in this jurisdiction, certainly after Lord Justice Jackson's Review, and even to the extent of undermining the reiteration of Jackson that the newly re-drafted CPR Part 36 was to operate as a self-contained code:

In the Court of Appeal *PGF II SA v OMFS Co 1 Ltd*[28] was a case in which Briggs LJ extended the *Halsey* jurisdiction in the sense that the court has the power to order the successful party to pay all or part of the unsuccessful party's costs in case of most serious and flagrant failures to mediate and that silence in the face of an invitation to mediate amounts to unreasonable refusal. It involved three dilapidations claims brought by the landlord, PGF, against the tenant, OMFS. Several Pt 36 offers were made by both parties during the course of proceedings. PGF invited OMFS to mediate on two separate occasions but were met with silence. The case settled one day before trial, with PGF accepting a Pt 36 offer made nine months earlier.

PGF contended that OMFS should not be given the benefit of the usual Part 36 costs protection because of their lack of response to the offer to mediate. PGF further argued that silence in response to an invitation to mediate was in itself unreasonable, regardless of whether there were grounds to refuse.

---

27 [2006] EWHC 12 (QB)

28 [2013] EWCA Civ 1288

Exercising his discretion, the Recorder agreed and refused OMFS's costs for the "relevant period" of 21 days from when the offer was made. OMFS appealed. Dismissing the appeal, Lord Justice Briggs said:

> "The time has now come for this court firmly to endorse the advice given in Chapter 11.56 of the *ADR Handbook*, that silence in the face of an invitation to participate in ADR is, as a general rule, of itself unreasonable...".

Later in the judgment, he said:

> "There are in my view sound practical and policy reasons for this modest extension to the principles and guidelines set out in the Halsey case...."

Parties who fail to reply to an invitation to mediate may face costs sanctions regardless of whether they would have accepted or not. It argues that the decision emphasised the importance of a principled approach to explain the inter-relationship among different Halsey factors and justify future amendments. As Lord Justice Briggs observed the 'advice may fairly be summarised as calling for constructive engagement in ADR rather than flat rejection, or silence.'

Since then, a growing body of case law has emerged on the subject, with the most recent addition being *Phillip Garritt-Critchley & Others v Andrew Ronnan and Solarpower PV Limited.*[29] This case went even further into defining the criteria as to when mediation should be considered, since it was held that being too far apart is not a reasonable answer for declining to mediate.

The case centred on claims that certain shares in a company had not been assigned under the terms of a disputed binding agreement. The claimants laid out their willingness to explore ADR in their letter of claim, while the defendants rejected mediation in both their response and the allocation questionnaire on the basis that the two sides were "too far apart". Likewise, the defendants are also said to have indicated their sureness in their own case, confident they would emerge the winning side in litigation.

The case was scheduled for trial, before which the claimants submitted a part 36 offer, which was not accepted, before a counter-offer to settle the dispute and contribute three quarters of legal costs was put forward by the defendants. A four-day trial was heard with judgment reserved, during which time the defendants revisited the part 36 offer with the view of accepting it, which duly occurred.

The lack of desire to mediate by the defendants prompted the claimants to seek indemnity costs, which Judge Waksman QC awarded in their favour,

29 [2014] EWHC 1774 (Ch)

making it apparent that the defendants' reluctance to engage with mediation was a central reason.

In his ruling, Judge Waksman QC made a host of observations about the nature of mediation that provides new key guidance to disputed parties. He said a building agreement dispute was a prime candidate for mediation because of the diversity of the scenarios involved, meaning the defendants' belief that the two sides were "too far apart" to reach any middle ground was unfounded. After all, how would they know there is no middle ground without discussing the situation?

Likewise, the bad feelings and misgiving between the two sides was also not a valid reason to rebuke an offer of mediation because that is the common dynamic in litigious disputes and, of course, the raison d'être of a mediator is to bring two diametrically opposed sides together. The judge also highlighted the defence's insistence in the strength of their case, which he found unrealistic because - if the case was so overwhelming - they would have sought a summary judgment.

Legal analysts have been quick to highlight the implications of the decision through house briefing notes. It "reinforces the message that mediation is strongly supported by the judiciary and that parties and practitioners need to carefully consider the potential ramifications of a refusal to engage in ADR," explained Peter Barnard from Pannone, which advised the claimants, while Edward Cooper from Taylor Wessing wrote if the other side offers to mediate or to engage in another form of ADR "it would be very risky in most cases to ignore or to refuse the offer".

From a practical point of view however, the authority is yet another example of case law providing disputed direction on when to mediate to avoid hefty court fees. There have already been rulings on the costs of participation in mediation, the recoverability of fees, when to engage with mediation and the legal standing of not responding to an offer of mediation was unreasonable.

Phillip Garritt-Critchley does provide more food for thought, including:

- The risk of over-confidence in the merits of a case, to the point of refusing to explore the idea of a settlement or not going for a full summary judgment;
- Even what appears to be the most ill-tempered and bitter of spats may not be enough to justify avoiding mediation because the job of a mediator is to bring sides together to overcome such disagreements;

- What may be seen as unreasonable by the parties, may not be by the court. The defendants' complete refusal to use mediation was not accepted even if they thought the other side was making unrealistic or unreasonable demands. If parties do not sit down to discuss their perceptions then there is no indication as to whether a claim is unreasonable.

A refusal to mediate may be a costly error. Even with a strong case, shirking mediation in order to get a victory or an improved settlement offer may come at a high price.

In *Laporte & Another v The Commissioner of Police of the Metropolis*[30] the claimant offered to mediate. The defendant, despite being prompted more than once by the claimant (and by the court) to consider ADR, did not accept the offer. At trial the defendant succeeded on every substantive issue. Further, the court found that, had there been a mediation, although there was a likely possibility of a settlement it would have been by no means certain.

When exercising its discretion on costs the court considered the defendant's conduct in the round, including the appropriate *Halsey* factors. The court awarded the defendant only two-thirds of its costs, thus imposing a cost sanction of one-third. (The fact that the defendant asked for £100,000 and the court awarded interim costs of £50,000 suggested that this sanction would have been a significant amount of money.)

- One of the 'conduct' factors considered by the court was although the court ordered the defendant to reply to the claimant's offer to mediate by a certain date, the defendant did not do so until well after that date.
- The judgment provides an insight into how a claimant, having offered mediation, should press for a response with "appropriate vigour".
- The defendant was found to have failed to engage with ADR ".....with proportionate commitment and focus". There was also a failure to "....fully and adequately...engage in the ADR process".
- It would probably have been a mistake for the claimant to have insisted on any preconditions for the mediation, but although they came close to doing this they did not actually do so.

30 [2015] EWHC 371(QB) (19 February 2015)

7.7 Potential Difficulties

In most cases, ascertaining the likelihood of a mediation succeeding is bound to be a speculative exercise. If the claim proceeds to trial then the court is likely to have access to any Calderbank correspondence but there is a risk that this will not provide a comprehensive picture as Jacob LJ observed in the *Reed Executive* case. Without more, the court is likely to be handicapped in its assessment of the prospects of success at mediation. Since few judges have extensive experience of mediation, their assessment of the likelihood of a mediation succeeding or any of the other *Halsey* factors may be less predictable.

Costs recoverability is almost always a key question in litigation strategy. The trending authorities suggest that a rejection of mediation now involves a high degree of risk for any practitioner advising on the management of a dispute. Given the age of *Halsey* there are very few occasions where mediation would be unsuitable, at least for consideration. It should never be rejected out of hand without explanation since plainly such an approach will be punished by the courts

Glossary of Common Mediation Terms

A

Adjudication A broad term describing a category of dispute resolution processes in which a third party neutral makes some form of decision on the outcome of the case. In England and Wales this specifically applies to construction disputes under the Housing Grants, Construction and Regeneration Act 1996 and successor statutory schemes where summary interim binding decisions on contractual disputes are made without following the procedures of litigation or arbitration.

ADR (Alternative Dispute Resolution) A range of procedures for the resolution of disputes that serve as alternatives to litigation through the courts. Commonly they involve the assistance of a neutral and impartial third party, either acting in a binding or non-binding arbitral capacity, or in a mediative or conciliatory capacity assisting the parties to their own solution. For some commentators, the encroaching proximity of court rules has meant a change in the use of the acronym to Amicable Dispute Resolution (ICC Rules), Appropriate Dispute Resolution (wide usage) or Accelerated Dispute Resolution (attributed to Grahame Aldous KC).

AI Artificial Intelligence in Mediation, e.g. ChatGPT as Mediator see https://mediate.com/artificial-intelligence-ai-in-mediation-chatgpt-as-mediator-4-0/

Arbitration A traditional and long-used private dispute process in which the parties agree to be bound by the decision of a neutral third party, the arbitrator, whose award is usually registrable and legally enforceable as a court judgment. Often structured to meet the needs of certain commercial bodies and industries, e.g. international trade, shipping and freight haulage, it has less formal procedures, with party participation in what these should be, abbreviated presentations and the undivided attention of the neutral(s). The arbitrator rules on discovery requests and disputes. The process can be binding or non-binding.

Assistant Mediator (Mediation Observer) A newly trained mediator attending a mediation session to gain experience of the process and act as a companion to the lead mediator. The specific role of the Assistant is determined by the lead mediator but often includes note-taking, observing, drafting, co-mediating and running messages.

B

BATNA (Best Alternative To A Negotiated Agreement) A measure developed by Roger Fisher and William Ury of the Harvard Negotiation Project which enables negotiating parties to evaluate their options. The BATNA is the best result that a party could hope for if it called off the negotiations. Parties are advised to know their BATNA in some detail before attending mediation, to understand the risk analysis of failing to obtain a settlement agreement. The BATNA should not be confined to the value of or risk in a legal claim and its costs, but should extend to valuing lost opportunity or lost business, damage to reputation, and anything else of importance.

C

Caucus Private meetings which take place between the mediator and a single party to a dispute or their professional advisers. These are confidential sessions where nothing discussed can be conveyed to the opposing party without the express permission of the originator. Caucus meetings are often used to examine the important issues and needs of each party, encourage openness about weaknesses as well as strengths and discuss options for settlement.

Civil/Commercial mediation The type of mediation commonly used in commercial disputes, for example, where two companies or other commercial/ statutory bodies may be in dispute with one another. In the UK it generally is a facilitative process, where the mediator is engaged with the parties for a single day and uses both joint ('plenary') and private ('caucus')meetings between the parties to enable the mediator to gather information, reality test, manage negotiations and oversee settlement. By contrast other forms of mediation may not admit caucus meetings, or be spread out over a few weeks.

Claimant, complainant A term used for a person/institution who advances a cause of action or expresses a problem.

Co-mediation A process using two or more mediators in the same mediation. Co-mediation enables the mediators to work as a team to identify the disputed issues, develop options, consider alternatives and endeavour to reach an agreement. They generally adopt a facilitative approach where the mediator has no advisory or determinative role on the content of the dispute or the outcome of its resolution, but may advise on or determine the process of mediation whereby resolution is attempted.

Combined or hybrid dispute resolution processes are those in which the neutral plays multiple roles. For example, in conciliation and in conferencing, the dispute resolution practitioner may facilitate discussions, as well as provide advice on the merits of the dispute. In hybrid processes, such as med-arb, the practitioner first uses one process (mediation – usually facilitative but then, potentially, evaluative) and then a different one (arbitration).

Community mediation Mediation applied to deal with conflict between individuals and/or groups in the community, or to deal with group or community-based issues.

Community Mediation Service A mediation service provided is by a non-government or community organisation.

Community mediator A mediator chosen from a panel representative of the community in general or from a panel provided by a local authority or NGO community mediation service provider.

Conciliation A dispute resolution process where the neutral third party takes an active role in a case by offering non-binding opinions or puts forward suggested terms of settlement. The term is used in mediation and distinguished by the advice or expression of opinion by the conciliator, rather than the mediator who may not offer an opinion. There is no international consistency over which process, mediation or conciliation, is the more activist and mediation is increasingly being adopted as the generic term for third-party facilitation in commercial disputes. The conciliator may make suggestions for terms of settlement, give expert advice on likely settlement terms, and have an advisory role on the content of the dispute or the outcome of its resolution, but not a determinative role.

Conferencing A general term, which refers to meetings in which the parties and/or their advocates and/or third parties discuss issues in dispute. It may also refer to the wider aspect of mediation in which a number of parties/stakeholders are involved, including supporters of others at the meeting and/or other individuals and relevant organisations to address issues and provide support (services) to uphold any agreement reached. Examples of agencies that may be involved in conferencing include the police, social services, and campaign groups, and those affected by settlement proposals.

Confidentiality The degree to which information given in the mediation cannot be passed on to others outside the process, with enforcement or protection given by operation of law.

Conflict Resolution The ending of conflict between parties. A process facilitated by communication, new understanding and sometimes formal agreement being reached.

Consensus building A process in which parties to a dispute, with the assistance of a facilitator, identify the facts and stakeholders, settle on the issues for discussion and consider options. This allows parties to build rapport through discussions that assist in developing better communication, relationships and agreed understanding of the issues.

Counselling A wide range of processes designed to assist people to solve personal and interpersonal issues and problems. Counselling has a specific meaning under the Family Law Act, where it is included as a Primary Dispute Resolution process (see PDR). Clients are individuals or organisations that engage dispute resolution service providers in a professional capacity. A client may not necessarily be a party to a dispute, but may engage a dispute resolution service provider to assist the resolution of a dispute between others.

D

Determinative dispute resolution a process in which a dispute resolution practitioner evaluates the dispute (which may include the hearing of formal evidence from the parties) and makes a determination. Examples of determinative dispute resolution processes are arbitration, expert determination and private judging.

Determinative case appraisal is a process in which the parties to a dispute present arguments and evidence to a neutral (the appraiser) who makes a determination as to the most effective means whereby the dispute may be resolved, without making any determination as to the facts of the dispute.

Digital Mediation Carrying out mediation by the use of technology, remote platforms, digital or electronic devices.

Dispute counselling is a process in which a dispute resolution practitioner (the dispute counsellor) investigates the dispute and provides the parties or a party to the dispute with advice on the issues which should be considered, possible and desirable outcomes and the means whereby these may be achieved.

Dispute resolution refers to all processes that are used to resolve disputes, whether within or outside court proceedings. Dispute resolution processes may be facilitative, advisory, evaluative, non-binding opinion or determinative. Dispute resolution processes other than judicial determination are often referred to as ADR.

Disputants People/organisations in dispute, whether solely with each other or with additional parties, and whether already in litigation or not.

E

ENE (Early Neutral Evaluation) A preliminary assessment of facts, evidence or legal merits. It is a process in which the parties to a dispute present arguments and evidence to a qualified, trained neutral, at an early stage, for his or her non-binding opinion of the likely outcome. From this determination on the key issues in dispute the parties can then attempt to resolve the dispute by further negotiation.

Evaluative Mediation An approach to mediation where the parties can seek and obtain the non-binding advice or opinion of the mediator. He or she takes a relatively active or interventionist role, making suggestions or putting forward views about the merits of the case or particular issues between parties at their request. Using this process, parties may "test" the potential outcomes of a case. The mediator allows the parties to present their factual and legal arguments. He or she may then offer his or her own assessment or predictions as to a trial outcome. It is often used for more difficult cases, in which the gap between the parties is large, the issues are somewhat complex and the stakes are high.

Executive Tribunal A process, sometimes called 'Mini-Trial', in which parties make formal but abbreviated presentations of their best legal case to a panel of senior executives from each party, usually with a mediator or expert as neutral chairperson. Following the presentations, the executives meet (with or without the mediator or expert) to negotiate a settlement on the basis of what they have heard.

Expert Determination A process in which an independent third party, acting as an expert rather than judge or arbitrator, is appointed by the parties to decide the dispute. There is no right of appeal, thereby giving parties finality.

F

Facilitative Mediation An approach to mediation where the neutral aids or assists the parties' own efforts to formulate a settlement. The mediator is in charge of the process but the parties are in charge of the content. This approach is sometimes referred to as 'interest-based' mediation. In this process, outcome control remains almost entirely in the hands of the parties and their representatives. A mediator enhances communication and helps to create options for resolution by ensuring that all relevant information is exchanged and heard by the parties. The mediator also helps to distinguish the parties' positions from their interests. Entry level training for all civil commercial mediators in the UK is in the facilitative model.

Face to Face (F2F) (Plenary/Joint Sessions) A meeting facilitated by a mediator which brings all those in dispute together to discuss issues and decide a way forward. This stage is not used during shuttle mediation.

Facilitative Dispute Resolution are processes in which a neutral assists the parties to a dispute to identify the disputed issues, develop options, consider alternatives and endeavour to reach an agreement about some issues or the whole dispute. Examples of facilitative processes are mediation, facilitation and facilitated negotiation.

Final Offer Arbitration ("baseball") – In this form of arbitration, which derives from the United States, the parties each separately submit a "final offer" to the arbitrator. The arbitrator chooses between the offer or the demand presented, based upon the arguments heard. It is called baseball arbitration because it was long used to resolve disputes between baseball players and teams.

H

Heads of Agreement The section of the settlement agreement in which the principal terms of the agreement are set forth.

I

Impartial A key principle that mediators must have no stake in the outcome of the process. Working without any investment in a solution.

Interventionist The degree of proactive involvement from a third party.

J

Joint Sessions (Plenary/Face to face) Stage in a mediation when the negotiating parties are brought together by the mediator. The Opening Joint Session takes the form of an introduction by the mediator and brief presentations by each party of their case at a round table meeting which may set the agenda and provide a vehicle for the controlled venting of emotional issues.

L

Litigation The process of bringing or contesting a law suit in which an impartial third party – the judge – receives evidence in support of the case and hears argument from each side after which a binding judgment is issued which can be enforced using the powers of the state. Litigation is an adversarial and usually public process that tends to create a winner and loser.

M

Med-Arb A process in which parties agree to mediate their dispute and, if unable to settle, they participate in binding arbitration using the same neutral. They contract to give the mediator power to 'convert' to being an arbitrator and make a legally binding award, in the event that mediated negotiations do not lead to a settlement.

Mediation A flexible process conducted confidentially by which an impartial, trained, mutually acceptable neutral third party helps two (or more) disputants work out how to resolve a conflict. The disputants, not the mediators, decide on the terms of any agreement reached. Mediation usually focuses on future rather than past behaviour, and is not concerned with blame or making findings of fact. Unlike judges or arbitrators, mediators have no authority to decide the dispute between the parties, although powerful mediators may bring to the table considerable capability to influence the outcome. Mediators may focus on facilitating communication and negotiation but they also may offer solutions and use leverage, including positive and negative incentives, to persuade the parties to achieve an agreement.

Mediation Agreement A document setting down the conditions under which the mediation will take place, including confidentiality, authority to settle, payment and role of the mediator.

Mediator An impartial, trained, mutually acceptable neutral person who helps disputing parties try to arrive at an agreed resolution of their dispute. Mediation cannot take place without a mediator, whose presence creates a new dynamic that is absent when parties undertake direct negotiation.

Multi-party Where a conflict or dispute involves more than two people, households, entities or organisations.

N

Negotiation A process in which disputants work out an agreement for themselves without the help of a third party, such as a mediator.

Neutral An individual who facilitates the ADR process, including mediators, arbitrators, adjudicators, private judges, facilitators, members of Dispute Boards and panellists.

Neutral Evaluation (**see ENE**) A process in which the parties to a dispute retain a neutral to provide a non-binding evaluation based solely on the merits of the case.

Neutral Expert Fact-Finding Used to help resolve a disputed technical issue, this may be a stand-alone, non-binding process or it can be part of a larger, non-binding process.

Non-Binding Arbitration A process that looks and feels like arbitration, but is advisory and non-binding.

O

ODR (**On-line Dispute Resolution, eADR, cyber-ADR**) are mediation or other dispute resolution services where a substantial part, or all, of the communication in the dispute resolution process takes place electronically, especially via online meeting platforms. This saves the parties and mediator from the cost of travel, cost of room hire and support, and is particularly useful where the participants are in different countries.

Opening Statements Oral presentations which are usually given in open plenary session after the Mediator's introductory address. These allow each party the chance to present an uninterrupted narrative of their case with the full force of feeling and certainty.

Ownership Ownership of an agreement is important in mediation, placing the emphasis on the fact that the parties themselves worked out a mutually satisfactory solution to their problem, and did not have it decided for or imposed upon them.

P

Parties are persons or bodies who are in a dispute that is handled through a dispute resolution process. In litigation the term is generally confined to people or entities in whom a cause of action is vested i.e. the claimant, and against whom the claim is brought, i.e. the defendant. In ADR the term is used in a wider sense to describe participants in the process.

Peer mediation Any use of mediation between peer groups, most usually when pupils and young people are trained to help others to try and resolve their disagreements. The term is also sometimes used to refer to mediators inside an organisation who mediate for their colleagues.

R

Reality Testing The method most commonly used by mediators to reduce party expectation. This tool involves attempting to get a party to understand the reality of his position by a self-evaluation of the strength of his case, his true BATNA, the costs consequences of the mediation failing, and the use of hypothesis in respect of outcomes. The use of the tool requires particular sensitivity, but can be vital for helping parties to adjust their position and become more flexible.

Reframing A tool used by mediators that involves changing party language by the use of more positive words, the complexion on words and circumstances and the order in which ideas are presented in order to allow a situation to be viewed more positively.

Reparation The act of making up for loss or injury. This may be financial, emotional or enacted through work. In Restorative Justice ADR processes, reparation is made either to the victim(s) of a crime, or to others within the community.

Respondent A person or organisation about whom a complaint is made.

Restorative Justice (RJ) A process in which mediative techniques are used to supports victims of crime, offenders and communities in seeking to repair the harm caused by crime, with mediation a favoured approach.

Round table meeting (RT) A meeting facilitated by a mediator or party representatives which brings all those in dispute together to discuss issues and decide a way forward. This stage is not used during shuttle mediation. In some disputes, for example personal injury claims or financial settlement of divorce, a round table meeting may precede mediation.

S

Settlement Agreement A brief document designed to set out in clear and understandable language the salient terms of a negotiated agreement. It has the effect in law of a contract, and therefore must be legal, sufficiently certain in its meaning, workable (i.e. the solution offered must be practicable) and enforceable.

Shuttle mediation A process in which the mediator/s talks separately to the parties, conveying their needs and suggestions to the others until a solution is found that is acceptable to all. This technique is also called caucusing, is sometimes used exclusively when the parties are reluctant to meet, although it may not be as effective in rebuilding relationships as joint meetings. The mediator may move between parties who are located in different rooms, or meet different parties at different times for all or part of the process.

Singapore Convention on Mediation 2019 Formerly the UNCITRAL Model Law on International Commercial Mediation and International Settlement Agreements Resulting from Mediation (2018). A multilateral treaty which offers a uniform and efficient framework for the enforcement and invocation of international settlement agreements resulting from mediation. It applies to international settlement agreements resulting from mediation, concluded by parties to resolve a commercial dispute.

T

Transformative mediation A model of mediation that focuses on the interaction between the parties, rather than resolution on favourable terms. The main function of the mediator is to provide an environment where empowerment and recognition between the parties can emerge and improve.

V

Victim-Offender mediation (see also **Restorative Justice**) is a process in which the parties to a dispute arising from the commission by one of a crime against the other come together with the assistance of a mediator.

W

Workplace mediation An informal way of resolving disputes at work which can be an alternative to formal grievance or disciplinary procedures, or employed before a case is referred to an employment tribunal to see if an agreed solution can be found. After cessation of employment the procedure is generally referred to as **Employment Mediation.**

Appendices

Appendix I: SCMA Standards.. 209

Appendix II Sample ADR Group Standard Mediation Agreement.. 237

Appendix III. Example Private Mediation Agreement...................... 253

Appendix IV. Example Settlement Agreement.................................. 257

Appendix I

The SCMA Standards

The Mediation Advocacy Standards

Printed: November 2015 in London, UK.

Publisher
The Standing Conference of Mediation Advocates Limited
71-75 Shelton Street
Covent Garden
London WC2H 9JQ

Author
Prof Andrew Goodman PhD

Technical Editors
Douglas Beckwith, Barrister
Roger Levitt, Solicitor

Team Coordinator
Isabella Borg

Layout and Photography
Richard Jackson

Reg No: 07721149.
Registered in England and Wales

Special thanks to:
All the people who contributed to this document.

Contents

1 The Business Case for Mediation Advocacy 2

2 Competency Criteria for Mediation Advocates 6
2.1 Introduction 6
2.2 Criteria 6
2.3 Nomenclature 6

3 General Requirements of Knowledge and Competence 8

4 Practical Skills Requirements 11
4.1 Pre Mediation Stage 11
4.1.1 Case diagnosis and process selection
4.1.2 Clarifying and initiating process
4.2 Selection of neutral and preparation stage 12
4.2.1 Identify, negotiate and select mediation process and mediator
4.2.1.1 Mediation process and mediator
4.2.1.2 Administrative, formal and legal aspects of coordinating a mediation
4.2.2 Preparation
4.3 Mediation Stage 14
4.3.1 General, monitoring process
4.3.2 Opening statement and agenda setting
4.3.3 Exploration
4.3.4 Generating options and negotiation
4.4 Closing and implementation 17
4.4.1 Closing
4.4.2 Implementation

5 Assessment programmes - Substantive Criteria 20
5.1 General requirements 20
5.1.1 Methodology
5.1.2 Transparency
5.1.3 Integrity
5.1.4 Ongoing monitoring of programme
5.1.5 Diversity
5.2 Evaluating the Standards 20
5.2.1 Experience of the mediation process
5.2.2 Knowledge of mediation advocacy
5.2.3 Practical mediation advocacy skills

6 Notes 23

1 The Business Case for Mediation Advocacy

For nearly 30 years, the market for mediation services has developed slowly:- even where governments, judiciaries, consumer groups and academics have welcomed the practical advantages in cost and time reduction, confidentiality, empowerment of participants, control and flexibility of outcome, and the preservation of reputation and relationships. Mediation is seen by the enlightened as a better, more productive and socially cohesive way to resolve disputes.

Why, then, hasn't there been such a demand for services from users to drive forward the substantial development needed by the industry to mature as a market? Why, even in jurisdictions where the courts make mediation compulsory, at least for low-value claims, has the take up and positive experience of Mediation not generated an irresistible momentum for change in civil justice?

Three factors appear to be the answer:

- Educating the market about a confidential process
- Getting media support to promote mediation; and
- Overcoming resistance to the process by the gatekeepers of disputes - usually lawyers -fearful of the loss of revenue from truncated litigation- particularly in jurisdictions where consumers of legal services have no control over time or cost.

The industry can push for the first two. The third requires stakeholder explanation, persuasion and acceptance of the business case for mediation advocacy.

Those who offer a professional practice representing parties in mediation understand that the process is more likely to succeed in effecting settlement and provide the client with a more desirable outcome by reference to their interests and needs, than a judge or arbitrator can deliver, and with far less risk. The practitioner/client relationship will be enhanced. The satisfied and happy client is the professional's best asset with repeat business and a free marketing device for your practice and your industry - so expanding your market in two ways.

The business case for mediation advocacy is also aspirational, since it leads to

- Enhanced public reputation in innovation and leadership
- Promotion of positive perceptions by customers, vendors, and other stakeholders - rather than the negativity associated with litigation profiting from the misfortune of others.

- Communicating a clear message that cost containment is wired into your ethos, and
- Meeting user expectation that providers and advisors of ADR services devise strategies to end disputes on acceptable terms as quickly and cost- effectively as possible

Reduced litigation spend is therefore transformed into a desirable aim for the development of solid client relations, rather than being seen as a short-term loss to the practice.
The International Mediation Institute reviews the approaches of major corporations to their dispute resolution strategy, and has published data which indicates that companies known to be "dispute-wise" (i.e. systemic and thoughtful in their approaches to dispute resolution) tend to have higher P/E ratios [1] than those that litigate to the end.

On October 29, 2014, an interactive convention in London entitled Shaping the Future of International Dispute Resolution was organised by the International Mediation Institute (IMI) for international entities and a wide range of global stakeholders . Over 150 delegates from more than 20 countries used interactive technology to vote on a number of key issues. The data generated was indicative of user demands of the mediation market, and suggested significant gaps may exist between what disputants expect and need, and what is currently provided by advisors, provider bodies, practitioners, educators and policy makers.

Consumers of mediation recognise its benefits and note the following, in order of importance -

- Certainty: risk reduction and control of outcome
- Expense: cost containment
- Efficiency: focussing on the key issues in the dispute
- Relationships: preventing conflict escalation and retaining relationships whenever possible
- Speed: securing the earliest possible outcome Enforceability of outcomes or awards
- Confidentiality

In any market the successful service provider is in tune with, and can deliver what his client wants. Yet mediation is still underused, mainly because one of the parties is not familiar enough or experienced with the process, or because external legal or other advisers do not propose mediation when circumstances suggest they should.

Trained mediation advocates are therefore market leaders and progressive thinkers, engaging their clients in a process that doesn't attribute fault or blame, looks forward rather than backwards, and is focussed on problem solving according to client needs. The IMI data suggests that the most important factors influencing how effectively a company uses alternative dispute resolution (ADR) are the skills and approach of the in-house lawyers, the knowledge and attitude of the company's senior management and the tactics of their external lawyers who all need to be informed in their decision-making. Mediation Advocates are educators, and can be management consultants in conflict avoidance and dispute strategy, providing substantial savings and business efficiency .

Mediation Advocates control the distribution of work to Mediators, by selecting and appointing an appropriate , competent, mutually acceptable Mediator. In sophisticated but expensive legal jurisdictions, or in developing countries with no effective process, Mediation Advocates deliver access to justice by providing added value - a key role for ADR in a modern world.

So the SCMA has established minimum criteria for Mediation Advocacy to engage in this new area of professional practice, or to add to your existing business. These criteria form standards which it is hoped will be recognised as a benchmark by the Inns of Court College of Advocacy, the Bar Standards Board, the Solicitors' Regulation Authority, RICS, ICAEW, CIArb and other institutions.

I have pleasure in enclosing a copy of the SCMA Mediation Advocacy Standards and would welcome the opportunity of discussing SCMA membership, training for and the application of the Standards.

Andrew Goodman

2 Competency Criteria for Mediation Advocates

2.1 Introduction

Mediation is most successful when the parties' advocates, advisors or representatives ("Mediation Advocates") are knowledgeable and skilled in the principles of the mediation process and negotiation theories. Mediations can fail when party representatives act as if they were in a courtroom rather than in a negotiation.

Mediation presents unique problem-solving opportunities in which representatives can assist their clients to reach faster, cheaper and/or better outcomes with the assistance of a mediator. They can help their clients achieve outcomes that may be unattainable in a courtroom or arbitration tribunal. To do that, they need a different set of knowledge and skills.

2.2 Criteria

SCMA assisted the International Mediation Institute in the design of criteria for programmes qualifying as competent Mediation Advocates in order to establish a professional and technical basis for enabling disputing parties to identify professionals experienced in advising and representing clients in the resolution of disputes through mediation and related dispute resolution processes. The Criteria are presented in two broad categories: The General Requirements for the programs are set out in Section 1 below (the "General Requirements") The Mediation Advocacy Practical Skills Requirements are set out in Section 2 below ("Practical Skills Requirements" and the substantive criteria for Mediation Advocates' Competency are set out in Section 3 below (the "Substantive Criteria").

SCMA now wishes to develop its own Standards to reflect the needs of this jurisdiction and to be commensurate with the recognised international Criteria.

2.3 Nomenclature

Mediation is a form of facilitated negotiation which does not necessarily take place as part of a judicial or other adjudicative process. Because mediation is an extra-legal process, not all professionals who may advise, represent and assist disputing parties in mediation are necessarily legally qualified.

In many countries, the term "advocate" and language equivalents of that word denotes or implies that a person is a qualified lawyer and should not (and in some cases can not) be used by a person not legally qualified. In some countries, however, that connotation does not arise. Nomenclature is therefore largely a jurisdiction-specific issue.

Moreover there are some proponents of mediation who believe the term 'mediation advocate' is an oxymoron, since mediation must be a non-adversarial process. The term is used for ease of reference by and to address the significant proportion of professionals in the mediation world, whose primary function is to assist clients resolve their disputes either as part of an orthodox adversarial system or within the shadow of the law.

3 General Requirements of Knowledge and Competence

The following areas of practical skills are required for effective mediation advocacy. This list is intended as guidance to those operating assessment programmes in designing knowledge assessments. The list is not necessarily exhaustive or mandatory.

1. Knowing when mediation may or may not be a suitable process to address particular issues.

2. Identifying procedural options and preferred processes for reaching optimal outcomes.

3. Knowledge of negotiation and solution-generating processes, as well as party and participant dynamics, as contextualised by the choice of mediation process/ vehicle.

4. Understanding the nature, theory, procedure, practical application, methodology, appropriateness, benefits and disadvantages of the available types of mediation, schemes or programmes, procedural rules and pertinent costs.

5. Understanding the role of a mediator, and the palette of mediator methodology, psychology, core training, and practices.

6. Knowledge of relevant laws affecting mediation practice including structure and enforceability of mediation and settlement agreements (where relevant), confidentiality and privilege /professional secrecy. Costs, (the impact of the increase in issue fees, contrast with litigation costs and the impact of case law and the approach of the judiciary) and costs budgeting for mediation.

7. Knowing how to use techniques for productively supporting the parties, their representatives, the mediator and the process to generate a mutually accepted outcome.

8. Knowing how to communicate effectively with the mediator, prior to, during and after the mediation sessions.

9. Being able to explain the nature, theory, procedure, practical application, methodology, appropriateness, benefits, advantages and drawbacks of available types of mediation within or between relevant jurisdictions, court-connected mediation schemes, ad-hoc or institutional procedural rules, applicable costs, and applicable professional ethics codes.

10. Knowledge of hybrid dispute resolution processes (e.g., Arb-Med, Med-Arb, Arb//Med, Med-Con, Med//Con, MEDALOA (a combination of Mediation and last offer Arbitration) and their potential advantages and drawbacks in different circumstances.

11. Understanding and applying the best timing for each dispute resolution process.

12. Familiarity with methods of formulating solutions, including assessing alternatives (BATNA, WATNA, PATNA, RATNA [2] & preparing client and self for joint/caucus mediation meetings.

13. Being able to assist parties in separating interests and needs from wants and positions.

14. Being able to seek and understand the motivations behind individual positions as distinguished from the issues in dispute.

15. Being familiar with techniques like questioning, summarizing, (active/ effective) listening, framing and re-framing, reformulating, reflecting and paraphrasing.

16. Being able to make strategic choices that can help strike a balance between positional claims that advance the clients' wants and creating value based on interests and needs.

17. Being familiar with cross-cultural settings and dynamics.

18. Understanding cross-border and multi-cultural mediation paradigms.

19. Being able to adapt procedural parameters when dealing with complex cases involving numerous participants.

20. Understanding and using professional and ethical standards and behaviours in generating, informing and/or setting norms.

21. Knowledge of problem-solving, interest-based negotiation techniques.

22. Knowledge of the distributive (adversarial) approach to negotiation, in addition to the problem-solving (interest-based) approach and knowing when and why to apply each. Knowing how to avoid and counter unhelpful adversarial attitudes, behaviour and language.

23. Being able to draft / approve settlement agreements as discussed by the parties to the mediation.

24. Being able to understand and interpret settlement agreements and procedural options.

25. Being able to use understandings and momentum derived from mediation to promote problem solving or dispute settlement where no concluded agreement takes place at the mediation itself.

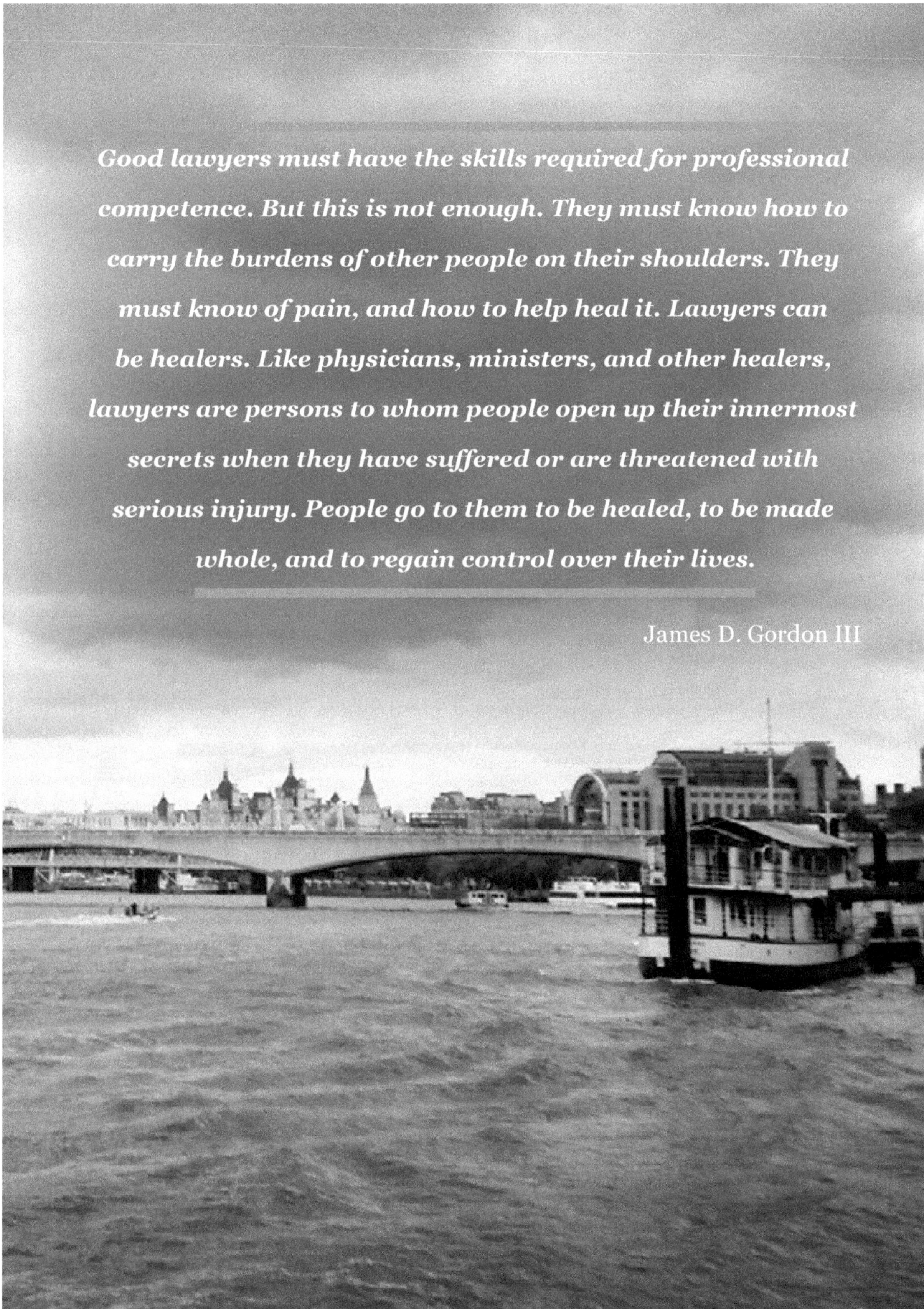
Good lawyers must have the skills required for professional competence. But this is not enough. They must know how to carry the burdens of other people on their shoulders. They must know of pain, and how to help heal it. Lawyers can be healers. Like physicians, ministers, and other healers, lawyers are persons to whom people open up their innermost secrets when they have suffered or are threatened with serious injury. People go to them to be healed, to be made whole, and to regain control over their lives.
James D. Gordon III

4 Practical Skills Requirements

The following areas of practical skills are required for effective Mediation Advocacy. The list is not necessarily exhaustive or mandatory and is offered as guidance. It is intended to aid in designing skills assessments.

4.1 Pre Mediation Stage

4.1.1 Case diagnosis and process selection

i.Conflict diagnosis, including conflict (de)escalation models.

ii.Understanding when a neutral third party can add value in a conflict and assessing the quality of that value compared with direct without prejudice negotiations. Being able convincingly to convey that understanding to the client.

iii.Using dispute assessment & risk analysis methodologies.

iv.Identification of relevant parties, stakeholders and participants to the process and identifying who not to invite and what to do if uninvited people seek to attend .

v.Identifying the most appropriate process. Skills to assess (contra-) indications, pros and cons, and strengths and risks of each method. Being able convincingly to convey that understanding to the client.

vi.Design, customization and implementation of appropriate conflict resolution processes.

vii.Considering possible application of hybrids and other process design options.

viii.Pre-mediation analysis.

ix.Application and interpretation of alternatives analysis, BATNA, WATNA, PATNA and RATNA

x.Whether or not to use norms to set ZOPA[3] and leverage such analyses.

xi.Defining time frames.

xii.Understanding different levels of readiness of the client to accept mediation and the ability to address their concerns effectively.

4.1.2 Clarifying and initiating process

i.Initiating contact with the other parties or their representatives, and/or with mediation institutions.

ii.Consider whether the parties wish to use norms, subjective interests, or a combination of the two to resolve the dispute, and what norms (if any) to use (e.g., laws, customs, community response).

iii.Consider the relevance of past, present or future events, and whether to focus on the past or the future as a basis for seeking resolution of the dispute.

iv.Counselling clients, principals, participants and relevant stakeholders, as appropriate to identify and resolve procedural issues and options separately from substantiveissuestobemediated,andifsowhenandhowtomediate. Explaining mediation goals and process.

v.Communicating effectively with the other side to bring them to mediation in the right frame of mind.

vi. Identifying and overcoming possible misperceptions (e.g., concerns of appearing to be weak if agreeing to negotiate).

vii.Collaborating and negotiating with other parties, their representatives and the mediator about process choice and design, logistics and timing. Setting, collaborating and negotiating about mediator selection criteria with the other parties and their representatives and where appropriate, working with the other parties to identify, set and implement each mediation parameter.

4.2 Selection of neutral and preparation stage

4.2.1 Identify, negotiate and select mediation process and mediator

4.2.1.1 Mediation process and mediator

i.Selecting the most suitable mediation procedure, style and approach (e.g. evaluative, transformative, facilitative, narrative, solution focused, eclectic, hybrid forms, co-mediation (when does this give added value?), joint sessions and/or caucus-based), including consideration of common mediation approaches used locally and elsewhere

ii.Determining whether mediation should be administered or self-administered. Applying specific aspects of court-connected mediation processes.

iii.Working with the participants and the mediator(s) to determine the need for a mediation agreement (if any), select a venue, identify participants, use opening statements (if any), time allocations (if any), prior written submissions (if any) both open and confidential , the mediator(s) role and conduct; discuss the use and frequency of joint sessions and/or caucuses (if any).

iv.Finding, selecting and appointing the most suitable competent mediator(s) for this case, these parties and the specific circumstances. Ensuring there is no conflict of interest with the appointment

v.Knowing when co-mediation is appropriate and how to select and convene a co- mediation team in collaboration with the other side.

vi.Knowing how to select a suitable mediator for a particular case, including subject knowledge, mediation style and skills, and identifying the need for a specialist or generalist.

vii.Collaborating and negotiating with other parties, their representatives and the mediator about process choice and design, logistics and timing.

4.2.1.2 Administrative, formal and legal aspects of coordinating a mediation

i.Negotiating and (where applicable) drafting the mediation agreement.

ii.Dealing productively with any obstructive or fencing behaviour of the other party or the party's representatives.

iii.Advising on mediation clauses, mediation rules and regulations of mediation providers and professional bodies, ethical guidelines, codes of conduct, complaint schemes, disciplinary processes, liability issues, confidentiality, privacy, refusals to participate, mandates, and authorities to settle.

4.2.2 Preparation

i.Composing mediation teams. Identifying/negotiating attendees on each side. Ensuring the ultimate decision maker is available to attend and/or be available by phone / skype

ii.Information strategy: when (and when not) to share what information with whom. Determining information that is needed.

iii.Identifying the necessary documents to be exchanged with the other side and confidentially with the Mediator, with knowledge of applicable confidentiality rules. Brief the mediator by initial conversation before sending documents. Facilitating conversations between the Mediator and your clients

iv.Timing of the revelation of interests and options.

v.Advising on the roles of client and advocate.

vi.Separating interests needs & positions / wants.

vii.SWOT analysis skills (own client and, , the other party).

viii.Preparation of self, client and the mediator.

ix.Drafting a Mediation Briefing or Position/Participation Statement and confidential note for the Mediator and a Strategic Mediation Representation plan for cases where such materials are required.

x Prepare a skeleton without prejudice subject to contract proposal for use at the Meeting xi Prepare a skeleton Tomlin Order / Settlement Agreement for use at the Meeting

4.3 Mediation Stage

4.3.1 General, monitoring process

i.Monitoring progress and checking whether the process needs to be adapted to the circumstances.

ii.Awareness of the key factors for success and failure in mediation.

iii.Collaboration with own client, the other party and the other party's representative to facilitate a constructive outcome based on problem-solving techniques.

iv.Counselling the client to obtain separate professional advice on financial, tax, social media, reputational, commercial and other relevant interests.

v.Making an informed choice between several approaches and options for resolving the issues, and knowing when to suggest each approach (including whether and when to terminate the mediation process as necessary).

vi.Balancing between (1) claiming value and advocating the client's interests and (2) creating value and motivating participants to reach a settlement.

vii.Acting as client coach and "reality check" to help them gain familiarity and confidence with the process, their relevant roles and whether their positions are compatible with their interests.

viii.Collaboration with the mediator, tasking the mediator, ensuring the mediator understands the client's core interests and constructively designing and implementing the mediation process from the perspective of all parties. Working with the Mediator to minimise 'down time' when the Mediator is with the other party and/or to ensure that time is used productively

4.3.2 Opening statement and agenda setting

i.Breaking the ice and creating constructive conditions for a productive mediation process. Identifying interests, topics for discussion, information to be exchanged (give and get) and possible impasses to be overcome.

ii.Agenda setting and time and expectation management.

iii.Coaching clients, where applicable, to prepare and deliver effective opening statements in accordance with the style of mediation or negotiation approach. Understanding what type and style of opening statement to use (e.g., argumentative, persuasive, explanatory, expressive etc.) as may be most effective, what to include and omit, and possibly proposing to defer to a later time or dispense with formal statements and/or initial open meeting when this would be more effective. Deciding who should deliver the opening statement.

iv.Supporting information exchange by summarizing facts and addressing queries from the other party, the other party's representative or from the mediator.
v.Interpreting the other party's opening statement and identifying key information, interests, opportunities and impediments.

4.3.3 Exploration
i.Generating effective negotiation approaches, explanations of first offers, package deals, concession strategies and negotiation techniques.

ii.Eliciting interests and distinguishing positions and wants from interests and needs .
iii.Applying communication skills such as active listening, reformulation and non-positional communication skills.

iv. Understanding and dealing with emotions, social and status issues, and international and cultural aspects and conveying this understanding to parties.

v. Identifying, analysing and dealing with impasses, breaking deadlocks and knowing how to support the client and mediator on these issues.

vi.Dealing with clients' instructions that may be difficult to reconcile with opportunities and options and resolving those inconsistencies.

vii.Balancing confidentiality and the need to provide the information necessary for resolving the dispute and reaching the best possible outcome.

viii.Dealing with difficult parties, party representatives, clients or inappropriate mediators.

ix.Applying reality-testing techniques to manage the expectations of the client and the other party.

x.Identifying the right time and work with the mediator to call for caucus, time- out, breaks, private client meetings, joint sessions, sessions with just professionals, changes of venue and changes of negotiation team members.

xi.Caucus:

a.Ensuring any caucus is handled ethically and confidentially.
b.Working with the client and mediator to provide information useful in resolving the dispute.
c.Exploring options with the mediator.
d.Seeking and providing positive and constructive feedback to/from the mediator.
e.Working with the mediator to identify the possible use of norms to generate, set and/or advocate possible outcomes.

4.3.4 Generating options and negotiation

i.Preparing the client effectively on how to react to, and consider, unlimited possibilities.

ii. Creating and prioritising interests and options.

iii.Where appropriate, assisting the client to be an effective negotiator (problem-solving, interest-based, positional, etc.).

iv. Formulating first/opening offers.
v.Responding to first/opening offers.

vi.Identifying topics for further discussion and information to be exchanged.

vii.Ensuring that the mediator presents the options proposed during private caucus accurately and maintains confidentiality.

viii.Working with the other party, the client, and the mediator to generate, develop, brainstorm and reality-test options. Ability to engage in and consult on several methods for generating options.

ix.Utilizing the processes of negotiation, and party and participant dynamics, as contextualised by the choice of mediation process.

x.Establishing mutually acceptable norms or reference criteria.

xi.Identifying objective and measurable criteria by which to assess feasibility and possible implementation of options.

xii.Responding to positional tactics.

xiii.Using mediator(s) for reality testing and/or for evaluative feedback where appropriate.

xiv.Using mediator(s) to support and lead the parties and/or to help them formulate offers or responses.

xv.Identifying and dealing with impediments, and enlisting the mediator's support.

xvi.Dealing with unexpected surprises or inconsistent negotiation styles. xvii. Maintaining momentum and dealing with decision fatigue. xviii.Dealing with reactive devaluation.

xix.Checking for confirmation bias.

xx.Clarifying intentions and motivations.

xxi.Adapting communication styles and strategies in accordance with progress made and other participants' conduct.

4.4 Closing and implementation

4.4.1 Closing

i.Securing the best available and workable outcomes that circumstances permit.

ii.Deciding whether to end or walk out of a mediation.

iii.Formulating final offers.

iv.Responding to final offers.

v.Dealing with incomplete settlements or inability to settle.

vi.Deciding whether and if so how to request a mediator's proposal.

vii.Maintaining positive momentum and leaving a window open.

viii.Generating joint or single communication strategies and dealing with possible reporting or reputational impacts.

ix.Facilitating the mediation to progress to a comprehensive, substantive, clear, valid and enforceable agreement (as SMART[4] as possible), preserving such relations as may be desired between the parties.

x.Managing setbacks in the final stage of the mediation if new issues emerge.

xi.Sustaining a constructive and amiable atmosphere to promote successful implementation of the agreement (keep the door and communication open).

xii.Assisting with the drafting of any publicity statements and contingency Questions & Answers, where appropriate.

xiii.Dealing with partial settlements and managing contingencies where applicable.

xiv.Dealing with parallel judicial, administrative, arbitral or other proceedings

xv.Closing documents and ceremonies (if any).

xvi.Possible rescheduling of additional mediation sessions with the same or different mediator(s), and when or where to conduct such sessions.

xvii.Considering possible final procedural options, hybrids and proposals.

xviii.Understanding that not all disputes result in a settlement directly after a mediation and knowing how to identify and establish possible next steps to retain positive momentum and reschedule the matter for future consideration and settlement as and when appropriate. Consider how best to stay in touch with the Mediator after the Meeting

4.4.2 Implementation

i.Considering possible compliance and enforcement requirements.

ii.Knowing the relevance of Consent/Tomlin Orders and, where applicable and possible, the means to ensure compliance.

iii.Monitoring compliance and dealing with any post-settlement issues.

iv.Maintaining a good-faith approach towards the mediated settlement agreement and dealing with possible surprises.

v.Ability to deal with and finalise any outstanding post-settlement issues.

vi.Dealing with any final settlement formalities and possible contingent documentation

vii.Securing such appropriate court or tribunal recognition for a settlement (e.g., use of consent orders).

5 Assessment programmes - Substantive Criteria

SCMA invites any professional practice, educational or professional institution to prepare a Mediation Advocacy Assessment or Accreditation Programme to meet these Standards. Once approved by the SCMA, professionals who pass the assessment of such Programme will be qualified for SCMA Certification in the SCMA Registry in accordance with its terms and conditions, including conditions of membership.

5.1 General requirements

5.1.1 Methodology

All Mediation Advocacy Programmes must implement a methodology for assessing whether each applicant's performance meets each of these SCMA Substantive Criteria.

The assessments may be based on written material, role-play or live action evaluations, other suitable methods, or any combination, and may include videotaped and online assessments such as web dramas, self-assessments, interviews, peer reviews, user feedback and other in-practice skill evaluations.

5.1.2 Transparency

The Substantive Criteria (i.e. assessment benchmarks applied for the Programme) must be published and be openly accessible to both candidates, intending candidates and the SCMA .

5.1.3 Integrity

Each Assessor must be experienced in representing clients in mediations and/or teaching/assessing mediation advocacy skills, and should preferably be members of a designated professional body established for the purpose, or of the Association of Mediation Assessors, Trainers and Instructors (AMATI).

5.1.4 Ongoing monitoring of programme

The Programme must include a process for the ongoing monitoring of the performance and practice of both the Trainers and Assessors. SCMA will liaise closely with all recognised programme organizers to maintain a sustainable quality control system.

5.1.5 Diversity

The Programme must be accessible on an equal basis to applicants regardless of their professional affiliations, gender, race, ethnicity, age, religion, sexual orientation or other personal characterization. This should be clearly stated by each programme provider to candidates and intending candidates.

5.2 Evaluating the Standards

Any Programme assessing or accrediting qualifying candidates for SCMA Mediation Advocacy Certification must meet the following minimum substantive criteria with respect to all applicants:

5.2.1 Experience of the mediation process

The Programme must include a methodology for ensuring that Applicants have demonstrated to the satisfaction of the Programme's Assessors experience of mediation as a Mediation Advocate in at least ten mediations.

Exemptions: Practising Mediators - Mediators having acted as sole paid mediator in at least 10 cases

5.2.2 Knowledge of mediation advocacy

The Programme must include a methodology for determining that candidates have demonstrated a strong understanding of general mediation advocacy theory and practice. Written tests, essays, reports, theses and interviews may be used to determine such knowledge. Applicants are expected to be tested on and exhibit a comprehensive understanding of Mediation and Mediation Advocacy theory derived from the listing of the General Requirements of Knowledge and Competency in Section 1 above or leading textbooks on the subject.

5.2.3 Practical mediation advocacy skills

The Programme must include a methodology for the assessment of performance as a Mediation Advocate against a variety of benchmarks that together demonstrate a high degree of Mediation Advocacy competency. The assessed benchmarks may be based on role-play or live action assessments, and may include videotaped and online assessments such as web dramas, self- assessments, interviews, peer reviews, user feedback and other in-practice skill evaluations. The methodology used will address all the Practical Skills Requirements in Section 2 above and will be sufficiently detailed to attest to an applicant's demonstrated high level of competency as a Mediation Advocate. However, it is not expected that all detailed Practical Skills Requirements in Section 2 above will be assessed in the same depth, and Programmes will be free to assess other practical skills not listed.

Given the comments under the Heading "Nomenclature" in Section 2, a Programme needs to clearly identify in the application which assessment will be accorded to successful candidates, whether Mediation Advocate or Mediation Advisor/ Representative.

6 Notes

[1] P/E = Price/Earnings ration; a measurement of the valueof a company that measures its current share price relative to its earning per share (EPS)

[2] BATNA = Best Alternative to a Negotiated Agreement; WATNA = Worst Alternative to a Negotiated Agreement; PATNA = Probable Alternative to a Negotiated Agreement; RATNA = Realistic Alternative to a Negotiated Agreement.

[3] ZOPA = Zone of Possible Agreement

[4] SMART = Specific, Measurable, Achievable, Relevant and Timely.

Appendix II

Agreement to Mediate

PARTIES:

1. ("Party A") represented by

2. ("Party B") represented by

("a Party" or collectively "the Parties")

3. ("the Mediator")

and

4. ADR Group Limited trading as the ADR Group of 1st Floor, 83 High Street, Rayleigh, Essex SS6 7EJ ("ADRg")

IN RELATION TO:

A. DISPUTE:
Matters which are subject to proceedings in Claim No.:
County Court / Chancery Division / High Court of Justice:
or *short description of the dispute*
("the Dispute")

B. The Mediation will be held at [venue] with the Mediator on [date] from [Time] for a duration of [?] hours or such longer period as may be agreed. ("the Mediation Session")

IT IS AGREED

The Parties and any person identified in Schedule 1 as an Observer agree in consideration of the mutual covenants between them that ADRg shall administer, the Mediator shall mediate (including all preparatory and post Mediation Session activity) and the Parties shall seek to resolve the Dispute through mediation on the following terms and conditions ("the Mediation").

1. THE RULES

The Mediation shall be held and conducted according to this Agreement to Mediate and the Rules of ADRg in effect ("the Rules"). The current version of the Rules are attached as Schedule 2.

2. COMMENCEMENT AND TERMINATION OF THE MEDIATION

2.1 The Mediation shall be deemed to have commenced on the date and time determined by the Mediator.

2.2 The Mediation shall be deemed to continue until any one of the following occurs:

2.2.1 when a written Settlement Agreement is executed and signed by the Parties;
2.2.2 a written notice of withdrawal is given by any Party;
2.2.3 the time set for the Mediation has expired without agreement for continuation or resumption;
2.2.4 the Mediator decides, at his/her absolute discretion, and notifies the Parties, that continuing the Mediation is unlikely to result in a settlement or is otherwise undesirable; or
2.2.5 the Mediator decides that he/she should retire for any of the reasons set out in the Code of Practice of ADRg.

2.3 The Dates and Times of the commencement and termination of the Mediation and the reason therefore shall be recorded by the Mediator in the Mediation Record.

2.4 The Parties or the Mediator may at any time adjourn the Mediation in order to consider further information or specific issues raised during the mediation, obtain further information or for any other reason which the Parties or the Mediator consider helpful in furthering the Mediation. ADRg will liaise with the Parties and the Mediator to reconvene or resume the Mediation.

3. PROCEDURES

3.1 Each Party shall supply the Mediator with an outline of their case and supporting documents at least 7 days before the Mediation.

3.2 A Party does not require legal representation to attend the Mediation. Where a Party is not legally represented, they are advised to obtain independent legal and tax advice before the Mediation and prior to finalising any agreement reached pursuant to the Mediation.

3.3 The Parties recognise that neither ADRg nor the Mediator will offer legal advice nor act as a legal advisor for any Party nor will they provide any Party with a legal analysis with respect to a Party's legal position or rights.

3.4 The Parties will participate in the Mediation personally or in the case of businesses, corporations or other legal entities, through their authorised representatives. The Parties will be represented in the Mediation as set out in Schedule 1.

3.5 Each Party warrants that at least one of its representatives has full and unlimited legal authority to bind that Party to settle the dispute on its behalf. Any restriction on this authority must be notified in writing to the Mediator and ADRg prior to commencement of the Mediation.

3.6 Any settlement reached in the Mediation will not be legally binding until it has been reduced to writing in a Settlement Agreement and signed by, or on behalf of, each of the Parties.

4. PRIVATE SESSIONS AND MEDIATOR CONFIDENTIALITY

4.1 The Mediator may hold private sessions with each Party and/or their representatives.

4.2 Subject to applicable provisions in The Rules information received by the Mediator through such sessions shall be and shall remain confidential with the Mediator save that (a) it is in any event publicly available or (b) the Mediator is specifically authorised by that Party to disclose it to the other Party and/or their representatives.

4.3 The Mediator may request of the Parties that he/she be permitted to bring an observer to the Mediation for mediator training purposes. ("the Observer"). It shall be at the sole discretion of each Party whether to grant that request. If an Observer does attend, then the Observer shall be bound by the terms and conditions of this Agreement to Mediate and the Rules on the same basis as the Mediator.

5. MEDIATION FEES, EXPENSES AND COSTS

5.1 ADRg's fees (which include the Mediator's fees) and any other expenses associated with the Mediation will be borne equally by the Parties, unless agreed otherwise.

5.2 The amount and payment conditions for such fees and expenses shall be as set out in the correspondence confirming the Mediation and ADRg's invoice.

5.3 The full fees shall be due and payable if the mediation is cancelled by either Party within 24 hours of the agreed scheduled date and time and 50% of the fees shall be due and payable if the mediation is cancelled by either Party within 7 days of the agreed scheduled date. Any expenses incurred by ADRg or the Mediator in anticipation of the mediation shall be reimbursed in full.

SIGNATURE OF THIS MEDIATION AGREEMENT

This Agreement to Mediate is to be signed by the Parties, any instructed legal representative of each Party attending the mediation (if represented) and Observer and is binding upon them as of the date of signature.

A. (represented by)

Signed: ______________________________ (Party A)

Name: ______________________________ (Party A)

Signed ______________________________ (Solicitor)

Name: ______________________________ (Solicitor)

Signed ______________________________ (Barrister)

Name: ______________________________ (Barrister)

B. (represented by)

Signed: ______________________________ (Party B)

Name: ______________________________ (Party B)

Signed ______________________________ (Solicitor)

Name: ______________________________ (Solicitor)

Signed ______________________________ (Barrister)

Name: ______________________________ (Barrister)

C. (The Mediator)

Signed: ______________________________

Name: ______________________________

Date: ______________________________

D. (The Observer)

Signed: ______________________________

Name: ______________________________

Date: ______________________________

Schedule 1
Mediation Attendance Schedule and Confidentiality Record

To be signed by the Parties, their legal representatives and other advisers, the Mediator, any Observer, and for any person attending the Mediation at the invitation of either party.

For any person attending the Mediation at the invitation of either party: although I am not a party to this Agreement to Mediate I nevertheless agree to be personally bound by clause 4.2 of this agreement and Rule 12 of the Mediation Rules of the ADR Group, respectively the confidentiality provisions.

NAME	SIGNATURE

Schedule 2
The Rules of ADR Group

1. The Concept

1.1 The parties will attempt in good faith to settle their dispute by Mediation in accordance with the Rules and an Agreement to Mediate ("Agreement to Mediate").

1.2 By entering into an Agreement to Mediate and proceeding with the Mediation in accordance with the Rules and that agreement, unless agreed otherwise, neither party is prevented from seeking to enforce or protect their legal rights through the courts or arbitration at any time.

2. Agreement to Mediate

2.1 The parties, their representatives, the Mediator and any Observer must sign an Agreement to Mediate prior to the commencement of the mediation

2.2 The Agreement to Mediate governs the relationship between the parties, all those attending the mediation and the Mediator before, during and after the Mediation Session.

3. Attendance and Authority of Parties

3.1 The parties and their representatives and advisers, if any, will attend the Mediation Session to be led by the Mediator.

3.2 The parties and their representatives, if any, must have the authority to settle the dispute. If a party is a natural person, that person must attend the mediation session. If a party is not a natural person, it must be represented at the Mediation Session by an officer or employee with authority to make binding agreements settling the dispute. If that person comes with limited authority, he or she must disclose the extent of their limitation to the Mediator prior to the commencement of the Mediation.

4. Selection of the Mediator

4.1 If so requested ADRg will provide to the parties' details of potential mediators selected from its panel of mediators. The provision of Mediators through ADR Group and the activities of the Mediators will be governed by the Rules and the Agreement to Mediate.

4.2 In making this selection consideration will be given to the subject matter of the dispute, the complexity, the value in dispute, the desired experience of the Mediator and the location of the parties.

5. The Mediator

5.1 The Mediator will:

5.1.1 communicate with the parties and/or their advisers jointly or separately prior to the Mediation as well as meet with them jointly or separately, if requested to do so, or if the Mediator deems it appropriate;

5.1.2 prior to the commencement of the Mediation Session read and familiarise him/herself with each party's Position Statement and any documents provided in accordance with paragraph 8.1;

5.1.3 determine the procedure for the Mediation;

5.1.4 maintain a Mediation Record stating the dates and times the Mediation commenced and concluded and the reasons for termination; and

5.1.5 abide by the terms and conditions of the Rules, the Agreement to Mediate and ADRg's Code of Conduct (European Code of Conduct for Mediators http://ec.europa.eu/civiljustice/adr/adr_ec_code_conduct_en.htm, as may be amended from time to time) (the "Code of Conduct").

5.2 The Mediator may:

5.2.1 if a settlement is not reached and if so requested and agreed by the Parties and the Mediator render a non-binding opinion or recommendation on how a settlement may be reached.

5.3 The Mediator will not:

5.3.1 impose a settlement on the parties; or

5.3.2 offer legal advice or act as legal adviser to any party at any time in connection with the dispute.

5.4 the parties and the Mediator acknowledge that the Mediator is an independent contractor and is not appointed as an agent or employee of any of the parties or ADRg. Neither the Mediator nor a member of his or her firm or business will act, or have acted, as a professional adviser, or in any other capacity, for any of the parties in connection with the dispute either before, during or after the Mediation Session.

6. Role of ADRg

6.1 ADRg will in consultation with the parties and the Mediator make the necessary arrangements for the Mediation including, as appropriate:

6.1.1 prepare the Agreement to Mediate;

6.1.2 liaise between the parties to agree a suitable date and venue;

6.1.3 provide the parties a Guide to Preparing Your Case for Mediation;

6.1.4 discuss or meet with any or all of the parties or their representatives (and the Mediator if appropriate), either together or separately, on any matter pursuant to the proposed mediation;

6.1.5 provide feedback on the Mediation to the Mediator as received from the Parties,

6.1.6 provide general administration in relation to the Mediation.

7. Representation

7.1 Parties do not require legal representation to attend the mediation.

7.2 Where a party is unrepresented, ADRg encourages such party to obtain independent legal advice in connection with the dispute and the mediation.

7.3 Each party will notify ADRg and other parties involved in the Mediation of the names of those people intended to be present at the Mediation Session and indicate their capacity at the Mediation as a principal, representative, adviser or any other capacity.

8. Position Statements and Documentation

8.1 Each party will prepare and deliver to the Mediator, seven (7) days prior to the mediation, a concise summary ('Position Statement') of the matter in dispute, copies of documents referred to in the Position Statement and those documents which the parties intend to refer to during the Mediation.

8.2 The Position Statement and the documents referred to therein are private and confidential and will not be disclosed by the Mediator to the other party or to any third party unless expressly authorised to do so by the party who has provided the Position Statement.

8.3 There is no obligation on the parties to exchange Position Statements however they are encouraged to do so.

8.4 Similarly, the parties are encouraged to prepare and agree a joint bundle of documents.

9. The Mediation

9.1 No formal record or transcript of the Mediation will be made.

9.2 The Mediation is for the purpose of attempting to achieve a negotiated settlement and all information provided during the Mediation is provided without prejudice and will be inadmissible in any litigation or arbitration of the dispute subject to the provisions of any applicable law.

9.3 Information, which would be otherwise admissible in any such litigation or arbitration, shall not be rendered inadmissible as a result of its use in the Mediation.

9.4 If the parties are unable to reach a settlement during the Mediation Session, the Mediator may, if requested to do so, facilitate further negotiation after the Mediation Session itself has ended.

10. Settlement Agreement

Any settlement reached in the Mediation will not be legally binding until it has been recorded in writing and signed by or on behalf of the parties.

11. Adjournment and Termination

11.1 The Parties or the Mediator may, at any time, adjourn the Mediation in order to consider further information or specific issues raised during the Mediation, obtain further information, or for any other reason which the Parties or the Mediator consider helpful in furthering the Mediation. ADRg will liaise with the Parties and the Mediator to reconvene or resume the Mediation.

11.2 The Mediation shall terminate in any of the following circumstances:

11.2.1 when a written settlement is executed and signed by the parties;

11.2.2 if any or all of the parties decide not to continue;

11.2.3 the time set for the Mediation has expired without agreement for continuation or resumption;

11.2.4 the Mediator decides, at his/her absolute discretion, and notifies the parties, that continuing the Mediation is unlikely to result in a settlement or is otherwise undesirable; or

11.2.5 the Mediator decides that he/she should retire for any of the reasons set out in the Code of Conduct.

11.3 The Mediator will provide the Parties with written confirmation of the termination of the Mediation when the Mediation extends past the Mediation Session.

12. Confidentiality

12.1 Every person involved in the Mediation and ADRg will keep confidential the fact that the Mediation is to take place or has taken place and all information (whether given orally or in writing) produced for or delivered as part of the Mediation including the settlement agreement (if any) except in so far as is necessary to implement and enforce any such settlement agreement or as required by any applicable law or the provisions of any applicable insurance policy or terms of any professional engagement.

12.2 All documents or other information produced for, or arising in relation to, the Mediation will be privileged and will not be admissible as evidence or discoverable in any litigation or arbitration connected with the dispute. This does not apply to any information which would in any event have been admissible for disclosure in such proceedings or as otherwise required by law including without limitation the Proceeds of Crime Act.

12.3 Subject to Rules 12.1 and 12.2 the parties will not subpoena or otherwise require the Mediator, any Observer, ADRg, any shareholder, director, employee, consultant or representative of ADRg ("ADRg Person") or any other person attending the mediation to testify or produce records, notes or any other information or material whatsoever in any future or continuing proceedings.

12.4 If a party does make such an application that party will fully indemnify the Mediator or an ADRg Person or any other person attending the Mediation in respect of any costs incurred in resisting and/ or responding to such an application, including reimbursement at the Mediator's standard hourly rate for the Mediator's time spent in resisting and/or responding to such an application.

12.5 Where the Mediation has taken place as a result of a Court order, the parties agree that the Court shall be notified of the fact that the case has been resolved through mediation. The notification will come from the parties and take the form of a letter agreed or draft Tomlin Order between the parties at the conclusion of the Mediation. The notification will not disclose the terms of any settlement, unless otherwise agreed by the parties.

13. Mediation Costs

13.1 Unless agreed otherwise the costs of the Mediation will be borne equally by the parties and as such may be taken into account in any further legal proceedings.

13.2 Each party to the Mediation will bear its own costs and expenses of its participation in the Mediation including the costs of its legal representative and advisers and unless agreed otherwise these costs will be costs in the case.

13.3 Where a party has a legal representative, that legal representative will be liable for their client's share of the costs of the Mediation in the same way as they are liable for disbursements incurred in any litigation.

13.4 Payment of the costs of the Mediation will be made to ADRg in advance of the mediation session and ADRg will be responsible for the payment of the fees of the Mediator. ADRg shall have the right to fix a cancellation policy with respect to costs and expenses which shall be set out in the Agreement to Mediate.

14. Inability or unwillingness of the parties to enter into an Agreement to Mediate

14.1 If the parties have entered into a written agreement which includes a clause referring any dispute arising thereunder to mediation in accordance with these Rules then in the event of either or both parties being unable or unwilling to enter into an Agreement to Mediate, the

then Managing Director of ADRg shall, without incurring any liability whatsoever towards any party on behalf of himself/herself or ADRg, determine the following elements of an Agreement to Mediate in his/her sole discretion:

14.1.1 choice of the Mediator;

14.1.2 date, time and place of the Mediation;

14.1.3 the applicability of all or any of the Rules to the mediation; and

14.1.4 the mediation shall proceed accordingly.

14.2 In choosing the Mediator the then Managing Director of ADRg shall apply the considerations set out in Rule 4.2 and these Rules shall apply in all respects to the chosen Mediator.

14.3 Should either or both parties not proceed in good faith with the mediation in accordance with Rule 14.1 then the parties shall be free to adduce evidence thereof in either court or arbitration proceedings provided they may not call as a witness or otherwise seek to take evidence from an ADRg Person or the Mediator

15. Exclusion of Liability

Nothing in these Rules shall limit or exclude the Mediator's, ADRg's, or the Observer's liability for any matter in respect of which it would be unlawful for the Mediator, ADRg or the Observer to exclude or restrict liability. Subject to that proviso, neither the Mediator, ADRg, or the Observer shall be liable to the parties for any act or omission in connection with the services provided by them in, or in relation to, the Mediation, unless the act or omission is fraudulent or involves wilful misconduct.

16. Human Rights

The referral of a dispute to Mediation in accordance with these Rules does not affect any rights that may exist under Article 6 or the European Convention of Human Rights.

17. Complaints Procedure

17.1 If any Party is dissatisfied with the service of ADRg and/or the conduct of the Mediator, a complaint must be filed in writing to the Managing Director of ADRg no later than 28 days from the date of the termination of the Mediation.

17.2 In the event a complaint is made in relation to the conduct of the Mediator ADRg reserves the right to withhold the Mediator's fee until such time as the complaint has been dealt with.

18. Governing Law

These Rules and any Agreement to Mediate entered into in which these Rules are incorporated by reference or attachment and any matter arising out them shall be governed by and construed in accordance with the laws of England and Wales.

19. Dispute Resolution

Any dispute relating to the Rules and any Agreement to Mediate entered into in which these Rules are incorporated by reference or attachment and any matter arising out of them which cannot be resolved by negotiation between the parties within 30 days of either party giving notice to the other party that a dispute has arisen shall be submitted to Mediation pursuant to the Rules and failing settlement of that dispute by mediation within 30 days thereafter, the dispute shall be determined by the appointment of a single arbitrator to be agreed between the parties, or failing agreement within fourteen days, after either party has given to the other a written request to concur in the appointment of an arbitrator, by an arbitrator to be appointed by the President or a Deputy President of the Chartered Institute of Arbitrators.

Appendix III

Private Agreement to Mediate

MEDIATION AGREEMENT-TO BE SIGNED BY ALL INVOLVED IN THE MEDIATION
This Agreement is made 202 between:-

The First Participants c/o	Solicitor [ ] of [ ] Solicitors ("the First Participant's Representatives")
The Second Participants c/o	TheSecondParticipants'Solicitorof(and any barrister, "the Second Participant's Representatives")
The Third Participants c/o	
Mediation Date and Time Booked	202 10.00 – 17.00
Mediation Venue	[ ] Site Visit [insert full address & postcode: 10.00 Mediation Meeting [TBC]
Mediator	
Dispute	[TBC] re
Mediators Briefing Email .... 202..	

IT IS AGREED by those signing this Agreement that:

1. The mediation services will be provided by the Mediator at the Mediation Venue in relation to the Dispute.

2. The Participants are taking part in this mediation in good faith with the aim of achieving common ground (and if time permits) a settlement of the Dispute. The Mediator's role is to help facilitate this. The First Participants and the Second Participants are authorised to agree terms of settlement and enter into a

binding written settlement agreement if agreed and following legal or other advice (as they are recommended to do).

3. This mediation and all communications relating to it are without prejudice and are to be kept confidential by the Participants, the First Participants Representatives and the Second Participants Representatives, the Mediator and any observer. This includes all documents and correspondence produced for or at the mediation save where disclosure is required by law to implement or enforce the terms of any settlement agreement. The Participants may discuss the mediation with their professional advisers and/or insurers and will provide such information as they are obliged to do by law.

4. The Mediator shall not be liable to any Participant for any loss, damage or expense whatsoever arising in connection with this mediation. In the case of alleged negligence the Mediator's liability is limited to the amount of the professional indemnity insurance of which he has the benefit.

5. The Participants agree that they will not call the Mediator as a witness or expert nor require him to produce in evidence any records or notes relating to the mediation, in any litigation or other process. If any Participant makes any such application that Participant will indemnify the Mediator in respect of any costs relating thereto to include (but not limited to) reimbursement at the Mediator's standard hourly rate for any time spent resisting or responding to any such application.

6. No recordings or transcripts of the mediation will be made.

7. A settlement will only be legally binding if and when set out in writing and signed by or on behalf of the Participants.

8. The fees payable to the Mediator have been agreed per the Mediator's Briefing Email. The agreed fees will have been paid in cleared funds to the Mediators bank account (specified in the Invoice sent) before the Mediation Meeting. Any overtime, at the rate agreed per the Mediator's Briefing Email. Each party will bear its own costs (if any) of participation in the mediation.

9. Form of Mediation

9.1 Facilitative Mediation

9.1.1 The Mediator will try to help resolve the Dispute by way of facilitative mediation, exploring issues, interests, needs and concerns of the Participants and assisting them independently and neutrally by generating options for a mutually agreed resolution of the matters in the Dispute. The Mediator Briefing Email explains what to expect at the mediation.

9.1.2 Mediation is a voluntary process and the Mediator will not, and cannot, compel the Participants to settle. Either the Mediator or the Participants may terminate the process at any time.

9.2 No Evaluative Mediation

9.2.1 The Mediator does not offer evaluative mediation.

9.2.2 The Mediator will not assess the merits of the Dispute or analyse or protect any Participant's legal position or rights.

9.2.3 The Participants must (if they require an opinion on the merits of an issue, settlement, or proposal; or if they require legal advice) seek advice from their own chosen solicitor, or counsel.

10. Cancellations and Adjournments

10.1 If the mediation is cancelled by any Participant more than 5 business days before the Mediation Date and is rescheduled, there is no cancellation fee for the first adjournment. Any time spent preparing for the Mediation Date will be noted and charged in the eventual billing. If more than one adjournment occurs, an adjournment fee of £250 may be charged at the discretion of the Mediator for each adjournment following the first payable before the Mediation Date.

10.2 If the mediation is cancelled within 5 business days before the Mediation Date and whether or not rescheduled, a cancellation fee of £400 plus preparation time notified (at £100 + vat per Participant) and any other incurred expenses is due and payable by the Solicitors for the Participants on or before the Mediation Date.

10.3 If the mediation is cancelled within 3 business days before the Mediation Date and whether or not rescheduled, a cancellation fee equal to the whole of the agreed mediation fee specified in the Mediator's Briefing Email including any other incurred expenses is due and payable on or before the Mediation Date.

10.4 Cancellations shall be in writing by the Solicitors for the Participants to the Mediator

11. This Agreement and the mediation is governed by the law of England and the Courts of England have exclusive jurisdiction to decide any matters arising out of or in connection with this Agreement or the mediation.

12. The referral of this dispute to mediation does not affect any rights under Article 6 of the European Convention of Human Rights, and if the dispute is not resolved through the mediation the Parties' right to a fair trial remains unaffected.

13. The Participants agree to an observer attending the mediation (usually a trainee mediator)

Signature of the First Participant: ....

Signature of the First Participant's Solicitor: ....

Signature of the Second Participant: ....

Signature of the Third Participant: ....

Signature of the Second Participant's Solicitor:..........................

Signature of the Mediator: ....

Signature of the Observer: ....

Appendix IV

Specimen Settlement Agreement

MADE ON [DATE] BETWEEN

(a) [Insert party name and details] and

(b) [Insert party name and details].

UPON THE PARTIES HAVING SETTLED THEIR DISPUTE BY MEDIATION ON [DATE]

IT IS AGREED THAT:

1. [Party name] shall pay [party name] the sum of [£x] by way of [cheque/bank transfer etc] by [time and date].

2. The sum referred to above is paid and received in full and final settlement of all claims and counterclaims [including where appropriate matters set out in the statements of case dated x/ matters set out in the letter dated x] between [party name] and [party name], including [e.g. VAT, interest and costs].

3. [Further, [party name] shall [as appropriate] by [date]].

4. [provisions as regards confidentiality].

5. [Notwithstanding paragraph 1 above, each party will pay/has paid the mediator's fees and the expenses of the mediation on [date] in accordance with the separate mediation agreement dated]

6. This settlement agreement shall be governed by, and construed in accordance with, English law.

7. In the event that any dispute arises in relation to the terms of this settlement agreement, the parties will endeavour in the first instance to settle it by mediation by reference to the mediator, [Name].

SIGNED:

Signed by [NAME]

for and on behalf of [PARTY NAME]

..

[TITLE]

Signed by [NAME]

for and on behalf of [PARTY NAME]

..

[TITLE]

Bibliography

Books and Articles

Abramson, Harold I. *Mediation Representation: Advocating as Problem Solver*, 3rd Edn, Aspen 2013

Allman, William F *Nice Guys Finish First* I Science(1984) vol 5 no 8 p25-31

Aubrey-Johnson, Kate and Curtis, Helen *Making Mediation Work for You* LAG 2012

Axelrod, Robert *The Evolution of Cooperation* Basic Books 1984

Beer, Jennifer and Packard, Caroline C. *Mediator's Handbook* 4th edn. New Society 2012

Birch, Elizabeth *New Sophistications in Commercial Mediation* ACI newsletter issue 9 Spring/Summer 2004

Blake, Susan, Browne, Julie and Sime, Stuart *The Jackson ADR Handbook* OUP 3rd edn 2021

Brown, Henry, Shipman, Shirley and Waters, Ben, Arthur *Brown & Marriott's ADR Principles and Practice*, 4th Edn, Sweet and Maxwell 2018

Carroll, Eileen and Mackie, Karl J *International Mediation: Breaking Business Deadlock* 3rd edn Bloomsbury 2016

CEDR First Mediators' Congress Workshop Session Report On Mediation Advocacy Resolutions issue 34 Winter 2003

Commercial Court Committee Working Party on ADR *Second Report* Nov 1998

Connerty, Anthony *ADR and the Lawyer* NLJ 147 Nov and Dec 1997

De Girolamo, Debbie *The Fugitive Identity of Mediation – Negotiations, Shift Changes and Allusionary Action* Routledge 2013

Dodson, Charles *Preparing for Mediation* Resolutions issue 17 Summer 1997

Elgin, Suzette Haden *The Gentle Art of Verbal Self-Defense at Work* Prentice-Hall 2003

Endispute *Making Alternative Dispute Resolution Work– A Guide for Practicing Lawyers and Business People* New York 1991

Fisher R., and Ury W, with Patton, Bruce *Getting to Yes: Negotiating an Agreement Without Giving In* Penguin 2012

Floyer-Acland, Bevan, Andrew Alex and Frayley Andrew *When to Use Mediation* IDR Europe 1990

Foskett, Sir David *The Law and Practice of Compromise* 9th edn Thomson Sweet & Maxwell 2024

Gilson, Ronald J *How Many Lawyers Does it take to Change an Economy* (1993) 17 Law & Social Enquiry 635-643

Goodman, Andrew *Preparing for Mediation – A Guide for Consumers* Mediation Publishing Dec. 2015

Ishikawa, Brendon, and Curtis, Dana *Appellate Mediation: A Guidebook for Attorneys and Mediators* ABA Dec 2016

Lempereur, Alain, Salzer, Jacques and three others *Mediation: Negotiation by Other Moves* Wiley 2021

Mackie, Karl, Miles, David, Marsh, William, Allen, Tony *ADR Practice Guide: Commercial Dispute Resolution* Tottel 3rd edn 2007

Mantle, Marjorie *Mediation: A Practical Guide for Lawyers* 2nd edn. Edinburgh University Press March 2017

Moore, Christopher W. *The Mediation Process: Practical Strategies for Resolving Conflict* 4th edn Jossey Bass 2014

Naughton QC, Philip *ADR Comes in from the cold* New Law Journal Practitioner March 17 1995

Newman, Paul *Keeping Secrets* Solicitors Journal 19.08.05 1007

Patton, Bruce, Stone, Douglas and Heen, Sheila *Difficult Conversations: How to Discuss What Matters Most* Penguin 2011

Pemble, Stuart and Whiteley, Miranda *It ain't necessarily so* (2004) EG 95

Rosenthal, D.E. *Lawyer and Client: Who's in Charge?* Russell Sage Foundation 1974

Shapiro, Daniel and Fisher Roger *Building Agreement: Using Emotions as You Negotiate* Random House 2007

Walker, Stephen *Mediation: An A-Z Guide* Bloomsbury Oct 2016

Walker, Stephen *Mediation Advocacy – Representing and Advising Clients in Mediation* 2nd edn. Bloomsbury 2018

Walker, Stephen *Mediation Behaviour: Why We Act Like We Do* Bloomsbury 2021

Walker, Stephen *Digital Mediation* Bloomsbury 2024

Williams, Gerald R *A Lawyer's Handbook for Effective Negotiation and Settlement* 1992

York, Stephen D *Preparing Your Client for Mediation* Resolutions issue 17 Summer 1997

Lecture and Seminar Materials

Birch, Elizabeth *Mediation in the Professional Negligence Sector* PNBA Back to Basics Course November 2003

Burgess, John *Looking In All Directions* Society of Construction Law 7 October 2003

Burgess, John *Mediation Skills: What the Mediator Wants from Advocates* 1 Serjeants Inn February 2005

Connerty, Anthony *ADR Tactics and ADR and the CPR* Bar Council Seminar, Inner Temple Hall 15 September 1999

Fraley, Andrew *Sharpening The Process – Tips And Techniques For Time Limited Mediation* CEDR First Mediators' Congress 20 November 2003

Goodman, Andrew *ADR Uses* 199 Strand 14 March 1996

Goodman, Andrew *ADR and Costs* PNBA Back to Basics Course November 2003

Goodman, Andrew *Mediation Advocacy* 1 Serjeants Inn February 2005

Honeywell, Martin *Mediation And Theories Of Change* CEDR Forum September 2005

Mackie, Karl *The Effective Mediator* CEDR seminar paper February 2002

Mackie, Karl *Breakthrough: The Myths and Magic of Mediation* CEDR Forum September 2005

Manning, Colin *The Lawyer's Role in Mediation* PNBA Back to Basics Course November 2003

Maynard, Francis *Handling time limited mediations* CEDR Forum August 1996

Naughton QC, Philip, *An Introduction to ADR* Bar Council Seminar, Inner Temple Hall 15 September 1999

Nesic, Miryana *Mediation advocacy: how to keep it on track for results*

CEDR First Mediators' Congress 20 November 2003

O'Sullivan, Gerry *The Mediator's Toolkit: Formulating and Asking Questions for Successful Outcomes* 2018

Richbell, David *How to Master Commercial Mediation* Bloomsbury 2014

Weatherill QC, Bernard *Effective Alternative Dispute Resolution* Chancery Bar Association Seminar 10 February 2000

Whatling, Tony *Mediation Skills and Strategies: A Practical Guide* Jessica Kingsley 2012

Whatling, Tony *Mediation and Dispute Resolution: Contemporary Issues and Developments* Jessica Kingsley 2021

Williams, Gerald R., *Lawyers as Healers and Warriors* CEDR Seminar September 1997

Further Reading

American Bar Association *Mediation Practice Guide: A Handbook for Resolving Business Disputes* 2004

Blackshaw, Ian S., *Mediating Sports Disputes* Springer 2002

Boulle, Laurence and Nesic, Miryana *Mediator Skills and Techniques: Triangle of Influence: Skills, Techniques and Strategies* 2nd edn Bloomsbury Professional 2023

Brazil, W. D. 'For Judges: *Suggestions about What to Say about ADR at CaseManagement Conferences - and How to Respond to Concerns or Objections Raised by Counsel*'. (2000) Ohio State Journal of Dispute Resolution, 16" 165.

Brooker, P. '*Survey of Construction Lawyers' Attitudes and Practice in the use of ADR in Contractors' Disputes*'. (1999) Construction Management and Economics, 17" 757-765.

Bush, Robert and Folger, Joseph *The Promise of Mediation: Responding to Conflict through Empowerment and Recognition* Jossey-Bass 2004

Cloke, Kenneth *The Magic in Mediation: A Search for Symmetries, Metaphors and Scale-Free Practices* 2023

Cohen, J. R. *'Adversaries? Partners? How about Counterparts? On Metaphors in the Practice and Teaching of Negotiation and Dispute Resolution'.* (2003) Conflict Resolution Quarterly, 20" 433-440.

Comvalius, Pascal *Mediation in Criminal Cases* 2022 Atmosphere Press

Crocker, Chester A., Hampson, Fen Osler; Aall, Pamela *Taming Intractable Conflicts: Mediation in the Hardest Cases* US Institute of Peace, 2004

Dingwall, R. & Eekelaar, J. (Eds.) *Divorce Mediation and the Legal Process.* Oxford Clarendon Press 1998

Feehily, Ronán International *Commercial Mediation: Law and Regulation in Comparative Context* Cambridge UP 2022

Field, T. G. & Rose, M. *'Prospects for ADR in Patent Disputes: An Empirical Assessment of Attorneys' Attitudes'.* (1991) IDEA, 32" 309.

Frey, M. A. *'Representing Clients Effectively in an ADR Environment'.* (1997) Tulsa Law Journal, 33rd 443.

Hanaway, Monica *Psychologically Informed Mediation: Studies in Conflict and Resolution Routledge* 2020

Intrater, K. A. & Gann, T. G. *'The Lawyer's Role in Institutionalizing ADR'.* (2000) Hofstra Labour and Employment Law Journal 18: 469.

Landau, Barbara; Bartoletti, Mario; Mesbur, Ruth. *Family Mediation Handbook* Butterworths, Canada 1999

Lebaron, M. & Zumeta, Z. D. *'Windows on Diversity: Lawyers, Cultures and Mediation Practice'*. (2003) Conflict Resolution Quarterly, 20" 463-472.

Lovenheim, Peter and Laurence, Bethany K. *Mediate, Don't Litigate: Strategies for Successful Mediation* Nolo, 2004

Mackie, Karl, Miles, David, Marsh Bill, Allen, Tony *Commercial Dispute Resolution: An ADR Practice Guide* 3rd edn Tottel 2007

Moore, Christopher W. *The Mediation Process: Practical Strategies for Resolving Conflict* 4th edn Jossey-Bass 2014

Mulcahy, L. *'Can leopards change their spots? An evaluation of the role of lawyers in medical negligence mediation'*. (2001) 8 International Journal of the Legal Profession, 203-224.

Nesic, Miryana *Mediation* Tottel 2001

Palmer, Michael and Roberts, Simon *Dispute Processes: ADR and the Primary Forms of Decision-Making* 3rd edn. CUP 2020

Phillips, G F. *'The Obligation of Attorneys to Inform Clients about ADR'*. (2003) 31" 239.

Plowman, Martin *Zen and the Art of Mediation* Law Brief Publishing 2019

Randolph, Paul *The Psychology of Conflict: Mediating in a Diverse World* Bloomsbury 25 Feb 2016

Sander, Frank E.A, Rogers, Nancy H., Rudolph Cole, Sarah, Goldberg, Stephen B ed. *Dispute Resolution: Negotiation, Mediation and Other Processes* Aspen Law and Business 2003

Schmitz, S. J. *'What Should We Teach in ADR Courses: Concepts and Skills for Lawyers Representing Clients in Mediation'*. (2001) Harvard Negotiation Law Review, 6" 189.

Strasser, Freddie and Randolph, Paul *Mediation: A New Psychological Insight into Conflict Resolution* Continuum 2004

Van Wezel, Katherine *Private Justice: The Law of Alternative Dispute Resolution* Stone Foundation 1999

Westcott, J. Ed. *Family Mediation in the UK* Jordan 2004

Wissler, R. L. *'When Does Familiarity Breed Content - A Study of the Role of Different Forms of ADR Education and Experience in Attorney's ADR Recommendations'*. (2002) 2." 199.

Wissler, R. L. *'Barriers to Attorneys' Discussion and the Use of ADR'*. (2003) Ohio State Journal of Dispute Resolution, 19: 459.

Wreston, M. A. 'Checks on Participant Conduct in Compulsory ADR: Reconciling the Tension in the Need for Good-Faith Participation, Autonomy and Confidentiality'. (2001) Indiana Law Journal, 76." 591.

Index

Acceptance, 139
Adjudicative model,
  Professional psyche and, 37
ADR Group, 65,237
ADR Pledge, 6
Adverse costs awards, 185
Advocate, role of, 30-49,126
  Lawyer or non-lawyer, 49
Agreement,
  Mediation, 86
  Sample, 237,253
  To mediate, 63
Alibaba complaints procedure, 7
Alternative Dispute Resolution *see* Mediation
Amazon complaints procedure, 7
Arguing against mediation, 67
Assessing suitability to mediate, 56
Attendees
  Choice, 94
  Non-attendees, 96
  Preparation, 99
  Role, 97
Authority to settle, 103

BATNA, 99,105,133
Benefits of mediation, 28
  Consumers, for, 34
Brief, working up, 104

CEDR, 28,37,50,65,170
CFA *see*
  Conditional Fee Agreements
Choosing a mediator, 71
Chronology, 92
Civil Procedure Rules, 3
  Ethics, mediation and, 100
Client
  Advice about mediation, 109
  Attendance, 94
  Control of, 154
Client *cont*
  Dealing with, as advocate, 151
  Goals, 101
  Interests, 39
  Introduction to mediation, 58
  Position statement, 91
  Questions, 60
  Reluctant, 62
Closed sessions, 124
Commercial Court Guide, 65
Conditional Fee Agreements,
  mediation costs and, 182
Confidentiality, 33,44,45,67,75,125,
  130,155,159-173,199,244
Consumers, mediation
  Benefits for, 34
  Government action, 35
Costs, 12,175-195
  Adverse costs awards, 185
  Conditional Fee Agreements, 182
  Court-directed mediation, 183
  Mediation and litigation, 178
  Predictability of outcome, 194
  Public funding, 182
  Recoverability, 180
Court-directed mediation, 183
Crisis, negotiations, 147

Deadlock, as stage of negotiation,
  147
Decision to mediate, 53-69
Decision-makers, attendance of, 94
Denial, 139
Document preparation, 88

E-bay complaints procedure, 7
Effective negotiation,
  Ten Rules, 143
Ethics, 100

Feelings, own, 153
Fixing date, 110

Glossary, 197

Hearing, the, 115-158
HMOC *see* Online Court

Instructing solicitor, agreeing to mediation, 63
International Mediation Institute (IMI), vii,7
- Decision Tree, 79

Inappropriate, mediation, 11-27

Jackson, Lord Justice, 3
Joint session, 119

Lawyers, using in mediation, 43
- Changing role, 2,48
- Opposing, 153
- Specialist mediators, 2

Legal box, 39

Mediation
- Adverse costs awards, 18
- Advocate, role of, 31-49,126
- Agreement, 86
  - Sample, 237,253
  - Standard Form, 86
- Arguing against, 67
- Assessing suitability for, 56
- Benefits, 28
- Costs, 12,177-195
- Decision to use, 58
- Definition, 9
- Development, 33
- Growth, 2
- Hearing, 115-158
- Inappropriate, 11-27
- Management, 134
- Market, 1
- Neutrality, 10
- Non-binding, 9
- Privacy, 10
- Privilege, 159-173
- Procedure, 118
- Professional psyche and, 37
- Ripe for, 57
- Settlement, 4,11,133
- Timetabling, 117
- Venue, 85
- Voluntary, 9

Mediation advocacy
- Forensic skills, 151
- Lawyers, 43

Mediation service providers, 81
Mediator
- Choosing, 71
  - Decision Tree, 79
  - Right individual, 74
  - Service providers, 80
- Dealing with, as advocate, 152
- Neutrality, 10
- Working with, at the hearing, 128
- Working with, before the hearing, 92

Movement in negotiations, 139,146

Negotiation processes
- Effective, 135,141
- Stages, 139,145
- Ten Rules, 143
- Tit-for-Tat, 150

Neutrality, mediator, 10
Non-binding, 9

Objectives, 101
ODR *see* Online mediation
Online Court, 7,36
Online mediation, 6,34
Open sessions, 123
Opening positions, 145
Opening statement, 121
Opponents
- Aggressive, 149
- Agreement to mediation, 64
- Lawyers, 153
- Obnoxious, 148

Plenary, 119
Position statement,
  Client's case, 91
  History, 91
  Identify participants, 91
  Outline dispute, 91
  Settlement gateway, 91
Pre-Action Protocols, 4
Pre-mediation phase, 83-113
  Ethics, 100
Preparation before hearing, 108
Privacy, 10
Private sessions, 123
Privilege, 159-173
  Challenges to mediation, 164
Procedure, 118

Role of advocate, mediation, 31-49
  At hearing, 126

Sacrifice, 140
SCMA, vii
  Standards, 207
Settlement, 4,11
  Agreement, 257
  Authority to, 103
  Pre-action protocols, 4
  Working towards, 133
Singapore Convention, 7
Small Claims Track Mediation, 6
Solicitor, getting agreement from, 63
Standard Form Agreements, 86,237, 253
Strategy
  Attendee choice, 94
  Contactability of non attendees, 96
  Fixing a date, 110
  Negotiation processes and, 135
  Team, 130
  Venue, 85

Tactics *see also* Strategy
  Working with mediator, 128
Team
  Strategy, 130
Telephone mediation, 6
Time-limited mediations, 156
Timetabling, 117
Tit for tat, 150
Tomlin Order, 107,155
Traits, effective negotiation, 141

UNCITRAL, 7
United Nations *see* Singapore Convention

Venue
  Choosing, 85
Voluntary, mediation, 9

WATNA, 99,133
Working up the brief, 104
Written statement of case
  See also Position Statement
  Role of, 90

www.ingramcontent.com/pod-product-compliance
Lightning Source LLC
LaVergne TN
LVHW070850210926
848482LV00016B/908
9781858116082